CW00920146

THE MANLY MAN MANUAL

Acknowledgements

Infinite Ideas would like to thank the following authors for their contributions to this book: Linda Bird, Eve Cameron, Kate Cook, Peter Cross, Sabina Dosani, Penny Ferguson, Sean Geer, Andrew Holmes, Giles Kime, Ken Langdon, John Middleton, Lizzie O'Prey, Marcelle Perks, Tim Phillips, Steve Shipside and Elisabeth Wilson.

First published in 2007 by
The Infinite Ideas Company Limited
36 St Giles
Oxford, OX1 3LD
United Kingdom
www.infideas.com

A CIP catalogue record for this book is available from the British Library

ISBN 978-1-905940-32-5

Designed and typeset by Baseline Arts Ltd, Oxford
Cover designed by Cylinder
Printed in China

THE MANLY MAN MANUAL

100 BRILLIANT IDEAS FOR BEING A TOP BLOKE

COMPILED BY **STEVE SHIPSIDE**

Brilliant ideas...

MAN OF STEEL

WORKLIFE – CLIMBING THE SLIPPERY POLE

THE OTHER HALF – HE SAYS... SHE SAYS

He says...The bloke's guide to lurve

GROOMING – SUITS YOU SIR!

Why should I read a manual on how to be a man?

There was a time when a man would no more look at a manual on manliness than he would ask for directions.

Real men didn't need books on how to be a man, indeed some would say that real men didn't need books, full stop. Men were simple, uncomplicated things for whom work was somewhere they larked about with the lads, food was something the little woman put on the table, and technical wizardry meant being able to change a tyre. Grooming consisted solely of the time-honoured ritual of shower and shave and the only product involved was an industrial strength 'aftershave' bought purely because it was advertised by some sportsman. The concept that women might not really fancy men who smelt like boxers never crossed a man's mind. If truth be told the thought that women had a say in how men should be would never have been taken seriously at all.

Times have changed. These days you can't just expect to sit in a job and get promoted every few years simply because you spend every lunchtime in the pub with the boss. You're still expected to twirl a tasty tyre iron but you'd better also be able to manipulate a mean mouse if you want to get ahead. The six pack has definitively replaced the bicep as the measure of a real man, and that means a balanced diet no longer means ordering dry roasted peanuts to go with your pint. Where once the longest you ever spent in front of the mirror was when deciding whether to grow a Magnum 'tache, now you're expected to know the relative merits of waxing or shaving.

However, you don't have to be a metrosexual (whatever that is) to understand the benefits of cologne and male moisturiser; frankly you just have to want to get lucky. And if you think luck is all it takes to get lucky these days then mate you have really taken your eye off the ball. The opposite sex is no longer impressed just because you own your own car, not least since it's not a patch on their BMW. At the same time, if for a moment you forget to treat that most modern woman with old-fashioned manners then it's the doghouse for you. And as for whether women have a say in how men should be? Well it's a fair bet that a member of the fair sex is the reason you're reading this – and pay particular note if she was the one who bought it.

Which is not to say that you can't win. Just that we could all do with a bit of help in our corner. Which is where the *Manly Man Manual* comes in. Get it right and even in this modern world of mixed messages you can still come out on top as the man who other men like and look up to and women want to lick all over.

Whether it's your work life, your love life, or your home life you'll find hints and tips on how to really get on top of manliness in the new millennium. Because there's nothing but nothing better than an insider tip we've also taken the trouble to ask women just what it is they really want – so you don't have to (see 'She says...Tips from the horse's mouth'). And because all work and no play makes Jack a very dull boy indeed, you'll also find chapters on how to have as much fun as ever, and get away with it. Just make sure you read the chapters on not getting caught out. And deny having ever noticed they were in there.

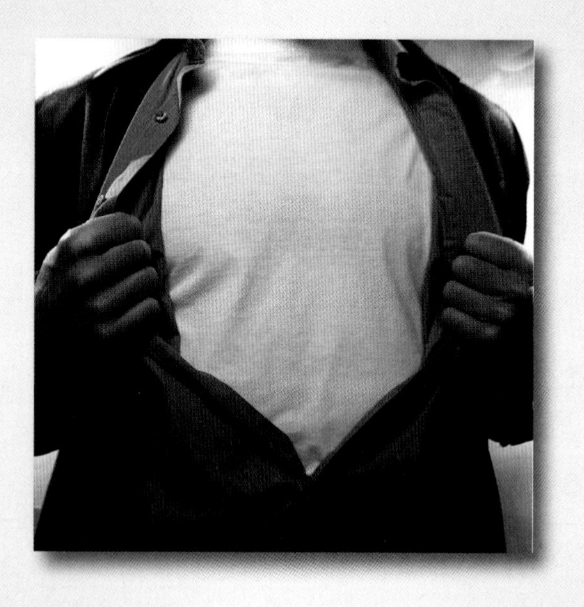

MAN OF STEEL

Because given the choice of achieving world peace or having women describe you as 'well fit' we all know what you'd really go for

Man of steel..

Find out in just 60 seconds.

How much time do you spend exercising each week?

1. Four hours or more
2. Fewer than four hours
3. Does changing channels count?

You're lounging by the pool when someone pulls out a camera, what do you do?

1. Tense your stomach muscles.
2. Suck your stomach in while smiling through gritted teeth.
3. No worries, your gut is hidden anyway by this conveniently placed cocktail bar.

The right response to the risk of 'free radicals' is to:

1. Increase your intake of antioxidants.
2. Shout 'swim radicals, swim'.
3. Reload and wait for the whites of their eyes.

or man of jelly?

Mainly 1s: Either you're Arnie or you're lying, but either way good on you for knowing your nutrition, caring about your appearance, and being prepared to put in the effort to make it happen.

Mainly 2s: You already know you should be doing something about your health and fitness, don't you? In fact you probably make resolutions each year/week/day but don't really find the time. Read on and see how to sneak those little changes that add up to a big difference into your routine.

Mainly 3s: You're a top bloke to go to the pub with but pretty soon you'll start to find that clothes don't fit, everything heads south, and jokes about man boobs aren't as funny as they once were. The baggy sweatshirts aren't fooling her either.

Read on for ideas to develop your six pack, boost your health (no, it's not just for girls) and make the most of your physique – all without trying too hard.

MAN OF STEEL

1. Why exercise makes you feel on top of the world

You may hate the idea of it, but taking exercise is life-changing and has real benefits for dieters. Once you get into the exercise habit, you won't want to stop.

I think the reason that so many of us are put off formal exercise as adults is a hangover from childhood. I detested Physical Education at school because I was useless at most sports.

At school there was cross country running on a cold winter's morning, followed by a cold shower. As I got older, however, I discovered exercise I liked. For me it was circuit training. I couldn't wait to get into my shorts and t-shirt and run around like crazy for an hour. That was over twenty years ago and I still go to the gym four or five times a week.

That's the key to incorporating exercise into your life – it has to be something you enjoy. I do believe there's something for everyone. Some of us love swimming. For others, it's running or tennis. These days gyms have a huge variety of classes on offer, ranging from the highly choreographed to gentle classes featuring very simple moves. There's no excuse for at least not trying some of them out. If you really don't like gyms, there is walking, which is a very good exercise indeed. It is easy to get into the habit of taking regular walks. Just one foot in front of the other, walk out of your door and keep going.

Here's an idea for you

Keep a log of your TV viewing time over a week. If you watch TV for more than four hours a day, you'll consume more calories than you need to because you'll have more opportunity to snack and you'll burn fewer calories while you are still.

Why bother to exercise? I'll give you seven compelling reasons:

- **Exercise uses up calories.** You will lose weight by cutting down on the calories you consume, but if you're active too, your weight loss will be faster. I love food and working out means I can eat more. It also means that I don't end up losing any weight, but just maintain the weight I am. When you exercise you build up muscle, which gives you shape; even thin people can use muscle tone. Muscle burns up more energy than fat tissue.
- **Exercise gives you a buzz.** You've probably heard of the runner's high, that happy, almost euphoric feeling during an exercise session. Experts put it down to a combination of factors: a release of endorphins, hormones that mask pain and produce a feeling of wellbeing; the secretion of neurotransmitters in the brain that control our mood and emotions; and a plain old sense of achievement. Whatever gives you the high, there's no doubting the feel-good glow it gives you.
- **Exercise boosts your confidence.** Every time you work out or play a sport, you're doing something positive for yourself, which is mood-enhancing in itself. When you start to see the results in the mirror, your self-esteem rockets. As soon as you see results, you will find it easier to stick to your weight loss plan too.
- **Exercise reduces your appetite.** As well as being a good distraction from the allure of the fridge, exercise slows the movement of food through your digestive system, so it takes longer for you to feel hungry.
- **Exercise helps you keep weight off.** The trouble with only tackling your weight loss from a dietary perspective is that it is usually quite hard to maintain your weight loss in the long term. Once you have reached your goal and are a little less strict with yourself, the weight can begin to come back. Studies have shown

that people who have successfully lost weight by taking exercise as well as a sensible approach to food are better at keeping their weight stable long-term.

- **Exercise really can be fun.** Depending on what you choose to do, you could discover a whole new social circle. I know a few people who met their partners on the Stairmaster at their gym! Don't imagine that everyone else at the gym will be gorgeous. Only the very expensive gyms are stocked with beautiful, thin and rich people – the heaviest weights they lift are their Louis Vuitton bags. Avoid them unless you're looking for someone beautiful, thin and rich.
- **According to studies** at the New England Research Institute, regular, vigorous exercise can be effective at lowering men's risk of impotence.

Having big muscles makes me feel like a real man...

2. Get your nutritional act together

Nutrition to win

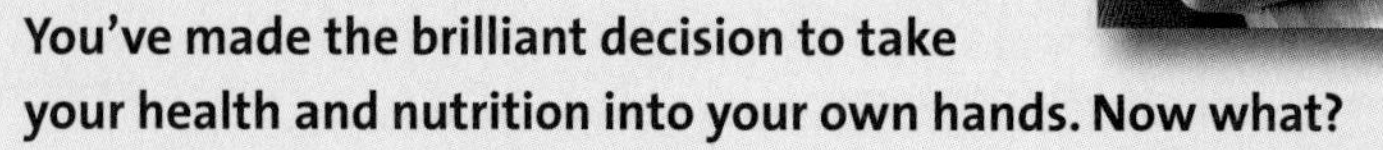

You've made the brilliant decision to take your health and nutrition into your own hands. Now what?

Put some solid systems in place to ensure that your good intentions actually get done. There's nothing more stressful than hundreds of 'I shoulds' running loose in your brain, like 'I really should buy fresh stuff instead of ready meals.'

My first tip is to write all these Shoulds down somewhere so that you can quit worrying about them. Break your Shoulds into sections, such as Diet Shoulds, Exercise Shoulds and Stress-busting Shoulds. Give each Should a priority rating from one to three and tackle the high scorers first. So, if 'I should stop having nine cups of coffee a day' is more of a priority than 'I should stop eating that extra square of chocolate a day', score it as a three and make it something you'll tackle this month. Only aim to take on three Shoulds a month – too many and you won't do them. Get the high-scoring ones under your belt before you take on the lower scorers.

Choose a day to start the healthy new you, but don't make it a Monday as it's always too depressing to start something at the beginning of the week, especially as the weekend is so far away. Take just one month at a time and say to yourself you'll stick to it for that month. In this way, you won't feel that what you're going to do will be forever. If you think that something is forever, you tend to rebel against it and are less likely to stick to it.

If there's one thing I detest it's anchovies...

Once you've got rid of all the old packets of food that are lurking around in your cupboards, it's time to go shopping for the basics. You'll need some of the following essential cupboard starters to get you going:

- Organic porridge oats and millet
- Rice milk – just for a change!
- Brown rice, quinoa (a wacky kind of grain) and wheat-free pasta
- Almonds, brazil nuts and cashew nuts
- Pumpkin seeds and sunflower seeds
- Oatcakes and rice cakes
- Tahini and houmous
- Extra virgin olive oil
- Tuna in olive oil
- Lentils and chickpeas
- Tinned tomatoes, sweetcorn, butterbeans and artichoke hearts
- Dried herbs, pepper, tamari (a kind of wheat-free soya sauce), olives, pesto, bragg liquid aminos (a bit like soya sauce)

Here's an idea for you

First go through your cupboards and throw out everything with unrecognisable ingredients on the back of the pack. The general rule is get rid of any ingredient that comprises more than three syllables as this usually means that it's a chemical ingredient that might not be a healthy option. You don't have to actually throw food away, just give it to less healthy friends who don't care that the ingredients are in a kind of chemical Greek.

These are only suggestions, of course. You'll probably want to add other stuff and take away anything you don't like.

Also, load the fridge with plenty of fresh vegetables. Ones that keep are broccoli, cauliflower, red cabbage and cabbage. Frozen vegetables can be useful too, so get some peas and spinach in.

I once had a client who asked me why I'd put tuna in olive oil on the list. This is simply because I really hate tuna in brine. But hey, each to his own! If you like tuna in brine or are worried about the extra calories the oil will add, then brine it is. An even better option would be tuna in spring water. Likewise, anchovies. If there's one thing I detest it's anchovies, but if you like them then by all means add them to your cupboard basics.

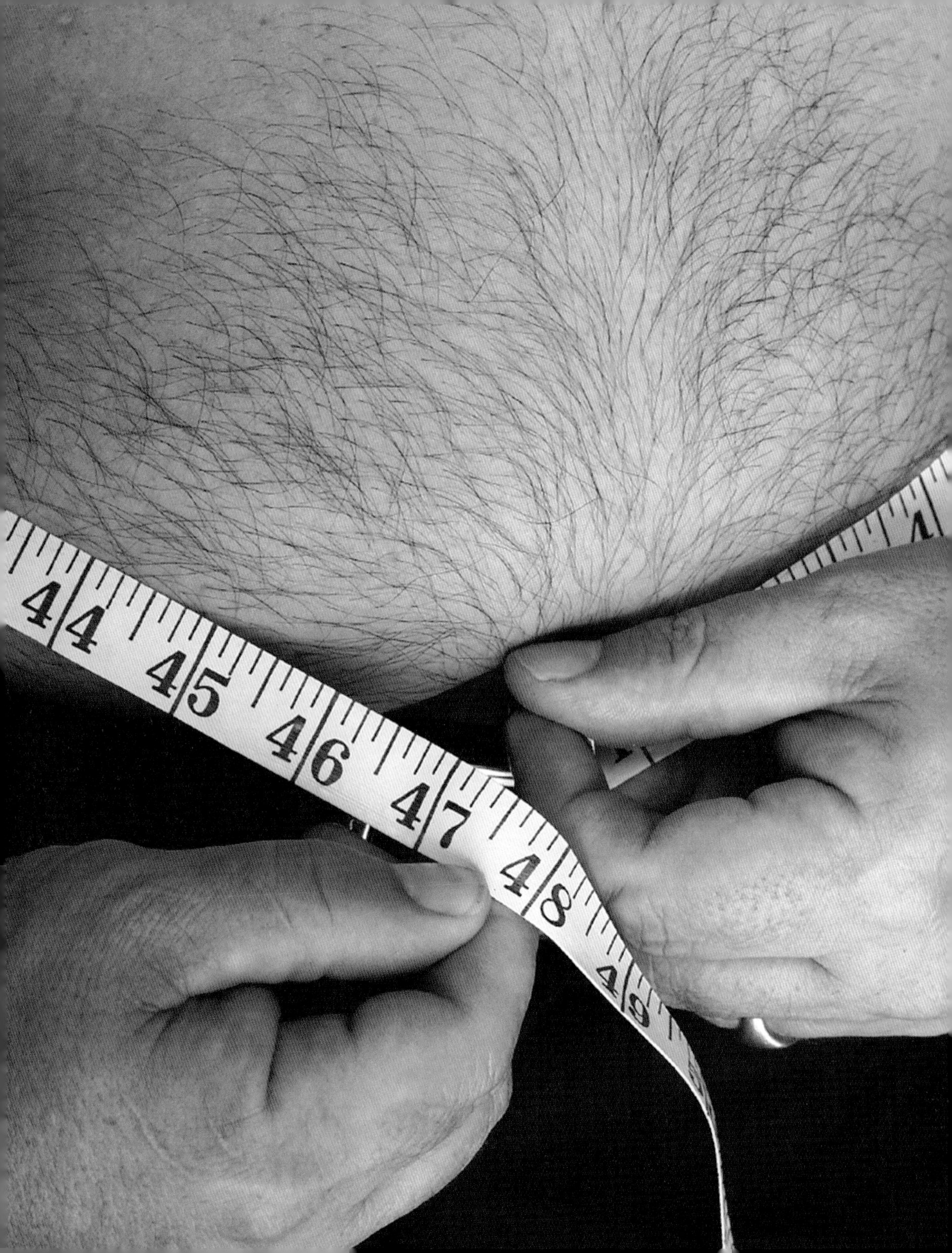
44
45
46
47
48
49

3. Fats, the good, the bad, and the ugly

Not to mention the downright unspeakable

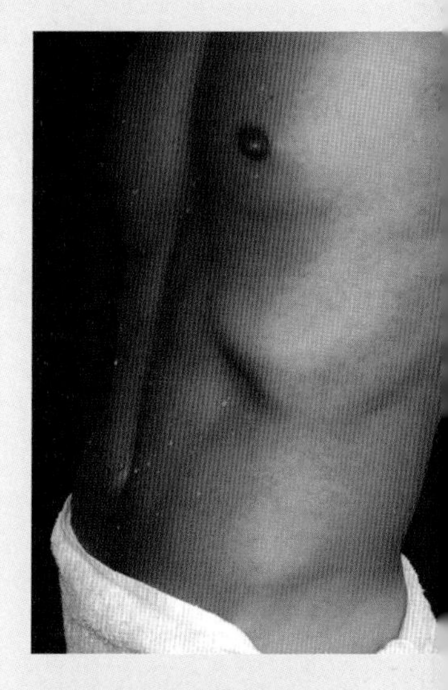

Fat friends and foes.

Eating too much of certain fats is definitely harmful to both your waistline and your health, so here are some handy hints on how to perform a bit of liposuction on your diet.

You need to know about fat in food because it's a rich source of calories. In fact, it contains more than twice as many calories, weight for weight, as carbohydrates and proteins.

As well as being a major cause of weight gain, a high-fat diet, particularly one that is high in saturated fats, can also increase your risk of heart disease and breast and bowel cancers.

Fat isn't all bad; our bodies need it. It delivers vitamins A, D, E and K and aids their absorption. It helps to regulate a variety of bodily functions. It makes food taste delicious and gives it a creamy, more-ish texture. The thing is not all fats are created equal and we typically consume too much of the wrong kind of fat and not enough of the good stuff. We should all know our rights from our

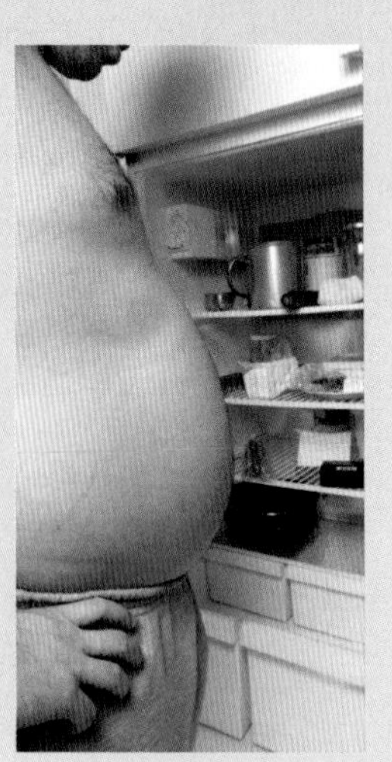

wrongs for the sake of our health, but there's even more reason to get clued up when there's weight to be lost. So here are the big fat facts to chew on:

- **Saturated fats** – Foods with high levels of saturated fatty acids include butter, lard, whole milk, hard cheeses, cream, meat and meat products, palm oil and coconut oil. These are the diet wreckers and you should aim to have only a very small amount of them in your daily diet. You can reduce your intake of these kinds of fats by buying leaner cuts of meat and chopping off visible fat. Grilling, baking or steaming foods is a more slimming way to cook than smothering everything in butter and cream.

You are what you eat!! Take note and reduce that gut!

- **Trans fats** – These are found in processed foods such as crisps, cakes, biscuits and pies and also in many brands of margarine. Cross the street to avoid them. Check food labels for these fats – they'll be listed as 'hydrogenated'.

- **Unsaturated fats** – These break down into monounsaturates and polyunsaturates. Monounsaturates are found in olive oil, nut oils, avocados and seeds, which have health benefits for your heart and so are a better choice than saturated fats. But they're still fattening, so use them sparingly. Polyunsaturates pop up in most vegetable oils (corn, sunflower, safflower), fish oils and oily fish. They are generally a good thing, particularly if you consume them in place of saturated fats, although they are still calorific.

Overall, fats should make up about a third of your total daily calorie intake, with saturated fats making up less than 10% of all the calories you consume. This rule is just for general health, but as most of us consume too much fat, it should help you lose a couple of kilos. It is quite safe to cut your total intake of all types of fat to about 20% of your daily calories. To reduce the fat you eat, you will probably need to play with the balance of fats in your diet. In the western world, especially in the UK and US, we generally consume a lot of saturated fat. People who live in southern Europe tend to have a better fat balance as they generally eat less dairy, more fish, more plant oils and much more fruit. Think of your favourite region of the Mediterranean and imagine being a local there. How do they eat? French, Italian and Spanish people who live in the countryside tend to eat well-balanced meals prepared from fresh ingredients, avoiding processed foods. If you must drink a lot of milk, try choosing skimmed or half-fat instead of whole milk.

Here's an idea for you

Reach for your extra virgin. A drizzle a day might keep the doctor away. I use olive oil in just about everything. The trouble is that I tend to use lots of it. Yes, it's a healthy oil, but if you eat a lot of it you are just adding unnecessary calories. The key is to measure it. A tablespoon is usually enough for everything.

4. Maintain your brain

Here's an idea for you

Open yourself to new experiences and insights by experimenting relentlessly (but legally, of course). Become a creature of un-habit: go to a Peter Gabriel concert; take a different route into work; try a different option off the menu; look for one thing, find something else; start a journal or an audio diary; buy a magazine you've never read before; check out a Girls Aloud gig (oops, probably went a bridge too far there).

Here are some tips for keeping your thinking gear in fine fettle.

What I'm about to say shouldn't come as any kind of surprise: your brain is a lifelong work-in-progress.

There's so much we all can do to develop our potential. Take it from me: given the amount of change we can expect to face over the coming decades, lifelong learning is not a trendy concept dreamt up by the human resources department, it's a survival necessity.

So, with an eye to the future, there are a few attributes you might want to consider working on if you're planning to go for more brain upgrades in the years to come. Here are a few suggestions:

Commit to lifelong learning

Recognise that the skills, knowledge and experience that got you where you are today won't be enough to get you where you want to be in the future.

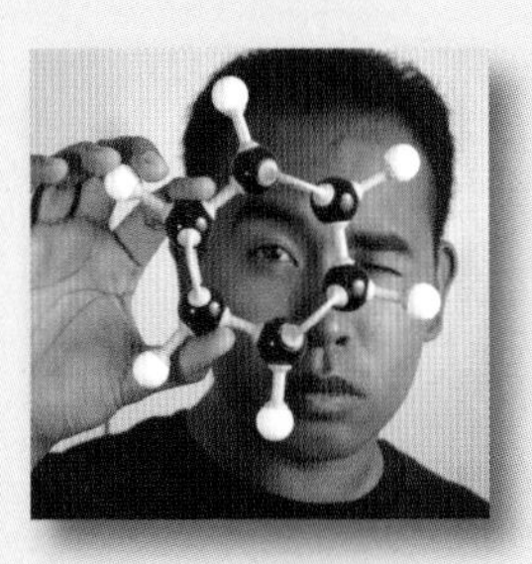

'Learning' does not always have to equal 'courses'. Read a book; talk to an expert; surf the net for information; just practise; take a secondment to another part of the business; go and do some work in the community.

Become a fluent communicator: verbally and in writing

Feel confident that you can give a prepared talk that has style, substance and clarity.

Aim to be 'media-friendly' at all times. It's now pretty much impossible for a politician to succeed without being a skilled communicator. People who are capable at their work but who don't come across well on TV or in person will struggle to move into senior roles in the future.

To polish your writing skills, try reading *The Pyramid Principle* by Barbara Minto, to my mind the best book around on how to present complex ideas in writing.

Work and re-work your CV – it's your career calling card.

Embrace technology

Fewer than half of Britain's senior directors can send and receive their own emails and 60 per cent are unable to log on to their company's website without help. There may be something faintly comical and endearing about the greybeards struggling to find the on/off switch. However, if you're a thirty- or forty-something with a disdain for new technology, be warned. You can run, but you can't hide.

Be opportunistic

When you're given the chance to try something new, make 'Why not' your default response.

Be spontaneous.

Don't think yourself to a standstill

Upgrading your brain involves a mixture of thinking and action. You need both – thinking without action is sterile, action without thinking lacks direction and mindfulness.

As Richard Pascale once put it, it's easier to act yourself into a new way of thinking than to think yourself into a new way of acting.

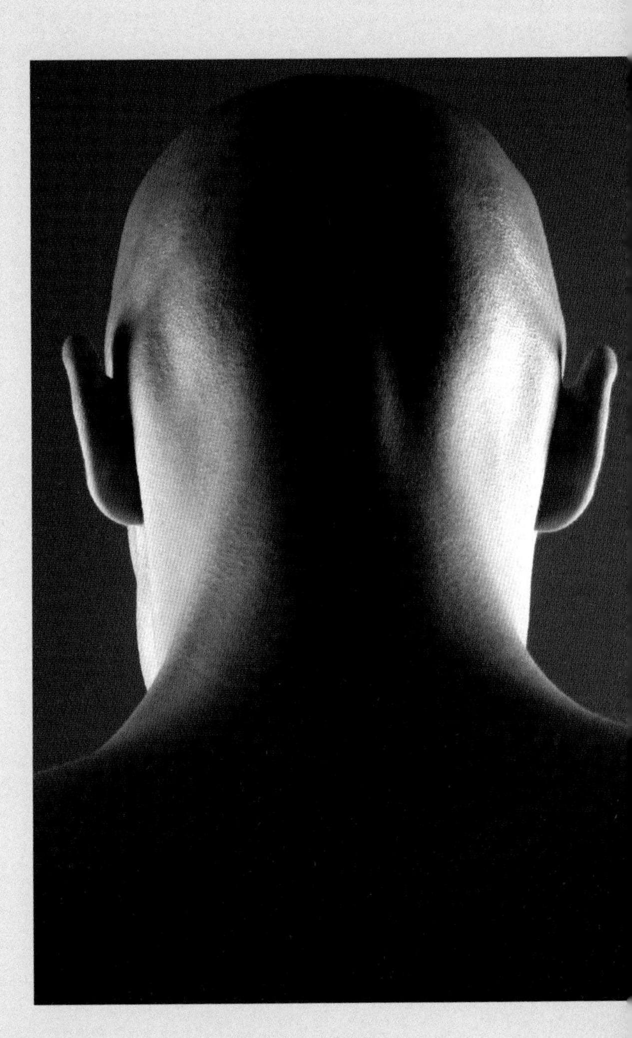

You've made a good start in picking up this book (and an even better start if you've read this far!), but in itself it means little. To tweak a cliché: today is your first day with your upgraded brain. So what are you going to do about it?

Stay curious

For a few nights back in June 2005, the moon appeared to be larger than normal in the night sky. Generally acknowledged as the world's largest optical illusion, even NASA couldn't explain the phenomenon. There's so much we don't know, so much we have yet to experience. Life can be just as entrancing whether you are eight or eighty.

Develop your goals, pursue your dreams, go out and grab your life.

Compose the life you want but don't ignore opportunities to be spontaneous.

Of course, this is nothing like a comprehensive tip-sheet. After all, your brain is a lifelong work-in-progress. So now go off and develop six more ideas of your very own!

Compose the life you want but don't ignore opportunities to be spontaneous.

5. Walk yourself thinner

If you're new to exercise or just don't fancy the gym, here's a simple way to drop some weight. It's easy to start, and requires no special clothing or equipment.

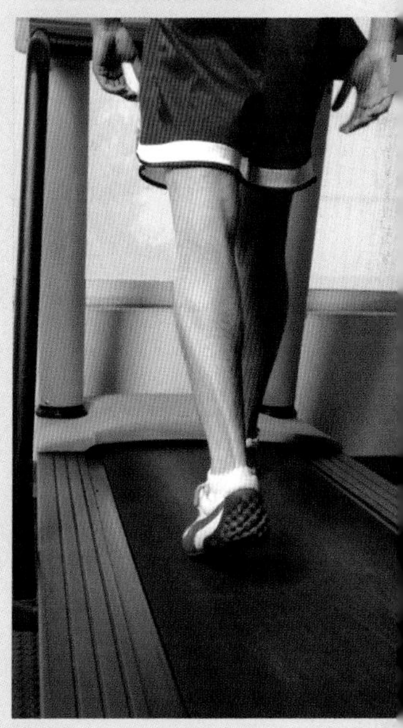

Most of us view walking as a way to get from A to B, and most of the time we'll choose to use the car or bus to get us to where we want to go.

There is a good reason to put one foot in front of the other more often: it's a great way to lose weight and stay in shape. It is not expensive, it is not complicated and you can do it anywhere.

Half an hour's walking will burn up an average of about two hundred calories and help to tone up your legs and bottom. There's a catch; you won't see results with a gentle stroll to work or the shops once or twice a week. To make a difference, you'll need to walk at least three times a week, building up to five times a week, for half an hour. You'll need to do it at a reasonable pace, one that warms you up, makes you feel ever so slightly sweaty and leaves you feeling slightly breathless, but not so breathless that you could not hold a conversation. If you walk up some hills or on an incline on the treadmill in the gym, you'll increase the challenge and burn up more calories. It is simple. Here are a few other pointers to bear in mind:

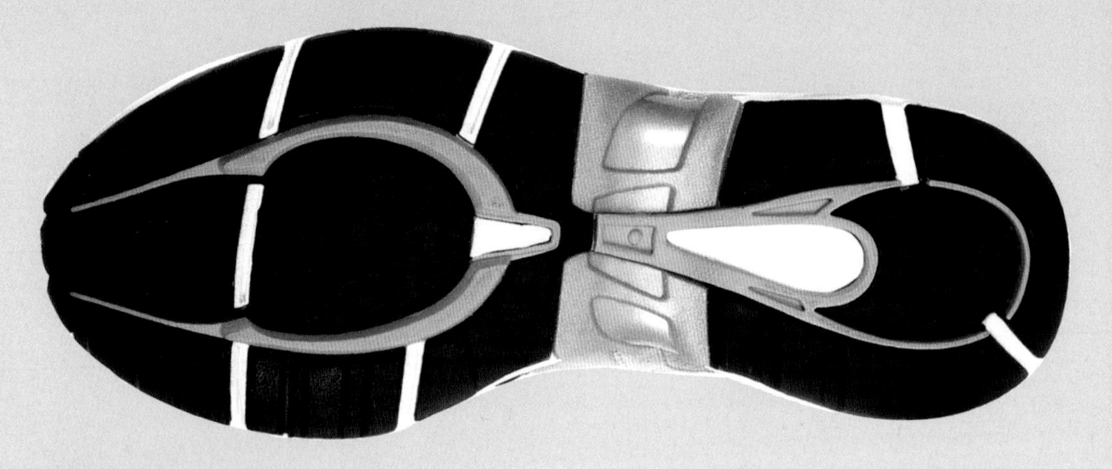

- You don't really need specialist gear for walking, but a decent pair of trainers will support you better than ordinary shoes. If you're planning to take up hill walking or hiking, you will need shoes or boots designed for the purpose, both for comfort and safety.

- You'll work harder outdoors than inside on a treadmill as you'll have to cope with changing terrain and wind resistance. This is a good thing as you'll burn calories faster and get extra toning benefits. Regularly spending time outside has been shown to keep you emotionally fit too, boosting feelings of well-being and staving off depression.

- Wear something comfortable! It might sound obvious, but if you get wet or too hot, you'll want to give up and go back home. High-tech sports fabrics are designed to draw away sweat and protect you from wind and rain without weighing you down.

...you'll burn calories faster and get extra toning benefits.

- When walking, keep your tummy muscles pulled in to work your abdominal muscles and protect your back. Walk tall, avoid slumping and use your natural stride.
- If you swing your arms while you walk, you'll increase your heart rate and get more of a workout.
- For the best technique, hit the ground with your heel first, roll through your foot and then push off with your toes.

Rather than just randomly walking when you feel like it, try to schedule a daily walk, or at least every other day. That way, you are more likely to stick with it and see results in conjunction with your healthier eating habits, plus you'll be able to monitor your progress.

To reap the greatest benefits, set yourself a plan, say over six weeks, gradually increasing the length of time you walk and its frequency and the speed. For example, in week one you could walk for half an hour three times a week, slowly for 15 minutes and briskly for 15 minutes. Over the next few weeks, you would aim to add another walking session and making each one 5 or 10 minutes longer, and you would walk briskly for 20 or 25 minutes and at a slower pace for the rest of the time. By the end of six weeks, you could be walking for 45 minutes to an hour four or five times a week, and mostly at the faster pace. You'll be seeing a slimmer you in the mirror.

Here's an idea for you

Make your dairy product intake low-fat. In research, obese volunteers lost 11% of their body weight over six months on a calorie-controlled diet that included three low-fat dairy portions a day.

6. Get the most out of your holiday

There's nothing like a fortnight in the sun to make you feel more wonderful, so why not book one today? It's therapy.

The key to a successful holiday is to extract the maximum benefit you possibly can from them, while paying very little yourself. Here's how.

Eat like a mediterranean

We all know that holidays can be great for our looks. There's usually a choice of delicious new foods to be sampled, so while you're away make a conscious effort to eat better – lots of wholegrains, fruit, vegetables and proteins such as lean meat and fish. That way you'll be getting a wider range of vitamins and minerals.

Make dining a special experience. Take pleasure in setting the table and preparing the food. If you really relish what you're eating you'll eat less, as it takes twenty minutes for the brain to learn that you're full. And no reading or watching TV or standing up while you're eating, or munching on the run. The idea is to savour the smells, sensations and colours of the food, and to slow down to help digestion.

Also, aim to drink more water. This shouldn't be hard as you'll want to stay cool poolside, but make sure you at least match every alcoholic drink with a glass of water. Try, too, to make time for breakfast. This shouldn't be difficult either as it is such a treat to linger over breakfast, rather than having to run out to work with a

piece of toast in your briefcase. Plus nutritionalists say that breakfast is one of the best ways to control your weight and boost your metabolism.

Explore, create, dream

There's nothing like a holiday somewhere exotic and/or romantic for firing up your passions. The sun, food, architecture, history or the region can all stir up your imagination and rekindle your *joie de vivre*. Capitalise on this and don't merely bury yourself in your Tom Clancy novel.

Use your holiday as a springboard for new beginnings. If you're thinking of making a career change or redecorating the spare room, now's the time to do the groundwork. While you're on your chaise longue, make a couple of to-do lists; things to do today, this month, this year, that you want to achieve before you're thirty/forty/married/infirm, whatever. It could be a safari in Africa, losing 5 kg or running a marathon. This is an extremely motivating exercise, plus you'll feel great as you tick things off your list. Think back to ambitions you had as a young 'un. Have they changed or have you neglected them? It's never too late to learn something new, see another continent, write your first novel, etc. The more fulfilled you are in life, the more confident and contented you'll appear – and 100% more attractive to boot!

Here's an idea for you

Eat like you're on a Caribbean holiday and spice up your home cooking by adding the herbs and spices used in exotic food. Spices also make a healthy alternative to salt. Cinnamon, allspice and cloves provide antioxidants, ginger aids digestion and garlic boosts heart health.

Move that beach body

We tend to spend most of our holiday outdoors, soaking up rays. However, rather than surgically attaching yourself to a deckchair, aim to incorporate at least thirty minutes of strenuous activity into your day. Swim, try windsurfing or diving, run on the beach, play Frisbee – anything that gets your heart rate pumping. And use your holiday to strengthen your relationship. Use the extra time you have for talking, sightseeing, taking up new hobbies together or inspecting the hotel linen together. Get motivated!

...take up new hobbies together or inspect the hotel linen together.

7. Are you sitting comfortably?

Comfort and tone at work or at home

Pilates isn't just for girls, and it's not just about classes or mat work either. Its principles can be applied to almost any situation, making it possible to do yourself some good wherever you are – in the office, on the bus or down the pub.

Life, I find, has an irritating habit of butting into my schedule of exercise and well-being. In theory I have an eight-hour regime of taking care of myself in the gym and Pilates studio, but in practice little things like work, family and friends tend to get in the way.

One of the beauties of Pilates is that it can be applied to almost any physical activity – or inactivity. You can be working out without anyone knowing. You really can be working out by sitting on your arse.

Sitting isn't as easy as it looks. Most of us manage to put stress on our shoulders, necks and backs just by the way we sit. Pilates posture can help.

First, make sure you're sitting back in your chair with your feet flat on the floor. Imagine that your coccyx (tailbone) is made of lead and pulling straight down into the chair. Make sure your spine is in neutral and you can feel the middle of your back lightly pressed against the seat back. Your shoulders should be relaxed but not slumped. To get a feel for that position try some leg lifts. Lift each knee alternately up, placing it smoothly down again with the foot

Here's an idea for you

'The lift' is another exercise you can do at your office chair or on the bus. The aim is to work on zipping up from the bottom of the pelvis towards your ribs. While sitting upright, imagine that there is a lift on your pelvic floor. As you breathe out try to take that lift 'up' to the next floor – you should feel your pelvic muscles go taut. As you take the 'lift' further up the floors from 'first' to 'second', you should feel your lower abdominals tighten. Higher than that and you risk the six-pack muscling in on the action.

flat on the floor. You should be totally stable. If you can feel your coccyx moving, then check that you are sitting back and in the neutral position – you may be sitting too far forward with your pelvis tilted. If you're not sure about neutral when sitting, then try lifting the knee right up towards your chest. As you do you'll reach a point where you can feel the pelvis tilt, and the coccyx slides towards the front of the seat. Hopefully that feel for being out of neutral should help you settle into neutral.

Hunching your shoulders upwards is a shortcut to tension and trouble...

With your pelvis and back sorted out, the next issue is your shoulders and the neck strain that all too easily results from tension and poor posture. Hunching your shoulders upwards is a shortcut to tension and trouble as it tightens the trapezius muscle at the top of your back and that transmits its strain into the back of the neck. If you feel tense (and who doesn't at some point in the working day) then try this.

Slide your shoulder blades towards each other and then down and at the same time extend your neck. You should feel an immediate easing of the pressure on your spinal column, shoulders and neck as well as feeling as if you've just grown an inch. Next time you want to shout at someone, try doing that first.

A really great time to try the sitting exercises is on the bus/tube or at the traffic lights on the way home. Because we're tired we're likely to slump and take all that tension back home with us. Try and make it part of your daily routine to ease that pressure out as a way of leaving work behind before you get home. Don't forget that it's just as effective in the pub or sat in front of the TV.

8. Backs to the wall

Who needs a gym when you have masonry?

Wall work provides a welcome break from the mat, a set of different sensations, and can be done pretty much anywhere and anytime.

While you might reasonably have reservations about lying down on the floor in most places, you can practise your wall work pretty much anywhere.

OK, I guess if you live and work in an igloo or a tent then there are certain practical hurdles to overcome but in general the beauty of wall work is that if you can lean, you can learn.

We're an upright sort of beastie so it comes as no surprise that there's a very primitive, primeval sense of vulnerability about lying down. The word prone (which in exercise means lying face down) has strong connotations of being open to attack and most of us are very reluctant to get down on the floor to exercise if there's any chance of someone walking in. Even people we know well. Being upright, however, feels less exposed so I find I'm far more likely to make use of a spare five minutes with a little wall work than I am to sit or lie down to stretch.

Not everyone's the same of course. There are always stories of businessmen setting down their suitcases in airport lounges and rolling like a ball. Start off by standing 30 cm (12 inches) or more from

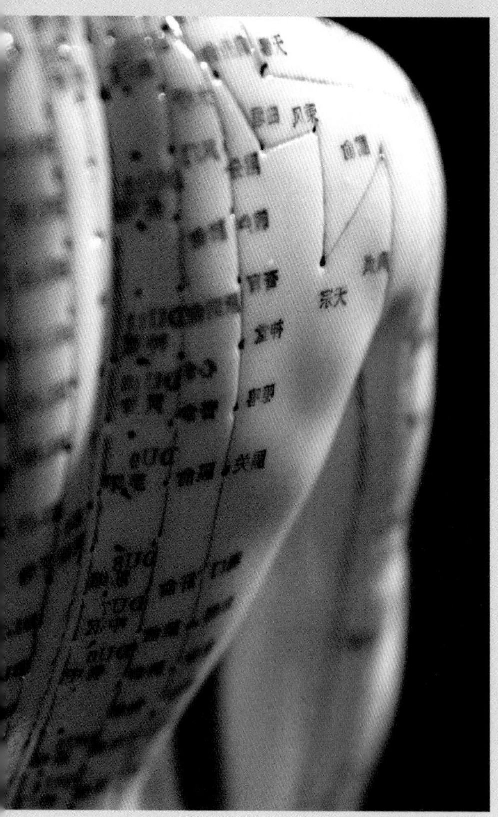

a wall with your feet hip-width apart and your knees slightly bent. Now lean back into the wall so your bum touches it and press your back against the wall, extending the upper body from the hips upwards as if you wanted to grow taller (without straightening your legs). Feel for your leg muscles and make the effort to relax them. In particular try to relax the thigh muscles (quads), which tend to tense, and the hamstring at the back of your leg, which will be stretched by this move. Scoop the stomach, park the pelvis and relax the shoulders without slumping them. Try to slide the shoulder blades down your back rather than pulling them backwards as this way you'll feel the wall over much more of your back area. Scooping your stomach should also mean that you can feel the small of your back flatten against the wall. This is, however, a matter of personal physique and if yours happens to prevent the small of your back from touching, then that's fine as long as your spine is in line.

Now breathe out and drop your chin to your chest. Start to peel yourself off the wall one vertebrae at a time. Try to feel each one as it leaves the wall and you bend ever further forwards. Let your upper body hang forward and loose so your head is down towards your knees and your arms are hanging down towards the floor. Some people can touch the floor at this point, don't worry if you're not one of them – they may be particularly supple, or they may just have arms like gorillas Just concentrate on releasing your own stress as you relax.

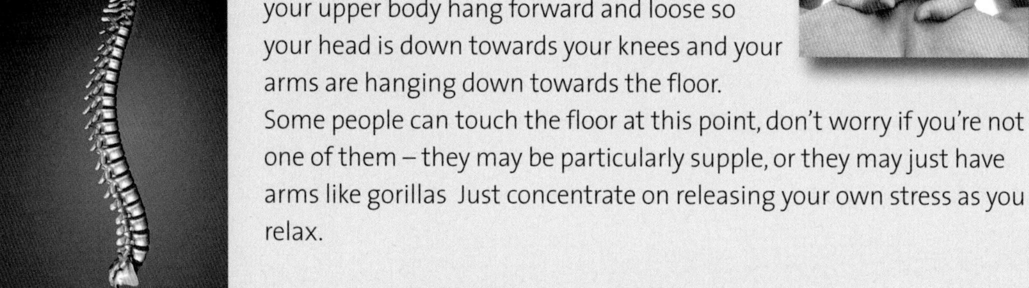

The return move starts with the tailbone and the pelvis. Breathing in, think of dropping your tailbone and pulling the pelvis back to place the vertebrae of the lower spine back against the wall. Carry on placing each and every one back against the wall one at a time until you are where you started. Repeat six times.

Here's an idea for you

You can combine the relaxing effects of rolling your spine off the wall with a strengthening exercise for your bum and the front of your thighs called The Chair. This is for when you've mastered rolling your spine and can concentrate on some strength work at the same time as unwinding. If you find the position interferes with the basic roll off the wall, then you should go back to the basic move until it is second nature. The move is exactly the same as rolling off the wall but your start position should be with the knees bent at right angles and the thighs parallel to the ground. Be careful that your knees don't project further forward than your feet, and that your bum doesn't drop below your knee level. From the side it should look as if you are sitting in an imaginary chair. Now complete your six repetitions of rolling your spine off the wall. The temptation will be to rush through the rolls, or cut corners because of the feeling of effort in your thighs. Try not to.

Now lean back into the wall so your bum touches it...

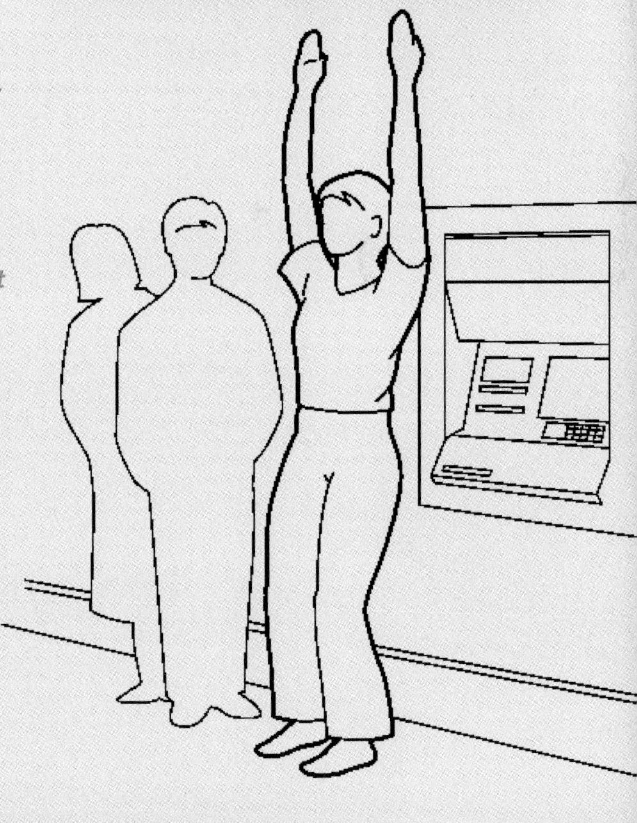

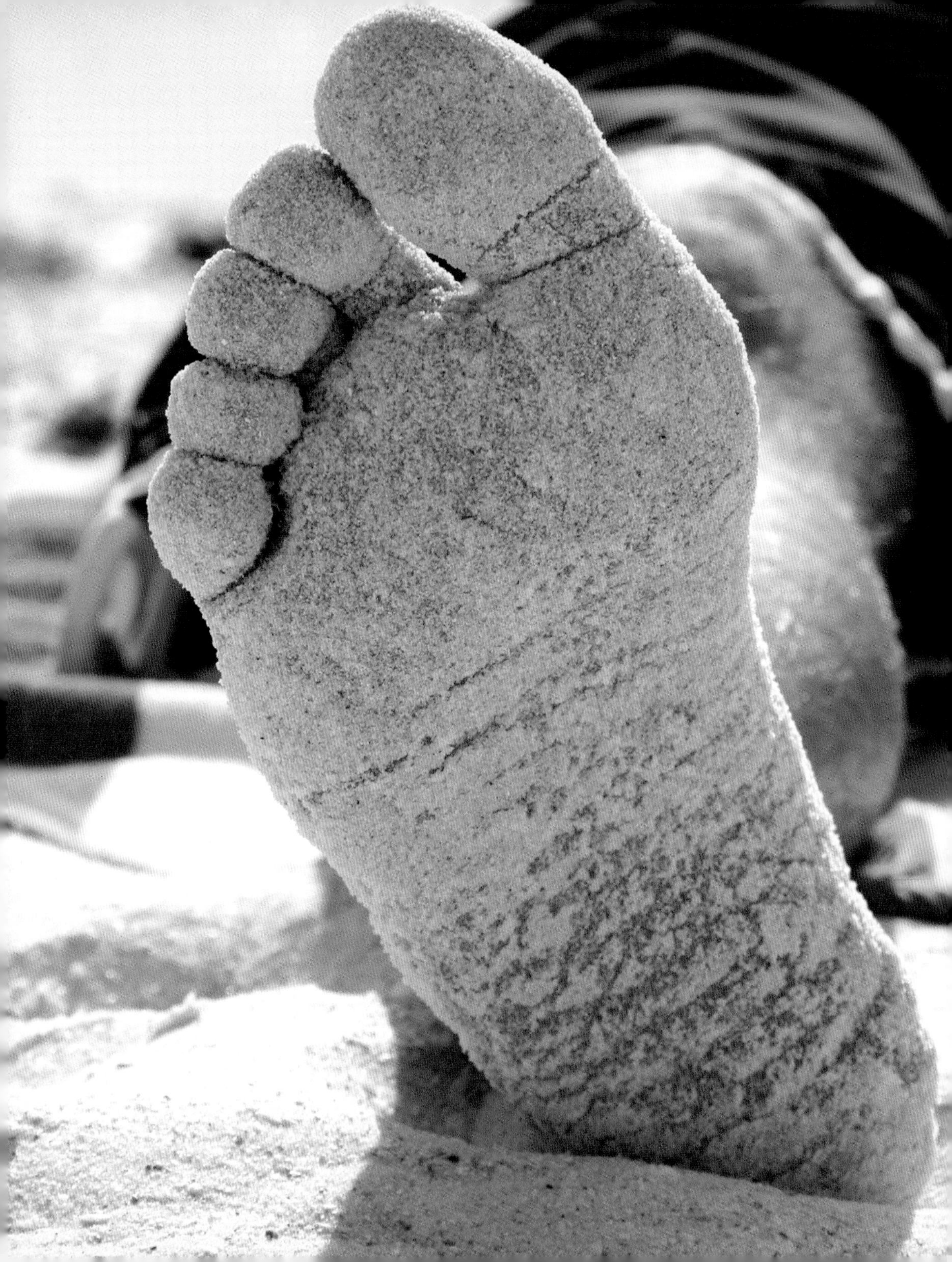

9. This little piggy does Pilates

Give your feet a break

Next time you put your feet up don't just give them a break – give them a workout.

I know, I know. People don't turn to Pilates for the chance to do their feet a favour. They usually turn to it in pursuit of that perfect athletic physique or as a means of recovering from injury.

Feet do not come into the equation. Like most adults you tend to hide your feet away and if we're going to be brutally honest you probably consider them a bit ugly. Time to change all that and for two very good reasons:

- You don't have to be a reflexologist to realise that the feet hold the key to easing stress and keeping the rest of the body happy.
- You might not think it as you apply that corn plaster, but the feet themselves are a miracle of anatomical engineering and deserve the best maintenance you can give them.

The first point is easy to prove. Next time you get back home from the match or from work, kick your shoes off, lose those socks and with your bare foot just try to grip the carpet, then relax. Doesn't that feel good? Doesn't that feel good right through to your shoulders? In fact it feels so good you should do it right now. I don't care if you're in the office, tell the boss I said it

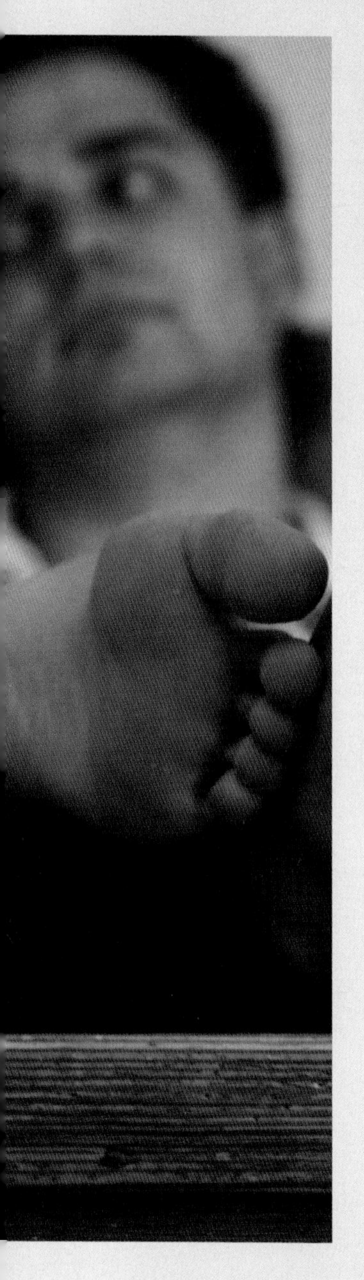

Here's an idea for you

Try playing imaginary piano scales with your toes (you'll need to be barefoot for this). Joseph H. Pilates was a great believer in body control and this is a great exercise for trying to re-establish the links between brain and body. With the soles of your feet flat on the ground, spread your toes as wide apart from each other as you can and then try to touch them to the ground one after another in order. It's not as easy as you might think. Remember they have to touch one at a time and in order. Got that? No problem? OK, then I'll bet you just did it starting with the little toe. Now try to reverse that and do it the other way, starting with the big toes.

was OK. We all know that daily stress makes its way into the shoulders, and while I'm not knocking the divine beauty that is the back rub, if you forget about your feet, then you're only dealing with the most obvious symptom of stress.

Your feet contain 52 bones, and more than 76 muscles and ligaments. More than a quarter of all the body's bones are in the feet, most of them are small and delicate, and yet everyday we expect them to handle the equivalent of hundreds of tons of force with barely a thought for their well-being.

Trust me, I'm a runner, which means I've done more than my fair share of foot abuse without a thought for any of the above. Until the day when something goes wrong of course. Once you've picked up a foot injury you start to realise how tough life is when walking becomes a problem, so take care of those feet.

Your feet contain 52 bones, and more than 76 muscles and ligaments.

A foot workout doesn't have to take long and will go a long way to easing stress. As ever, even though you're thinking of your toes you shouldn't neglect your posture. As you sit, park your pelvis in neutral, and pull your head and spine upright as if being pulled up by a string running right through your spine and out through the top of your head. Scoop your stomach and now focus on your feet.

Start with a little ankle rotation to ease swelling and increase mobility. Rotate each foot in a circle while keeping the knee and lower leg still. Now try rotating them both together but in opposite directions and then change direction to circle the other way. If you've been walking all day, and especially if you've been carrying heavy bags, then this should ease the pressure immediately.

Now try pointing and flexing both feet together. Pointing means pushing your toes as far away from you as you can but try not to curl the toes, instead keep them straight and in line with the foot. Flexing means turning the ankle the other way so that the toes point back towards you, again the toes should be in line with the foot rather than trying to bend right back.

10. Keyboard keep fit

Pilates is a great way of avoiding injury and you don't have to be a woman to benefit – the average desk jockey risks quite enough damage at work, and a few simple moves can ease the pain of the working day.

Pilates first found fame as a way for injured dancers to recover their strength and mobility. With its emphasis on building up tone with low stress and few repetitions it proved a great way of recovering dynamically – essential for those aiming to get back to full fitness as fast as possible.

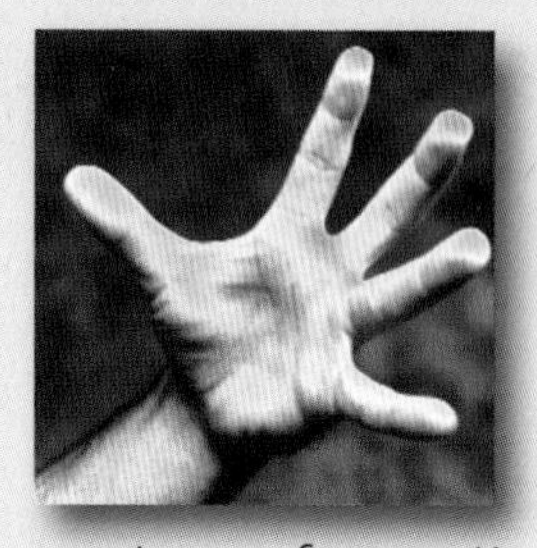

These days the walking wounded that turn to it are just as likely to be office workers with back pain and stiff necks. Ironically many of them will perform their Pilates moves with great care and attention in the studio, then go back to doing exactly what caused the problem once they're back in the familiar surroundings of the office. While the studio is undoubtedly the place to learn new moves, you can practise them just about anywhere on the planet, and Pilates in the office is a great way of preventing those problems from showing up in the first place. Take it from me. I found out the hard way. A professional life slaving over a hot keyboard left me with chronic back pain, stiff hands and an amusingly lop-sided neck from clutching a phone under my chin. These days I make sure I get away from the keyboard often enough to give my body a break, but when deadlines are tight, or the boss is hanging over your shoulder, you don't have to leave your seat to perform simple exercises to release those muscles, help your posture and above all ease the stress.

Since we tend to store up stress in the shoulders, try to roll it out again with shoulder rotations. Mobility exercises – taking the joints through their full range of movement – are a staple of most forms of modern exercising and Joseph H. was a great fan as can be seen from exercises like the one leg circle which was one of the first he taught in *Return to Life through Contrology*. Your shoulder, like your hip, is a ball and socket joint, meaning it can rotate in any direction, so every now and again you should let it. Sitting in neutral, with your feet flat on the floor and your shoulders relaxed but not slumped, bend your elbows and rest your fingertips on your shoulder (right on right, left on left). Now circle them forwards and upwards so your elbows touch, then lift up above your ears, pull back to be in line with your shoulders and finally come forward again. Now perform the same circle but in the opposite direction – remember the importance of working every equal and opposite muscle so that for every pull there is a push.

Here's an idea for you

Put your arm up in the air, bend your elbow and allow your hand to rest on the top of your head with your fingers on the side just touching your ear. Now gently ease into a stretch by pulling very lightly with the hand while resisting gently with the head and neck muscles as if you were trying to straighten your neck against the pull of your hand. Don't overdo it: this is a gentle release of the muscles in the neck for just a few seconds. Now reverse arms and do the other side. Now roll your head back and circle. There, feel slightly less homicidal now?

The best office destressing exercise is to land a right hook on the boss, but...

The best office destressing exercise is undoubtedly to land a clean right hook on the boss, but since this may lead to ugliness it's worth looking at other options. Stress balls – those squidgy balls you can squash in your fist when anxiety rises – are a good exercise for your hand muscles. The problem is people often tense the trapezius muscle that leads to the shoulders when they do. If you use a stress ball, then make sure you perform the shoulder roll above.

Now work on the fingers – if you've been typing, then they're probably tense and tired. Despite the publicity about RSI you only have to look around any office for a couple of minutes and you'll find keyboards without wrist wrests, keyboards set up at the wrong height for the seat and keyboards right at the edge of the desk so there's nowhere to rest your elbows. Concentrated mouse work, even with elegantly shaped ergonomic mice, can also put real pressure on your fingers. Remember that before you start your fiftieth game of minesweeper.

To release tension in the fingers start by turning your hands palm upwards and bring the tip of each finger in turn to the tip of your thumb then repeat the sequence. Just to make things a little more interesting, try starting with the little finger on one hand at the same time as you start at the index finger on the other so the two hands are out of synch.

Next, hold all your fingers our flat together and then open up the gap between the second and third fingers so that the first and second pull away in one direction and the third and fourth in the other. Sci-fi fans will immediately recognise this as the Vulcan greeting. Now bring the second and third fingers together and keep them together and this time open up the gaps between the first and second, and third and fourth. Try not to do this if the self-appointed office wit is around, otherwise Spock/Mork and Mindy gags will follow you around forever.

11. Bus-stop body builder

You spend five years of your life queuing, so make use of them

The Full Monty showed us how queuing should really be done – twirls, hip thrusts and all – but for those of us who don't have the moves or the music there are other ways of playing the waiting game to win.

You will spend five years of your life standing in line. That's not including all that time on the bus/tube spent glaring at the youth of today in the hope that one of them will crack and offer you his seat.

In Britain queuing is the unofficial national sport. It's being proposed as a relay event to the Olympic Committee and the discipline of Last Orders at the Bar Full Contact Queuing may soon be recognised as a formal martial art. In the meantime you might as well use some of that time on your feet to keep your body on its toes, as it were.

It doesn't matter if you're standing in line for stamps, waiting for a bus or queuing for the border at Burkina Faso, you can always use the time to check your neutral stance and tone your torso.

First make sure you're standing with your feet hip-width apart, facing directly forward, knees very slightly bent and your shoulders nice and relaxed but not slumped. Check that your pelvis is in neutral by tilting it forwards and backwards until you find the midpoint. If you genuinely are in line for an immigration official, police checkpoint or anything at all when in prison, then it's best not to rock your pelvis forward and back too vigorously. You might be sending out the wrong signals.

Without bending your neck forwards, tilt your head so that your chin drops very slightly forward to extend the neck and help elongate the spine.

Breathe deeply. Really deeply, right down into your lower abdomen. Time to contemplate

The aim is not to have your stomach clenched like a fist...

Here's an idea for you
To help you maintain that taut but elastic approach try two things:

- *Don't focus on the rectus abdominis (or 'abs') that make up the six-pack we all see in the magazines. Think instead of the transversus abdominis, the sheet of muscle that lies underneath the abs. Instead of seeking to scrunch up your six-pack, think about tensing your transversus.*
- *Lightly place the tips of your fingers between your navel and your underwear as you breath. Feel the navel being pulled in and the tautness of your abdominal muscles as they rise and fall with the incoming breath.*

your navel. Focusing on your belly button, use your abdominal muscles to pull it right in towards your spine and up towards your ribs. Keep breathing in deep into the abdomen – it may seem a little strange at first but you should be able to do this without relaxing your stomach muscles. The aim is not to have your stomach clenched like a fist, but instead taut and elastic so that it is flattened but still rises as you draw air into your body.

Now breathe into your stomach, and gently out again for ten long, slow breaths. Of course you don't actually breathe into your stomach, but that's how it should feel.

Concentrate on that stomach, on keeping your shoulders relaxed, and on emptying all the air out of your lungs as you breath out.

As well as practising your Pilates stance, toning your tum and taking your mind off the wait, this should also help calm you down and reduce your stress levels. Perfect for when the muppet at the front of the queue walks up to the counter and asks for 'six first-class stamps ... and a complete change of name and nationality, please'.

12. Row like Redgrave

Strength, stamina and smoothness are the promise of the rowing machine. So why do so many users look less like Steve Redgrave and more like Mr Bean? As with so many things, it's all down to style.

Rowing is right up there with swimming as one of the best all-round exercises you can do – but with the handy difference that you don't have to navigate shrieking ten-year-olds at half term and you're unlikely to end up with a nose full of chlorinated piss.

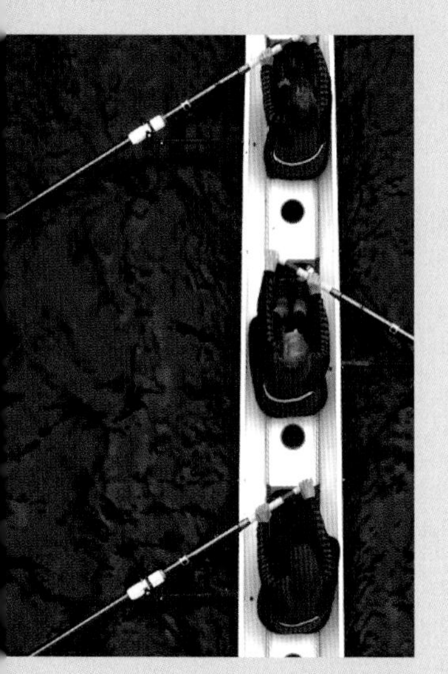

Done properly, rowing is a great calorie burner, combining weight control with strength development and a cardio workout. It works your legs, your arms, shoulders and back muscles. Do it badly, however, and you end up staggering away from the machine bent over double in those 'ooooh me lumbago' poses beloved of ancient TV sitcoms. So here's the low-down on rowing like Redgrave – how to build strength and stamina with smoothness and precision.

Breaking it down

Beginners look at the rowing action and see two parts: the pull back, which is the hard bit where they grunt and sweat; and the flop forwards again, which is the easy bit – at least until they put their backs out. Pros, however, break the action down into four distinct movements:

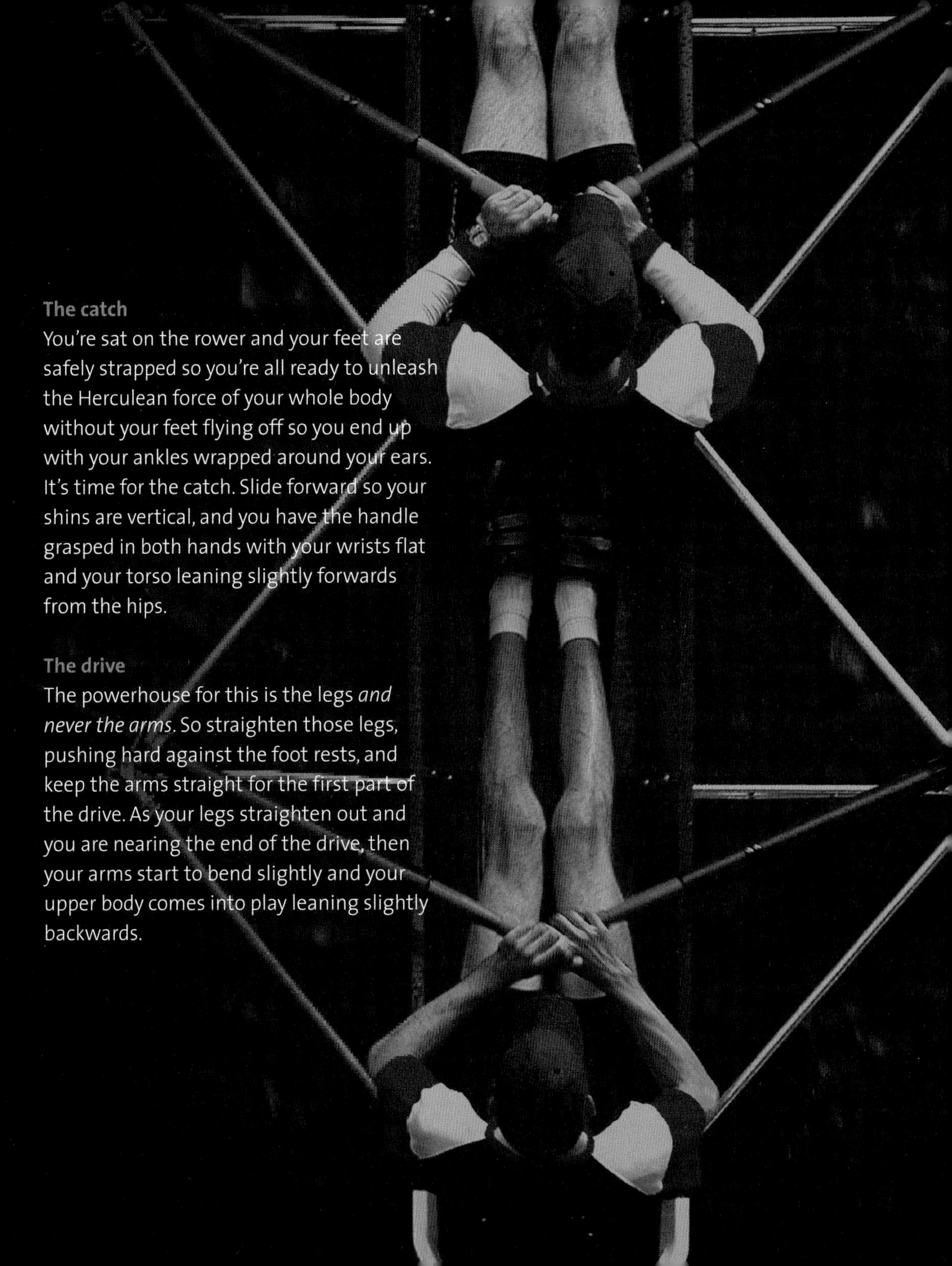

The catch

You're sat on the rower and your feet are safely strapped so you're all ready to unleash the Herculean force of your whole body without your feet flying off so you end up with your ankles wrapped around your ears. It's time for the catch. Slide forward so your shins are vertical, and you have the handle grasped in both hands with your wrists flat and your torso leaning slightly forwards from the hips.

The drive

The powerhouse for this is the legs *and never the arms*. So straighten those legs, pushing hard against the foot rests, and keep the arms straight for the first part of the drive. As your legs straighten out and you are nearing the end of the drive, then your arms start to bend slightly and your upper body comes into play leaning slightly backwards.

The finish

Legs straighten completely, upper body leans lightly backwards, and you pull the handle in towards your stomach just below your rib cage. At the end of the pull your elbows should be tucked in close to your body and behind your back, not sticking out sideways as if you're doing the Birdie Song.

The recovery

First the arms extend forwards, then your upper body leans lightly forward, and your legs bend as you slide smoothly back towards the flywheel down by your feet.

And back to the catch ...

It sounds simple enough, but if you bear the above in mind and take a good look at your fellow gym rowers you'll see that there are plenty of people who snatch at the handle, and try to pull back with their arms. Others end the whole movement still hunched forward or learning backwards, even as they recover. There's always one, and yes, it's usually a bloke, who thinks that they will get the best benefit by flogging themselves to death regardless of form in a triumph of strength over style. Get it right, however, and not only do you reduce soreness and the risk of injury, but you will effortlessly increase both your speed and endurance.

...you will effortlessly increase both your speed and endurance...

Here's an idea for you

See the lever on the flywheel that sets the difficulty level? On pretty much all the machines you'll see in the gym it can be set from anywhere between 1 and 10. Pros call it the 'damper', and if you're using a standard air flywheel it lets air in or out. Set it at 1 and it keeps the air trapped in the wheel cage. Since the resistance you feel is the air being turned, and trapped air is already spinning from the last stroke, this gives least resistance. Shove it up to 10 and the air that you've just grunted to spin around is released and replaced with fresh air that you have to get moving again from scratch – hence the extra effort. Not many people know that. In fact few of us really understand resistance levels at all, with the result that the unsure slot the lever down to 1 and most blokes whack it up to 10 in case anyone should think they're not Olympic heroes. Real Olympic heroes tend to go for the feel that is most like a real boat, which according to Terry O'Neill, former Olympic rowing coach, means a level of 3 or 4. Then they concentrate on stroke rate, aiming for about 35 strokes a minute. Next time, instead of thrashing away at the maximum setting, try taking a leaf from the real-life water warriors, and see how long you can keep up the same pace.

13. Great balls of rubber

Ever wondered what those oversized beach ball things are doing in the gym? Well here's where you find out what they're for, and why a bit of ball-play can help create a better you.

Swiss balls are just wonderful. They're big, they're soft, they're squidgy, they come in rainbow colours and they smell great.

Only you're going to have to take my word on what they smell like because they're so obviously meant to appeal to kids that you probably haven't dared use one yet. Well here's the good news: you can get comfy, play ball and roll around on the floor with confidence because those balls are the key to great stretches and core strength. Which translates to a flat stomach – something that at least half the people in any gym are working towards, only they don't know how to use the balls.

The first thing to know about the balls is that they aren't all the same size. Different balls are suitable for different sized people. The key is being able to sit comfortably on top of the ball with your knees bent and your feet flat on the floor. Roughly speaking a 45 cm diameter ball suits people 1.40–1.52 m tall (4 feet 7 inches–5 feet in old money); 55 cm balls are for those 1.55–1.68 m tall (5 feet 1 inch–5 feet 6 inches), and 65 cm for people who are 1.70–1.80 m tall (5 feet 7 inches to 5 feet 11 inches). There are 75 cm balls for the six-footers (1.83 m) and even an 85 cm ball for basketballers but you will probably have to buy one from the US. Generally the balls you see in gyms are 65 cm with a few smaller ones

Here's an idea for you

If you find the side stretch comfortable, then at the top of the stretch, when you are resting on your side, try twisting your torso to turn face down onto the ball so that your chest and both arms are resting on it.

around. Manufacturers colour code their balls by size, but beware: your gym may have bought from different manufacturers so that nice small yellow ball that was just right may turn out to be oddly larger next time you reach for it. Two important things to know about the ball. One: they are tougher than you think and can take a full-grown man and all the weight he can heft on a pair of dumbbells. Two: although you can burst them if you press them onto something sharp they don't explode, but just deflate pathetically, so don't be afraid to bounce on them.

Swiss balls are soft and supportive, as you will feel as you lay yourself out across one, which means you can trust yourself to one and stretch in comfort. Balls being balls, however, are round and so everything you do perched on the ball involves a little bit of balancing, and this means working the muscles that control your core stability, even if all you're doing is sitting on the thing.

...the exercise is surprisingly hard on the stomach muscles.

Exercises to try

You may be tempted just to sit on the ball while watching telly, but there are more effective ways to exercise to develop stretches, core stability and strength.

Side stretch

Kneel with the ball next to you and your arm resting on it. Now with the leg that's furthest from the ball stretch straight out sideways and gently shift the weight onto the ball so you are draped over it sideways on. The hand that's not on the ball should now stretch up and over your head towards the ball.

Back stretch

Sit on the centre of the ball, making sure that your feet are a little apart to keep you rock solid and stable. Then very gently walk your feet away so that you lie back and both your back and neck come down to be supported on the ball. You may want to have a hand behind your head to take the weight off your neck until it is resting on the ball. With your feet flat on the floor, now open your arms on each side and feel the stretch across your back. To open it up a bit more, stretch your arms over your head and down as if reaching for the floor behind your head.

Forward roll out

Kneel on the floor in front of your ball and lean forward very slightly to rest your forearms on the ball with your hands together. Now, keeping the abs good 'n' tight, gently roll the ball forward until your arms are straight. Hold that for a moment, then roll it back to the start position. Repeat. Most people find that although the body position is very comfortable, the exercise is surprisingly hard on their stomach muscles.

14. Static crackle: get a strong mid- section

Sit-ups, crunches, reverse crunches – have you ever wondered if there was another way to a strong mid-section without all the bobbing up and down? Well there is, and oddly enough it involves not moving at all. Time to get static.

Whether it's about body building or fitness training, the emphasis down the gym tends to be on moving things. Moving heavy things very slowly.

Moving light things very fast. Or simply moving yourself as fast or slowly as you are able. What tends to be forgotten in all this is the potential strength benefits of not moving at all. Welcome to the wonderful world of isometric exercise.

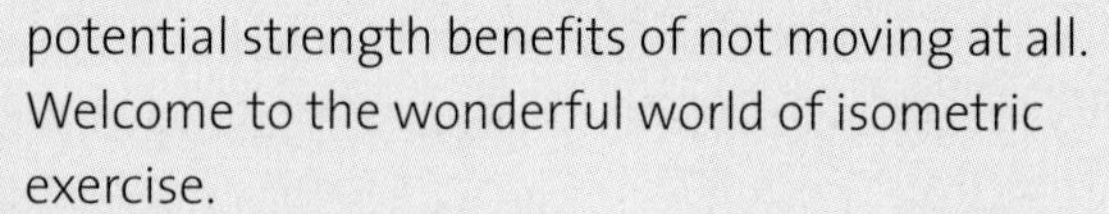

Most exercises are dynamic, and consist of a force moving an object whether that is a weight, some kind of resistance device or just hauling our own sorry selves around. That makes perfect sense because we are moving beasties and good exercise mimics the tasks we have to do in daily life. Or at least the ones we used to do when daily life involved running after mammoths, fleeing things with big pointy teeth and so on. But movement isn't the only way to build muscle, and that's where isometric exercises come in.

Isometrics really mean tensing a muscle without moving anything – either just by contracting it, or by applying a force to something that simply can't go anywhere. Stand in a doorway and try to push the frame apart Samson style. Nothing is moving (hopefully) but, my, can you feel the squeeze. Because it is seen as better to exercise a muscle through its full range of movement, isometric exercises aren't usually recommended for fitness fans unless they've suffered injury to a joint and want to maintain strength. There is, however, one exception. The plank. With the plank and its sideways-on variants the whole point is to hold the body perfectly still. Because it's only supported on the ground at a couple of points, however, this requires quite a lot of muscular effort. Unlike crunches, which mainly work the

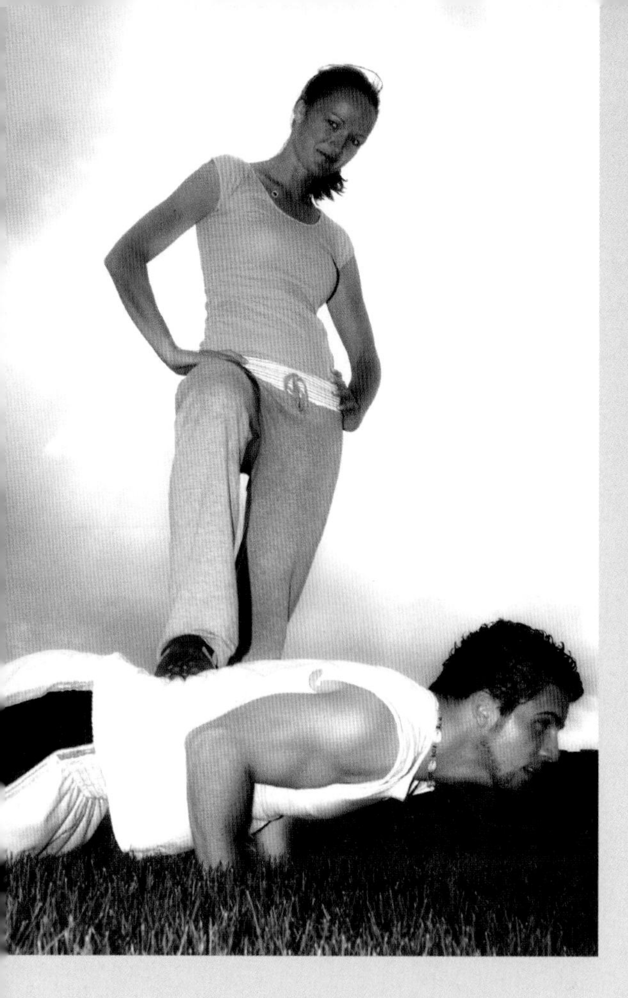

rectus abdominis, the effort of keeping the stomach straight (and off the ground) requires the work of all the muscles including the obliques and the transversus abdominis. Which makes for a strong midsection.

Purists argue that this isn't really isometric exercise because the muscles are resisting something that can move – as you find out when you stop resisting and collapse like a burst balloon – but who has time for nit-picking when there's gym-fun to be had?

The plank

Couldn't be simpler. Lie face down on a mat and then lift up so you are resting your weight on your forearms and your toes o(or your knees if toes proves too hard). Now hold that position absolutely rigidly. Your

Here's an idea for you

Enjoy the side plank but find it too easy? OK, then to put a bit of a stretch down the other side of the body assume the position and stick your 'spare' arm straight out sideways so it points at the ceiling. Now stretch the arm further over your head so you look something like a sugar plum fairy ballerina who has fallen over sideways in mid pirouette and is too shocked to get up. Hold the position for as long as you can.

back should be straight – if your bum is sticking up, pull it back into line. If your hips or belly are sagging, then whip them back into line too. You are straight as a ramrod, and by now probably starting to feel about as stiff. Keep going for as long as you can – time yourself and see if you can get any better.

Isometrics really mean tensing a muscle without moving anything...

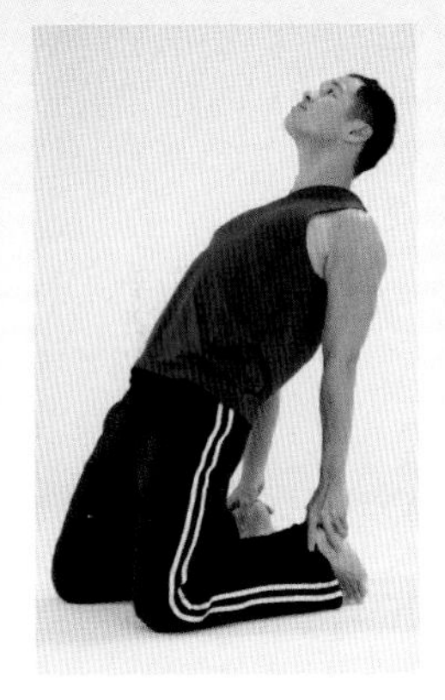

The side plank

This time you start on your side and raise yourself onto your elbow with your body dead straight so that there is a long wedge of daylight underneath you from your elbow (which should be directly under your shoulder) right down to your feet. This puts more of the stress on the sides (surprise) and thus the obliques. If you want to add a bit of extra interest (go on, you know you want to) then stretch the arm that's away from the floor straight out so it sticks up in the air. When you can't hold it anymore roll over to your other side and repeat the process.

15. Good morning superman

Get a back like Atlas

Working hard for a flat stomach but neglecting your back muscles? Well neglect your back and no one will see your six-pack or admire your navel piercing because you'll be hunched up like Quasimodo doing his shoelaces.

It's one of the simplest but smartest features of our body that most muscles have an opposite muscle that's just as important. Where one pulls, the other pushes.

Your biceps bend your arm, your triceps straighten it out. Most exercises are designed to work both, either in tandem or one after the other, so as not to create an imbalance. In one key area, however, that rule seems to go out of the window. In the quest for the hard body we tend to spend a lot of time worrying about rock-hard bellies, but forget that unless we strengthen the spinal muscles to cope we could be sowing the seeds of serious back trouble. It's a tribute to the awesome power of vanity really – we all know what a six-pack is, but when was the last time you saw someone on *Baywatch* with just, like, awesome erector spinae? The first most of us know about our back muscles is when they fail on us. Building up the stomach muscles can actually help provoke that by adding to the imbalance between the muscles that curl up the back and the muscles that straighten it. So even if they're not going to win you admiring glances from the opposite sex it pays to put a bit of effort into your back.

...working the lats helps give a V-shaped torso.

Putting your back into it

When people talk about the back muscles they usually mean the ones that show towards the tops of the shoulders. Men in particular are fond of working the lats (laterals) that help give a V-shaped torso. The muscles that get ignored, however, are the erector spinae which run up the length of the spine and help hold up and straighten the back. It's your erector spinae you reach for when you feel something go in your back. For most of us it's only at that moment that we even think of exercising our back muscles. Which is part of the phenomena that sees some four out of five adults suffering from lower back pain. The more you're working the rest of your body, the more you need a strong back to hold it all together. Just one thing though. Kill or cure is not the way to work in a gym, so before working your back you should be sure to have sought out qualified medical advice and talked it over with the gym instructors. You have? Promise? OK, over to you.

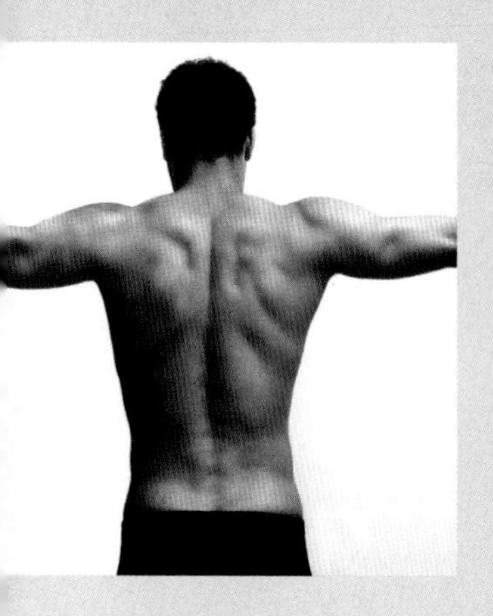

Here's an idea for you

Try doing the Superman-style back extension on a Swiss ball. With your feet firmly on the floor (well, as firmly as you're going to get balanced on a ball) lie face down on the ball so it supports your stomach and ribs. Now lift your head and shoulders off the ball and curve your back upwards. As a variation you can try this with either your hands on your head or, to make it slightly harder, stretch your arms out ahead of you. For a little more effort you can hold light dumbbells in your hands.

Superman

Lie flat on your front on a mat and smoothly lift both your arms and your feet off the mat as if you were trying to curl your whole body into a bow shape with only your stomach, ribs and hips left on the mat. Keep it steady, hold it for a moment, then return. Now add a slight twist to that by slowly raising your right arm with your left leg, then your left arm with your right leg. This should be comfortable enough to do ten or twenty times without feeling difficulty.

Good morning

The name of this exercise suggests that it goes back to a particularly courteous bygone age since really what you are about to do is take a bow. Stand with your feet shoulder-width apart and your knees slightly bent. Bend forward from the waist until your torso is parallel to the floor and hold this position for a moment before gently rising back up. If you feel great doing this, then you can add weight to the exercise with either a very light barbell across your shoulders or a light dumbbell in each hand with the weight resting on each shoulder. If you are a beginner to back workouts or feel anything that could remotely be described as a twinge, then don't even think about the weights.

16. In the swim: splash with style

Swimming is one of the best all-round exercises known, but most of us, if we're honest, are no better at swimming than we were at school. Learn to cut a dash as you splash.

Swimming involves your whole body. It works your heart and lungs, it increases strength, flexibility and endurance, but involves very little risk of injury.

It is often picked out as one of the few exercises where even a very hard workout leaves you feeling good and ready for the rest of the day.

When you signed up for your gym a lot was made of the fact that it has a swimming pool, right? It's a big selling point for gyms, and often one of the reasons given for choosing one over another by new members all picturing themselves enjoying a refreshing dip and cutting a dashing figure as they surge up and down the lanes.

Six months later and those would-be dolphins are either forming hippo herds in the shallow end, or avoiding the pool altogether in favour of the cardio machines they understand better. Unless you're one of the dedicated few fish people it can be hard to make progress in the pool. The default option is just to flounder up and down a bit the same as ever. Which is fine but limited since it doesn't lead to any improvement in style or strength. The real answer is a swimming coach, but since these aren't always an option here are some thoughts about how to examine your own swimming, and some exercises you can do to improve it. At the very least they will make a change from the end-to-end plodding.

Break it down

Whether your favourite stroke is front crawl, back crawl, breaststroke or butterfly it has both an arm action and a leg action. Coordinating both actions was one of the hurdles you had to overcome when you first learnt that stroke but now if you want to get better you're going to have to get uncoordinated, just for the moment. Swimming is a fairly complex set of movements and rhythms and it sometimes helps to break them down in order to focus on individual elements. Here we're going to focus on just the arm, and then just the leg movements in isolation.

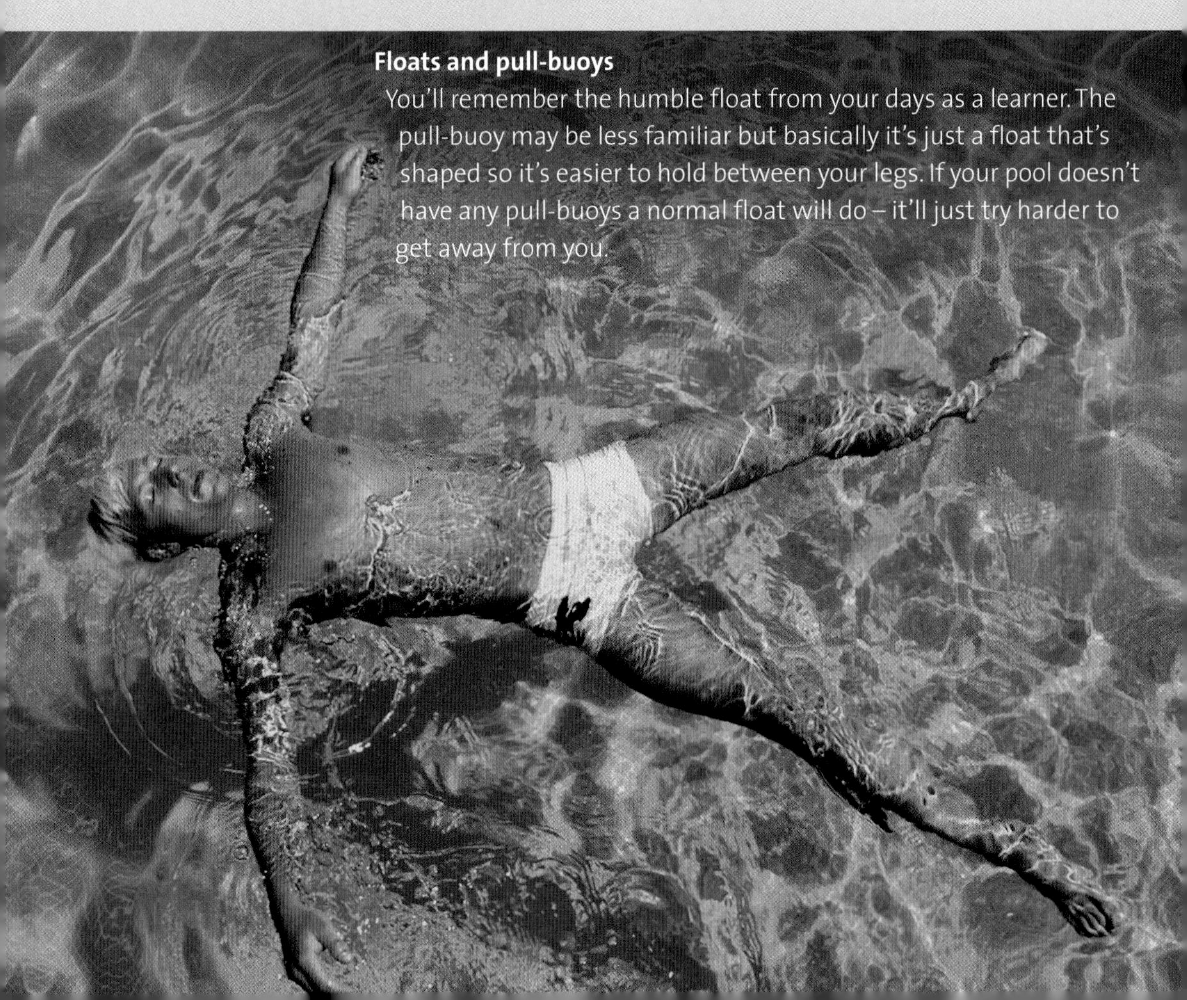

Floats and pull-buoys

You'll remember the humble float from your days as a learner. The pull-buoy may be less familiar but basically it's just a float that's shaped so it's easier to hold between your legs. If your pool doesn't have any pull-buoys a normal float will do – it'll just try harder to get away from you.

Legs

Scissors kick, butterfly kick or frog leg strokes should all be enough on their own to propel you from one end of the pool to the other. Grab a float, hold it out in front of you with both hands and use only your legs to swim.

Arms

As with legs, only in reverse. Lodge a pull buoy or a float (you may need two depending on your natural buoyancy or lack of it) between your thighs. Now set off up the pool using only your arm stroke.

In both of these cases the aim is not to be fast, but to be comfortable. If you are tired after a length, then you may want to work on putting less effort into the stroke, and instead getting more out by means of better form.

Forming hippo herds in the shallows, or avoiding the pool altogether?

Here's an idea for you

As you focus more on making your stroke efficient it becomes time to take up a new sport – stroke golf. Swim a length and count the number of strokes it takes you to complete it. Now using what you've learnt from swimming with arms or legs only try to swim the length using fewer strokes. See how far you can bring down your score by concentrating on getting the most progress out of the fewest number of strokes.

30
2
4
6
8
10
32
34
36
38
40
15
3
6
9
12

17. Timesaving tips

Maximize your workout time

Too pressed for time to have time for presses? Try a few of these tips to maximise those fleeting moments in the gym.

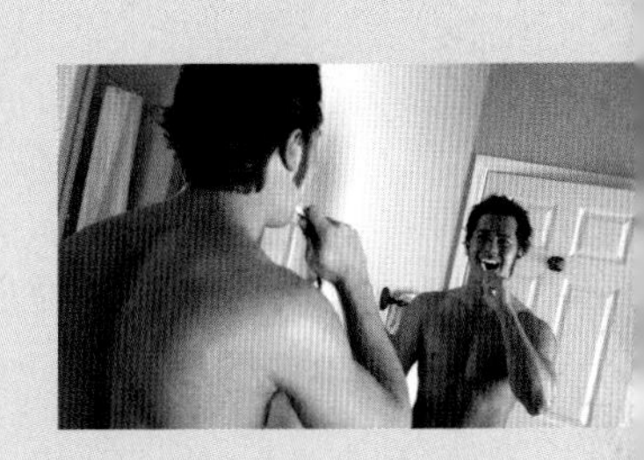

Modern life is hectic, no one has enough time, there are a gazillion things demanding your attention and since fitness isn't your profession or your first love it's the gym time that ends up suffering.

This is only natural. We're all forever promising ourselves that we'll do an extra long session next time just as soon as we've finished with this budget/school holiday/international arms deal. Little and often, however, is a much better way to exercise than sporadic blitzing. For a start it means you're less likely to half-cripple yourself by launching an under-prepared body into an overambitious workout. It's also easier mentally to keep up the momentum and the feel-good factor, not least since mega sessions with long gaps in between quickly become daunting and may lead eventually to cancelled gym memberships. Little and often makes it easier to monitor progress – a motivational bonus – plus frequent short spells in the gym will do more to raise your metabolism on a daily basis than a once-a-fortnight gut-wrenching osteopath special.

So how can you make sure you get a decent workout when you only have a few precious minutes to dedicate to the temple of toning?

Try the following:

Have your kit ready, packed up, and by the door
Einstein used to line up seven sets of clothes on the hangers each week so he never wasted precious brainpower deciding what to wear or trying to find it. Take his lead. When you pull stuff out of the dryer, match it up into complete sets of kit, then make sure you have a gym bag ready to go for every day. Leave it sitting by the door like a patient dog hoping to go walkies and it will be both convenient to grab and a helpful reminder to your conscience.

Plan your workout, work your plan
Nobody has enough time at the gym so who are all those people wandering around from cardio room to weights and back? Be clear in advance what your workout goals are. Don't fix on a single machine – it may be in use – but decide in advance how much cardio you're going to do or what weight session you have in mind.

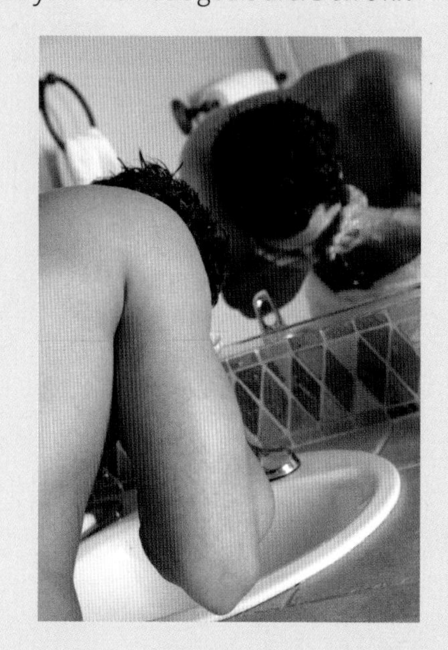

Try going early
What? Like in the morning? Working out before the day gets its claws into you means you start out feeling good and get your metabolism up and running. There are also fewer people and it's hard not to feel virtuous which makes it more likely you'll be back for more tomorrow.

Train with your beloved/kids/mates
Don't force fitness to compete with friendships and lovelife – it will come a sad second and if it doesn't you will become a sad individual. See if you can mix gym/social life by training with friends and family.

This may mean thinking a little laterally. You may have trouble getting your spouse to show up to an abs class, for example, but swap it for something more fun like a core class and you can frolic with the whole family.

...if you're doing weights rest at least 30 seconds in between sets.

Don't rest, cross-train

Your gym tells you to spend no more than 20 minutes on a machine? Fine, just leap straight off it and onto another one. Take ten on each if you like. Forty minutes working on a mix of rower/treadmill/bike will give you a more thorough workout than the same time spent plodding away at the same machine. It uses different muscles and psychologically allows you to put more effort because you know you're changing soon.

Don't rest, superset

Normal practice if you're doing weights is to rest at least 30 seconds in between sets. Well don't. Instead switch straight to an exercise that works the opposite set of muscles and cut to and fro between the two with no rest time at all. For example, if you're working biceps, then alternate with a triceps press. Pair chest press exercises with lateral pull downs. Hamstrings with quads, etc.

Here's an idea for you

We spend half our time in the weights room waiting for someone else to get off the machine we want. Meanwhile there's a rack of dumbbells sitting unused in front of a mirror somewhere. Learn the range of dumbbell exercises and you'll be able to get a whole upper-body workout without moving from the spot, or doing the gym 'excuse-me' mamba around the machines.

18. Getting smart with dumbbells for your upper body

There's more to dumbbells than biceps curls. Combined with some simple accessories, like a bench and your body, they offer one of the simplest and most effective workouts. Plus there's never a queue for them.

Dumbbells have a bad name from years of association with muscle-bound freaks doing endless biceps curls.

What's easily forgotten is that they offer more range of movement than any other weights apparatus (you try waving a barbell over your head with one hand) and are also great for chest, abs, legs and back. What's more I can virtually guarantee that you'll never have to queue for them. If one set of dumbbells is in use, there's bound to be another pair of a different weight that you can use for another exercise in your extensive dumbbell repertoire. You don't have a repertoire of dumbbell moves? Then read on.

All of these moves are best done in front of a mirror. Primarily this is to watch for good form but we all know that it's really so you can admire your fab new muscle vest.

Arms

It would be churlish not to mention the biceps curl so – just as a reminder – stand feet shoulder-width apart, don't move your shoulder, and keep the smooth control on both lift and descent. For a bit of variety try a hammer grip in which you hold the dumbbell so it's vertical in your hand at the top of the lift, as if hefting a hammer.

If you have a bench to hand, then sit on it facing the mirror and rest your right elbow on your right inner thigh just behind the knee. Now you should have completely isolated the biceps during the movement with no shoulder involvement at all.

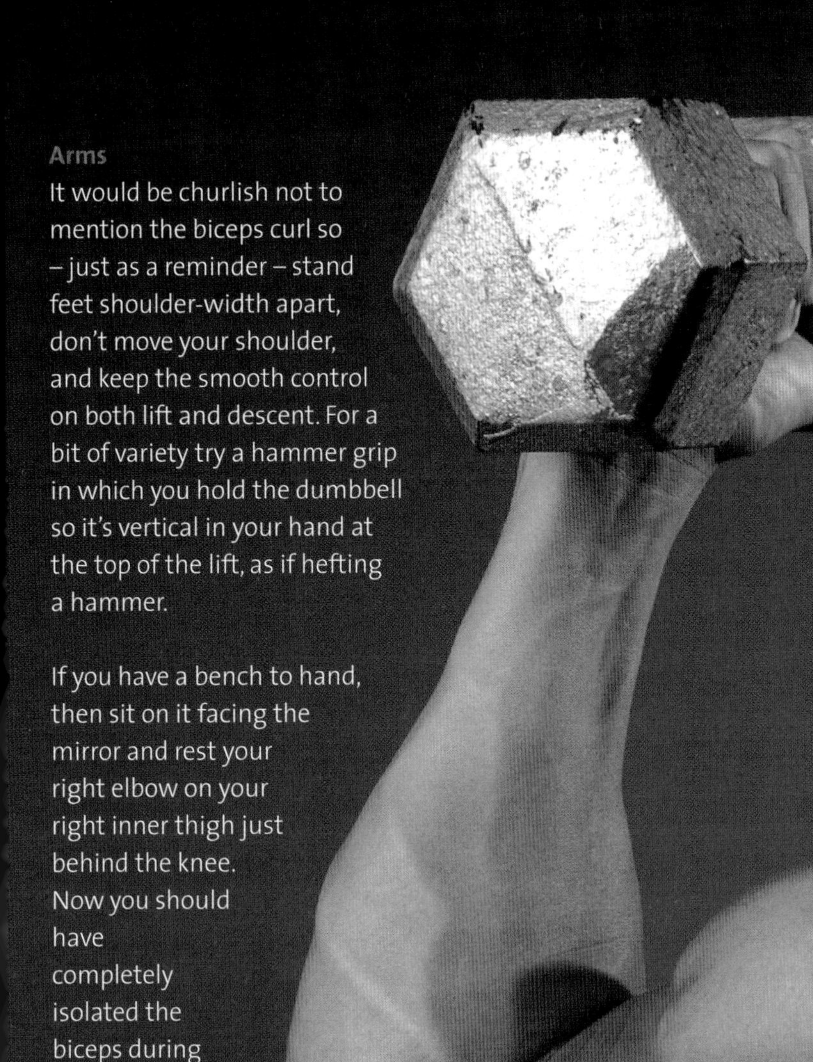

Triceps time. Standing up, hold the dumbbell in one hand, straighten your arm above you and then gently bend your elbow so the weight comes to rest just behind your neck. Now, without moving anything but your forearm at the elbow, straighten and relax the arm to work the triceps.

Remember that bench? Great, if you have a bench then keep your left leg on the floor and put your right knee on the bench. Lean forward and grip the bench with your right arm. With the dumbbell in your left hand, pull your elbow up so your upper arm is parallel to the floor. Now extend your forearm out straight behind you and back to work those tris.

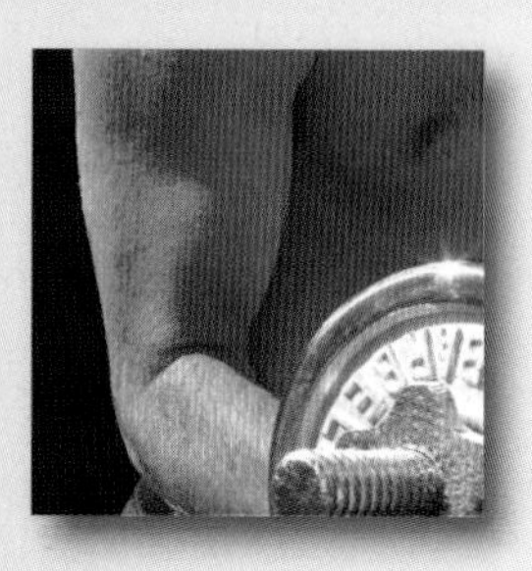

Shoulders

Dumbbells really are the thing when it comes to the deltoids in the shoulders. With a light weight in each hand, stand with feet shoulder-width apart and knees slightly bent and arms by sides. Now lift both arms out straight up to shoulder height. Relax and lift again but this time with arms straight up to the front so you end up in the classic 'sleepwalker' position. Repeat. Lots.

Chest

Try the close-grip bench press – Take a dumbbell in each hand and lie on the bench. Extend both arms straight up above your chest. Lower the weights with your elbows sliding past your sides and stop before the dumbbells reach your chest. Repeat.

Chest fly – Using a lighter pair of dumbbells than those you used for the above exercise, lie on the bench with the weights extended straight up over your chest. Now bend your elbows slightly (and keep them bent) and lower the dumbbells out and to the sides so your arms are out sideways like someone throwing the shutters open in the morning. Bring the dumbbells down until your upper arms are parallel to the floor – don't take it down any further as it will stress the connecting tissue in the front of your shoulders. Smoothly return to start position. Repeat.

Take a dumbbell in each hand and lie on the bench.

Back Reverse fly – Effectively this is the fly move for the chest but flipped over so you're face down. Start face down on the bench with the dumbbells hanging down, then, keeping your arms lightly bent, pull your shoulder blades together and lift the arms out wide to each side. Keep the movement slow and return back to the start position. Don't let the weights drop onto the floor or be tempted to drop your arms suddenly after reaching the top of the lift.

Here's an idea for you

Enjoying the weights work and want to get a bit fancy? Most of these moves can be done swapping the bench for the Swiss ball to add a little imbalance to the move and bring the core muscles of the midsection into the action. Don't be tempted to start off with overly heavy dumbbells though, as you will look a right muppet if you overbalance and fall off the ball spilling dumbbells in all directions.

19. Getting smart with dumbbells for your lower body

Dumbbells aren't just for arms. Here's how hand-held weights can work your thighs, hamstrings, calves and buttocks.

Those looking to work their lower bodies rarely give the dumbbells a thought, but you don't need huge weights to work the larger muscles, just good technique and some dumbbells.

Saunter over to the dumbbell rack, make sure you have a bench nearby and take the time to check yourself out in the mirror. By concentrating on smaller weights and better form you are about to work out and reduce your risk of injury.

Squats

It's not a pretty name for an exercise which should lead to leggy perfection, but it does sum up the move so precisely that it would take a good marketing team to rename it.

Go too low and you risk overextending and straining your muscles.

Here's an idea for you

Looking for a bit of variety in your lunges? Try the Bulgarian split. Drag a bench over and position it behind you. Now when you stand with your knees slightly bent and feet shoulder-width apart, stretch your rear leg out so you can rest the top of your foot on the bench behind you instead of placing it on the floor as you normally would. Now lower your body as normal in to the lunge and straighten up again. Use a very light weight, or no weight at all, when you first try this as you'll feel a stretch down your quads that will make normal lunges feel like child's play.

To hit your hip flexors try a sideways lunge. Start in the usual position but with lighter than usual weights (at least until you're used to the exercise) then take a very big step sideways as far as you can reach. Lower yourself by bending the leg that stepped out, keeping your knee moving in the same line as the foot. Smoothly straighten your knee to bring you back, and then step back to the start position.

Start with two dumbbells (you can go fairly heavy on this one), one in each hand, at your sides, your feet shoulder-width apart, knees very slightly bent. The point of dumbbell squats is not to imitate Russian weightlifters so keep the whole movement smooth and controlled. No bouncing. No grunting.

With your shoulders pulled back, bend your knees and ease your body down as if you were slipping into a comfy chair.

Don't go so far down that either your knees move further forward, then your toes, or your bum is so low that your thighs dip down instead of being parallel to the floor. Go too low and you risk overextending and straining your muscles. Smoothly raise yourself back up to the start position.

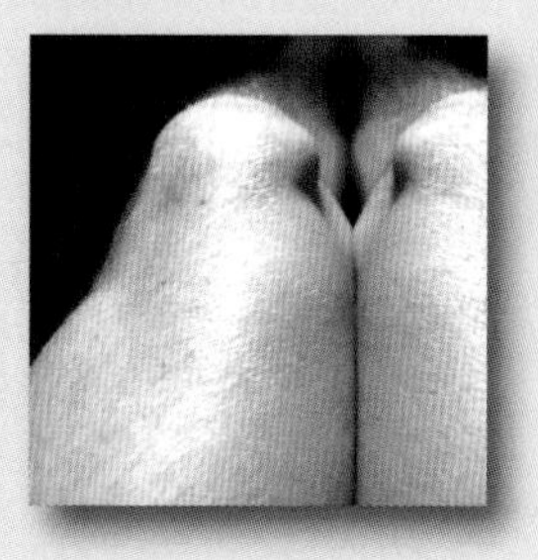

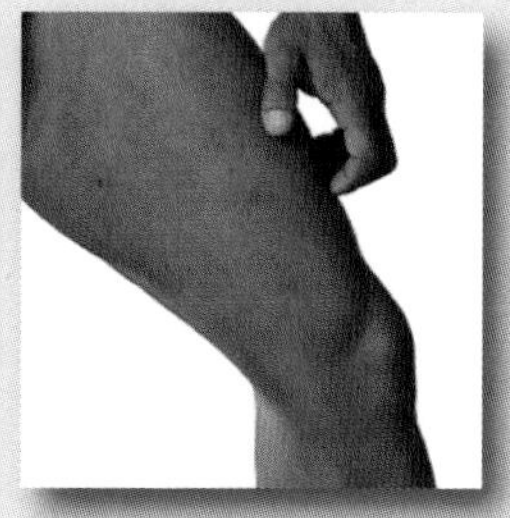

Taking the lunge

Start as with the squat, but this time take a long step forward so your front foot is now about a yard from your back one. Keeping your torso bolt upright, lower your body by bending your legs. Your front knee shouldn't go past your toes (this is a sensible precaution for most exercises or stretches where you bend your knees). Even though you may feel a burning sensation down the length of your back leg it's the muscles of the front thigh that should be doing the work as you now lift your body back up by straightening the front leg.

For a bit of variety, and to hit the calf muscles a little more, try to switch from forward lunges, where you step forwards with one leg before lunging, and backward lunges, where you, erm, step backwards with one leg before lunging.

20. This time it's personal

The benefits of a personal trainer

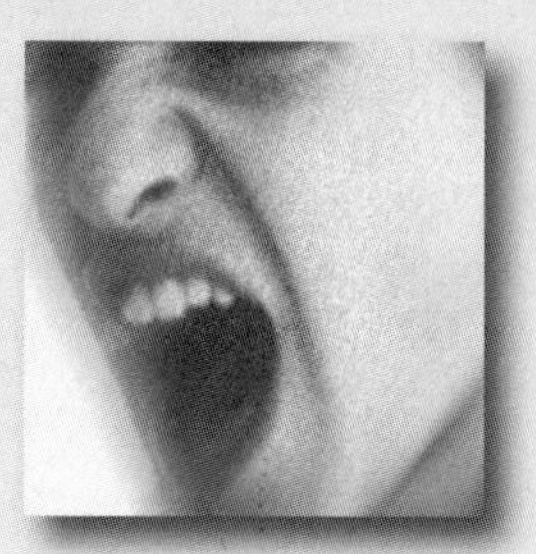

Personal trainers – fashion accessory for the cash-rich and time poor? Or failsafe route to fitness?

Most gyms these days offer personal training as part of their portfolio and probably promote it with all the zeal of timeshare salespeople.

At some point you will consider it, if not now, then later when you hit a motivation or performance plateau that you don't know how to get over. So what will you get for your money? And how can you decide if a personal trainer is for you?

Let's be clear about what a personal trainer means. We're not talking about having someone knock up a tailored training routine for you when you first start – all gyms should do that as a matter of course. Personal trainers will dedicate themselves to you and you alone for each hour that you book. They should assess your fitness level, set up a programme complete with goals and waypoints, and provide the motivation to achieve them.

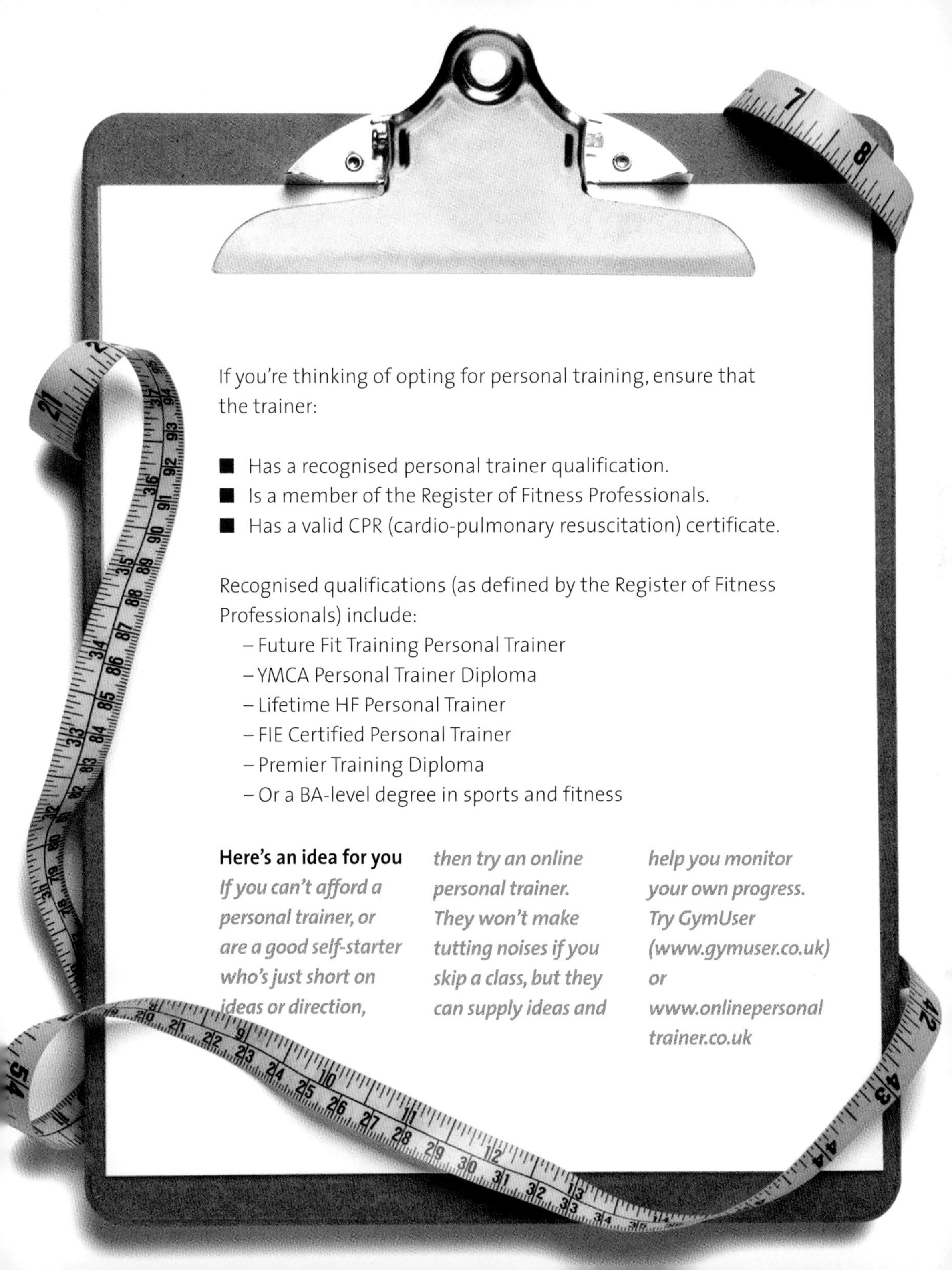

If you're thinking of opting for personal training, ensure that the trainer:

- Has a recognised personal trainer qualification.
- Is a member of the Register of Fitness Professionals.
- Has a valid CPR (cardio-pulmonary resuscitation) certificate.

Recognised qualifications (as defined by the Register of Fitness Professionals) include:

- Future Fit Training Personal Trainer
- YMCA Personal Trainer Diploma
- Lifetime HF Personal Trainer
- FIE Certified Personal Trainer
- Premier Training Diploma
- Or a BA-level degree in sports and fitness

Here's an idea for you

If you can't afford a personal trainer, or are a good self-starter who's just short on ideas or direction, then try an online personal trainer. They won't make tutting noises if you skip a class, but they can supply ideas and help you monitor your own progress. Try GymUser (www.gymuser.co.uk) or www.onlinepersonaltrainer.co.uk

Why would you pay the extra?

Given what you're already forking out for the gym, why would you pay extra for a personal trainer? If you have a clear idea of your fitness targets, the knowledge of how to hit them and a high level of self-motivation, then the honest answer is that you don't need a trainer. If, however, you find that motivation is a big problem, or you have an unusual target (say a new sport), or you're going nowhere and don't know what to try, then a personal trainer could be exactly what the doctor ordered.

What can I expect?

Depends entirely on what your agreed goals are. If your aim is to lose weight and tone up, then you can expect to start off with a cardio warm-up before going onto weights and moves that you wouldn't normally do.

In the process you will learn a lot about form, posture, technique and the use of different pieces of equipment. It also makes the gym session an appointment, a commitment that you can't back out of, and introduces the trainer as a kind of external conscience nagging you if you let things slip. Sort of like Jiminy Cricket in tracksuit bottoms.

Your aim is to lose weight and tone up...

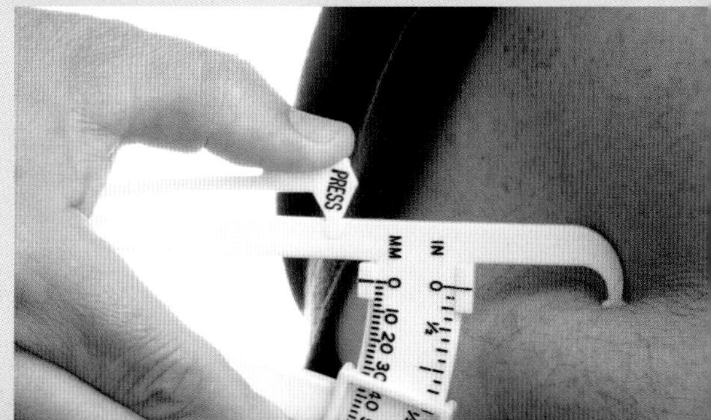

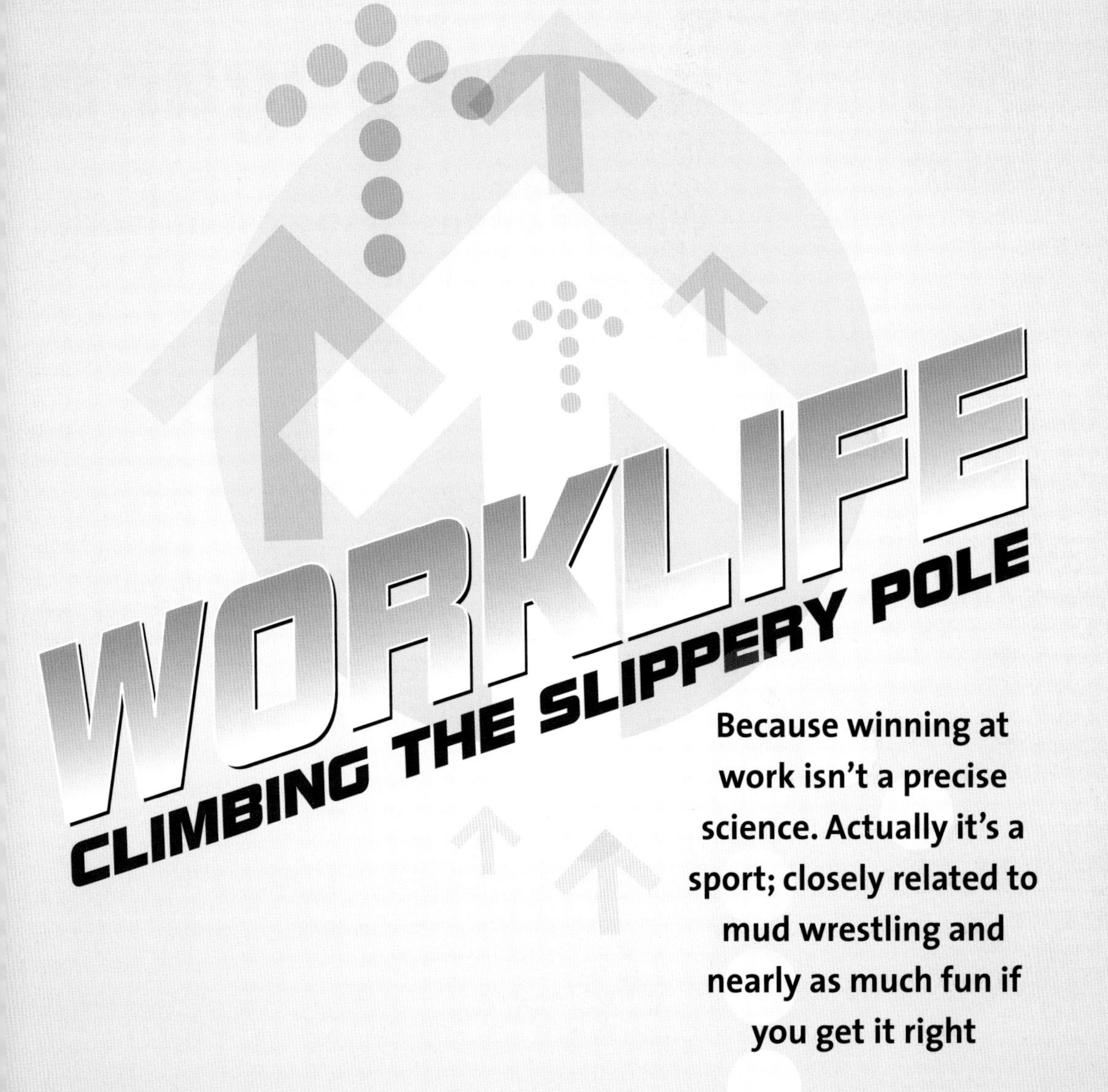

WORKLIFE

CLIMBING THE SLIPPERY POLE

Because winning at work isn't a precise science. Actually it's a sport; closely related to mud wrestling and nearly as much fun if you get it right

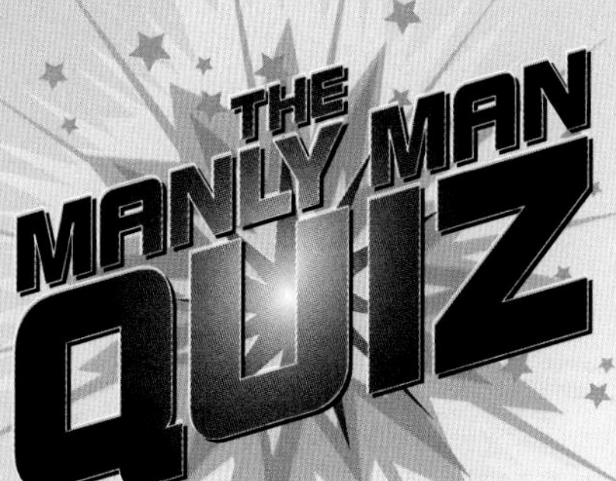

Alan Sugar or

When it comes to success at work, which one are you?

Office politics are:

1. For winners

2. For losers

3. For people stupid enough to go into the office

If someone asks you what you do for a living, do you

1. Feel happy at the chance to talk about your job?

2. Get that familiar sinking feeling?

3. Find someone else to talk to?

Your work philosophy is:

1. Don't work hard, work smart

2. Put the hours in and keep your head down

3. These burgers don't flip themselves you know

Homer Simpson?

Mainly 1s: You're a player, you know that the system is there to be used and if you read on you will find some tips you hadn't thought of.

Mainly 2s: Be honest, when you were a child did you play at being a 'middle manager'. Thought not; so find out how to sharpen your game and get out of that rut.

Mainly 3s: For you being in a rut would actually be a step up. Being too cool for school only works while you're still young enough to look good in surfer shorts. When those days are done you'll find that you either you win at work or you end up working for losers.

21. Playing politics – and winning

Show us someone who says they're not interested in office politics and we'll show you someone who's not going up the organisation as far as their talent deserves.

Good office politicians keep the competition, their management and colleagues on the back foot by never accepting the existing organisation as it is. Two great ways to win here – abolish your job and/or create a completely new one.

Promotions never come as fast as the average person wants. The organisation settles down, your boss is comfortable with your performance but has no intention of promoting you because, you know, they'll have to find a replacement. And they certainly don't want you to get their job.

The time has come for you to play some office politics and make that new job happen. After all, you need to do more than survive in this area.

Job description, what job description?

One of the things you can do is to make your job redundant. This may seem a risky process, but it's a great mistake in career planning to assume that the current management structure is the one in which you have to succeed. Indeed, the opposite is often the case – and you'll probably get away with it.

Here's the reasoning. Many jobs exist because they have always done so, rather than because they represent the best way of getting things done successfully. If you go into a new job and do it the best way for your organisation to succeed, you'll probably find yourself going way outside the original job description. So, your way of operating gets better results. Now delegate as much of the job as you can in your new way of working, and guess what?

When you explain what has happened to your boss, he or she will realise that they need to change the structure of their operation. If you've done this ploy well, they'll also realise that your tasks are now handled much more efficiently and they don't need you in your old role. You've got away with it. Time to move onwards and upwards.

Here's an idea for you

Look around at how you and your colleagues work. Now ask yourself this question: 'If I owned this business, what changes would I make to my part of the organisation to make a big improvement?' This should give you loads of ammunition to put up a paper that suggests the changes which sensibly should be made. Now you're off and running towards inventing and then taking the new job that you really want.

The fundamental lesson here is to use your influence and authority to get the best results possible without paying much attention to how things were done in the past.

Oh, the obvious person for the job seems to be me

The corollary of abolishing your job, namely inventing a new one, also holds true. People who succeed are the ones who help the organisation keep up to date and help to prevent it ossifying.

It is easier to create a new job if the change helps the organisation achieve better performance, but it's possible to do it for your own purposes alone. Probably started by putting up an unsolicited paper, the creation of a new job is in two parts. First describe the new way of doing business that will ensure that the job of your dreams is going to exist. Then sell the idea. What you're doing here is showing

...use your influence and authority to get the best results possible...

what your new plan will do in business terms rather than in structural or people terms. Don't reveal your whole hand at this stage because it's too early. Don't give anyone the opportunity to say that what you're doing is for your own greater glory rather than the advancement of the organisation. Having sold the change, produce your implementation plan and, of course, include the new positions required.

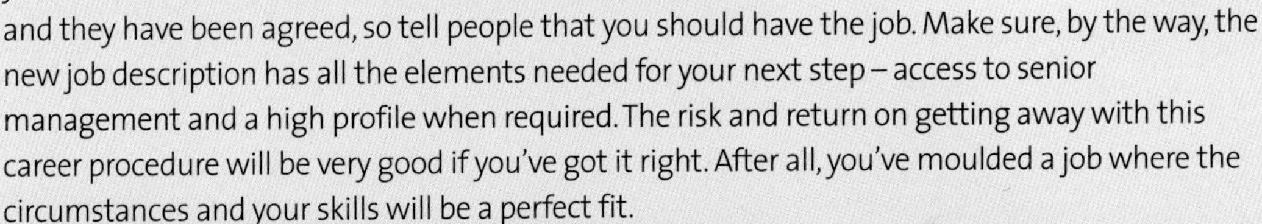

Next, it's time to go for it. Do not at this stage play any kind of shrinking violet game; clearly show that you are the person for the promoted role you've chosen and defined. You have the business benefits behind you and they have been agreed, so tell people that you should have the job. Make sure, by the way, the new job description has all the elements needed for your next step – access to senior management and a high profile when required. The risk and return on getting away with this career procedure will be very good if you've got it right. After all, you've moulded a job where the circumstances and your skills will be a perfect fit.

22. Passing an exam without revising

Spending hours and hours studying, wasting your life – social life at that – all for a piece of paper seems ludicrous, doesn't it? Well perhaps you don't have to.

Studying is, at the best of times, an exceptionally dull process. We use so little of what we retain in the real world that it hardly seems worth all the effort. The reality is, of course, we have no choice, unless we fancy ending up on the bap heap, at the bottom of the economic pile, flipping burgers for below-subsistence wages.

Why on earth do they make us study during the summer? When it's hot and sunny all you want to do is chase the opposite sex and frolic in the hay; the last thing on your mind is that all-important exam you have to prepare for. Perhaps it's a government-imposed mechanism for avoiding teen pregnancies. Or maybe it's the sadists in the exam system who want to make your life a misery. (We favour the latter.) So you find yourself in a bit of a bind. On one hand you know you have got to do at least the bare minimum to pass your exams; on the other, you want to escape the thin air of your bedroom. So what can you do to maximise the amount of time you get to play and ensure you do okay in the exams? Well, with the judicious use of a handful of techniques and tools you ought to satisfy your desires while still passing your exams. Of course, the balance you choose to place on both is entirely up to you!

Here's an idea for you

Make a list of the exam techniques you can think of and decide which ones could offer you the greatest return for the least amount of effort. Certainly give question spotting a go – although it's a bit high-risk, so is doing nothing. Once you have got your list, give each technique a try and focus on a small subset that allows you to maximise your frolicking.

Some of the best revision reducers (as we like to call them) include:

- Subliminal learning – who needs books when you can have a few tapes with the key facts on them? After a day's lazing around in the sun, all you have to do is lie on your bed, pop on the Walkman and let your subconscious brain do the work. How's about that for an approach!?

- Use study aids – why reinvent the wheel when you can draw on all the advice and support you need from the experts? A lot of what you need to know for the exam can be condensed into a few pages of text contained within a study guide you can buy for a few pounds.

- Time management – if you can focus your efforts into a couple of hours a day, and we do mean focus here, then you can maximise the time you have for fun. It requires the self-discipline of a self-flagellant but without the scarring.

- Buy some time from someone else – if you are one of these lucky people who have plenty of cash or rich parents who would rather throw money at a problem than deal with it directly, then you are in luck. There are plenty of people out there who will prostitute themselves to get you through the exams: teachers, failed academics and smart-arses desperate for cash. Passing the buck to someone who knows the system is a sure-fire way to reduce the amount of time you need to be spending on revising.

- Tune in to your natural way of learning – yes, we all have preferences, and sadly most of us are oblivious to them. You can waste literally weeks trying to get stuff into your skull to no avail. The simple reason why you fail is that you may have completely missed the way your brain prefers to learn. To absorb as much information as possible, as effortlessly as possible, means that you have to get to the root of how you learn, be it in pictures, words or feelings.

So there you have it, a collection of smart ways you can try out to limit the amount of study time. Don't get too carried away, though. This doesn't mean you can do nothing at all. And remember that spending too much time out in the sun shrivels your skin and gives you cancer, so maybe study is good for you after all.

AUGUST
SEPTEMBER
OCTOBER
NOVEMBER
DECEMBER

SUNDAY

MONDAY

TUESDAY

4

5

6

12

13

23. Missing a deadline

From school until retirement, we spend our lives struggling to hit deadlines. And all too often we miss. Missing with panache is the route to a more contented existence.

Think about it: many of us will be repeatedly missing deadlines for well over half a century. There are only two ways to deal with the situation: do everything on time or try and get away with being late. If you want to achieve the former, take a time management course. Oh, and abandon your plans for the weekend, because you'll be working. If you want to get away with it, read on.

Like the other unsustainable lies we tell ('the cheque's in the post', 'she's just a friend' and 'I was going to pay for it officer, I've no idea how it got into my pocket'), 'I'm just finishing it now, I should have it on your desk by the end of the day' is little more than a delaying tactic. It exists to give us breathing space, but it can't change reality. You are no more likely to get the report on the desk tonight than you are to don a tutu and dance on that desk. The stark truth is this: you will miss your deadline.

Once you have accepted this, there are two tasks you have to achieve: keeping your boss off your back until you do deliver and the creation of an environment that means you will get away with the repercussions of your tardiness.

...when the blame is handed out, losers catch it and winners don't.

Succeeding in these tasks grooms you for higher office. We all miss deadlines; it's just that when the blame is handed out, losers catch it and winners don't. Execute the skills below effectively and one day you may be senior enough to set deadlines for other people. At this point, a good understanding of what their excuses are likely to be when they miss those deadlines will be your secret weapon.

When missing deadlines, thorough preparatory work is vital. If you intend to be late, put in a flurry of activity – or what passes for it – as early as possible. Requests for clarification of the brief; regular status reports to people who don't need to know; well-thumbed, clearly labelled files of relevant documents in your in-tray all show that you mean business, while you pop out to the cinema or get away early.

Closer to deadline time, don't hide. You can finesse a few extra days simply by subtly nudging the deadline in casual conversations that you initiate. 'I should have it Wednesday, or Thursday morning at the latest' is followed the next day by 'No problem with Thursday as a delivery day', which commits you to Thursday 5 p.m. With a little effort, you can shunt the delivery into Friday, and once you get to Friday lunchtime, no one expects it until Monday. This very effective way of missing deadlines is known as 'managing expectations'.

Use third parties as fall guys. This relies on what is known as 'workflow', which is defined as 'The ability of other people missing deadlines to make you miss yours'. Don't pretend you don't actually have the information they are supplying, because then someone might check. Instead pretend that you need more time, because you only just got it.

Unexpect the expected. If you know in advance you will be stuck in the usual two-hour traffic queue, keep it to yourself, and then call from the car to say that for some reason you are in a two-hour traffic queue, which is a shame because it means you won't be able to finish the project today. The same goes for meetings that predictably over-run, and if you have to cover for people when you knew for weeks they would be out of the office. Practise being sorrowful and surprised. Shrug a bit. Shake your head. Who knew?

Finally, make office alliances. If several of you have to meet the same deadline, make a pact that you are all going to miss it by the same margin. It adds credibility to all the above tactics if you all use them. This also gives you an opportunity: if you agree with your, erm, mates that you will all be three days late, be two days late. It'll seem like you are one day early.

Here's an idea for you

Use these deadline-missing excuses when you're not running late, then surprise everyone with a punctual delivery. It means you get a chance to hone your skills in a no-risk situation, and the mild disappointment that your boss feels when you announce you will be late is eclipsed many times over by the delight they feel when you are on time.

24. I think I'm coming down with something

When you're going to skive off by pretending you aren't well, there are some dos and don'ts to ensure you get sympathy, not the sack. Malinger with merit.

Occasionally in our working lives, we need to push on, buck up, be strong and go to work when we don't feel like it because we are 'can do' people. Tips for how to do that are in a different book, because it's statistically more likely that you are a 'can't do' person, and in this situation you'll need to know how to convincingly fake an illness – or how to 'throw a sickie'.

People have been throwing sickies ever since there were difficult jobs that needed to be done which other people could do for you. As soon as the alpha male in primitive society developed the language to say, 'Let's go hunting, there's a mammoth out there with really sharp tusks,' the beta male developed words for 'You go ahead, I think I'm coming down with a bit of a sniffle'.

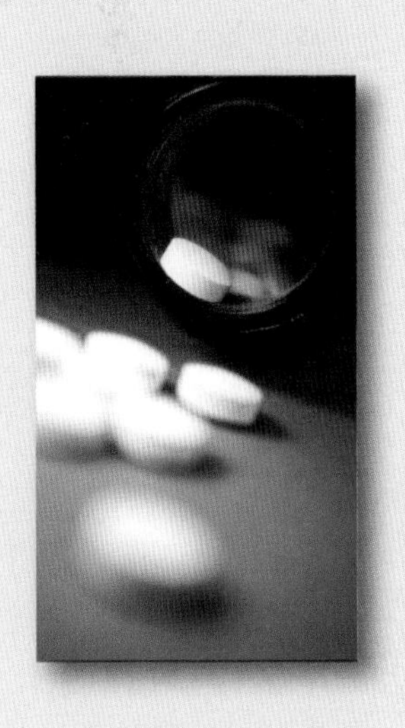

Despite having generations of previously unwritten knowledge to fall back on, the modern worker – that's you – has not learned many of the principles of throwing a sickie, resulting in some poor performances. This is one aspect of your job that you simply have

Here's an idea for you

Get in touch with your feelings and don't over-complicate your calls with fancy words. Describe the symptoms that you should be feeling instead of calling in with the name of your supposed condition. Compare 'I just can't stop vomiting ... oh dear, here it comes again ...' with the more usual 'I think I have gastric flu'. Say the first, and no one wants you in the same county. Say the second, and we instinctively assume you are lying.

Don't speak or drink in the morning before you make the call...

to excel at if you want to get on. If you are unconvincing, your boss may fire you and your colleagues will hate you. After all, they get to do the work you are avoiding.

If you only remember one piece of advice, it should be this: keep it simple. We learn from television shows that some rare diseases are very spectacular and complicated. Doctors spend years learning about them, and the five minutes you spent looking up the symptoms on the Internet are no substitute. Use illnesses with which you are familiar. When friends, relatives and loved ones are sick, look on the bright side: when they are better, you will be able to copy their symptoms and get a few days off as well.

When reporting in for your sickie, do the job yourself. A handy tip is not to speak or drink in the morning before you make the call, especially if you smoke. Your huskiness will be mistaken for laryngitis. Also, make the call from a quiet place. The following are not recommended in this category: train stations, rock concerts, bars. Except when trying to cut the call short (see below) don't put on an act. Ill people play down their symptoms, because they are too ill to make a fuss.

On the other hand, don't undersell your sickness. A common mistake is calling in with something serious because you missed your train or you have a job interview. One hour later, you arrive at the office miraculously cured. A good rule of thumb is that illnesses should last two days, injuries at least one – though don't forget to limp for at least two days afterwards.

This raises the final point that separates the amateurs from the professionals. It is highly recommended that you assemble supporting evidence and stay in character. A doctor's certificate may be hard to obtain unless your problem is one of the classic untreatables (think backache), but a spousal alibi is excellent. If your significant other can call later in the day to report that your temperature is still high, you're sleeping now but she thought it was best if everyone knew, you are both acting responsibly.

Ultimately, it's not hard to throw a sickie in the short term. It is harder to throw them convincingly over a period of months or years. Think of this strategically: cycle your ailments, keep a log, recruit friends to support your arguments. And keep watching those hospital TV shows for your raw material: every actor who plays a patient in them is throwing a sickie. If they can, you can.

25. Doing nothing at work – bosses

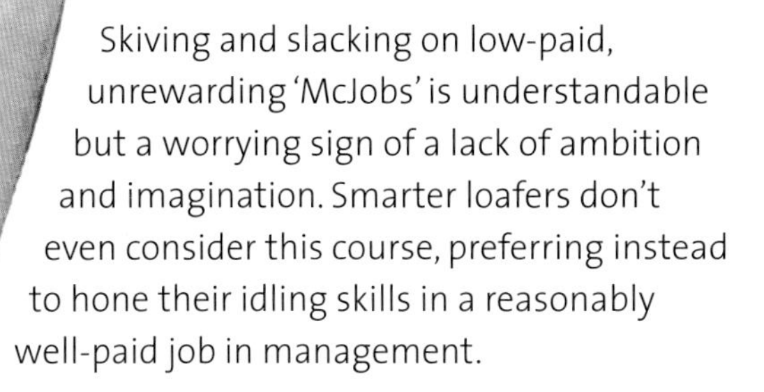

Like the muddy tropical river to the hippo, or the lush rainforest to the sloth, middle management is the natural environment of choice for the serious slacker.

Skiving and slacking on low-paid, unrewarding 'McJobs' is understandable but a worrying sign of a lack of ambition and imagination. Smarter loafers don't even consider this course, preferring instead to hone their idling skills in a reasonably well-paid job in management.

A survey by Investors in People recently found that 84% of workers in organisations with more than 1,000 employees thought they had a lazy colleague. That compared with only 50% in companies with fewer than fifty staff. There are many ways of explaining that figure, including the fact that smaller companies inspire more loyalty and have fewer places to hide. More precisely, it probably comes down to the simple truth that small companies don't have middle management.

Here's an idea for you

To really make the grade as a slacker boss, you will need a 'treasure' – an assistant who actually does some of the things you should do, keeps your boss at bay and also enjoys an excellent work environment. In many companies the treasure is so well respected that other managers eventually don't bother approaching the slacker (that's you) at all. Tread carefully, though, because lots of slackers are rumbled and the ones that lose their jobs are those who have lost the trust of their treasure. Fail to ensure your treasure gets what they need, or start to act Ab Fab, sweetie, and you're on a hiding to hard work.

...the team does the work, you do the loafing.

In France there was an outrage over Corinne Maier's book *Hello Laziness* (Bonjour Paresse) and its subtitle, *The Art and the Importance of Doing the Least Possible in the Workplace*. Ms Maier's main point was that most 'work' is pointless posturing, politics and meeting mania and so the only real response was to go with the flow and do the least possible. To your savvy slacker, this will have been very old news. Maier's suggestion that the best rewards come from 'the most useless sort of job ... consultant, expert, or adviser' might make a couple of consultants feel uneasy but hardly come as a shock to anyone who has ever set foot in any company big enough to have an atrium. So how do you get yourself into this skiving sweet spot? Simple. You're going to need two main things: charm and a team of other people to do the work for you.

Really top-notch loafing requires teamwork: the team does the work, you do the loafing. The key to that is making sure that the people who actually work closest to you see that it's in their interest to protect you. To do that you're going to have to weave that magic charm on them, let them know you're on their side, and that you have the key to their future happiness. If you don't have a hope in hell of pulling that one off, then it's equally effective (though harder to achieve) to let them know that you have the key to their very best skeleton closets. Since the best

skeletons tend to be hidden safely beyond the reach of the full-time layabout, then the first option is the best and that means that you will have to put a bit of effort into getting your staff grades, salaries, and perks

above the norm. It may sound like hard work but in the long run you'll be doing yourself a favour. A team in line is half the job done.

Truly accomplished slackers then ensure that they spend a vast amount of time with clients/on the road/etc. to explain their prolonged absence. Be careful about the old 'working from home' ruse – it suggests that there will be evidence of work done, and that is never the object. Team building, client relationships and marketing are much safer bets for spending days out of the building without anyone expecting you to have anything to show for it.

One other word of advice: for every top-drawer loafer, there is a nemesis, usually in the form of an ambitious colleague eager to get on, possibly at your expense. This inspires panic in substandard slackers, who may be galvanised into extreme responses, even including doing some work. Don't fall into this trap. The fact is that the average ambitious middle manager spends less than two years in the same job so if you've got it sweet then don't move on and start again; instead, sit tight and look to your team, not to your new threat.

26. Doing nothing at work – employees

For run-of-the-mill workers, the key to loafing is to create an illusion of purpose and industry that deflects the scrutiny of superiors.

The late, great Spike Milligan used to tell a tale of his army years, during which one inspired loafer took to wandering around with a tin of DDT (insecticide). If ever anyone challenged him to explain what he was doing he snapped sharply to attention and replied 'de-lousing sir'. Nobody ever enquired further and he would be free to carry on doing precisely nothing in peace.

We're not saying that you should take to schlepping around large containers of poison (although this may still work in the military, prisons, and fast-food outlets) but the key points to this technique are as true today as they ever were. The first is that if you want to spend all day doing sweet Fanny Adams then you'd better have a cover story. The second is that whatever that story is you must be prepared to launch into it with conviction and the kind of enthusiasm that suggests nothing would please you more than to explain it in incomprehensible detail until your interrogator's ears bleed.

Here's an idea for you

Get yourself a key friend in geekdom. Someone savvy on the systems side is needed to tell you crucial info such as whether the company has keystroke monitoring systems to record effort and detect games players. Bunking off to see a systems person is also a universally accepted ploy, even in the future. It's reassuring to note that in the high-tech futuristic vision The Island, Ewan McGregor regularly shouts 'computer down' and slides off to see his mate Steve Buscemi in tech support. Note also that the long-term result of this behaviour is that he gets to hang out on yachts and shack up in a playboy mansion with Scarlett Johannson.

When it comes to a cover story there's nothing like a good prop and we've come a long way from the DDT tin. Today's loafers have at their fingertips an armoury of high-tech tools.

Once the great trick was to always be seen with a clipboard. Clipboards speak volumes about business, importance, and those endless 'jobs' like 'stocktaking' and 'time and motion studies' that were always nothing more than the inventions of loafers looking to do as little as possible before knocking-off time came around again. The trusty clipboard (and its executive brother, the bulging file) can still come in handy but if you really want to get away with it these days it's time to go digital. Digital devices add a whole new dimension to loafing because their very presence intimidates the Luddites and their multi-tasking flexibility makes it hard for even the initiate to call your bluff. Proof positive of this is the evolution of the uber-loafer – the king of the freeloading food chain. Posing as 'systems administrator', 'network engineer' or any one of a dozen similarly meaningless monikers, these geek gods have reached the noodling nirvana where they can face down anybody from line managers to the CEO. This is done with nothing more than a withering look and a sarcastic outpouring of gobbledygeek. A typical example would go as follows:

...there's nothing like a good prop...

Baffled CEO/MD/HR exec: 'So what exactly have you been doing for the last three weeks?'Uber-loafer [sighing at the pathetic inadequacy of the question/questioner]: 'Patching the Unix kernel.' CEO/MD/HR exec [even more baffled]: 'Patching the colonel?' Uber-loafer [with the exaggerated patience normally reserved for small children]: 'Upgrade, protocol, security, TCP/IP, parallel-processing, cluster, hacker, hexadecimal, three-speed, cupcakes ...'' [the final words of which are normally delivered to the back of an already retreating questioner].

You don't have to be an uber-loafer to take a leaf from their book. Even the humblest warehouse worker, if wielding one of those brilliant, handheld data input devices, is in a position of strength because nobody, not even the person who bought them, really knows all the things you might be doing with them. Other examples include Blackberries ('of course I'm not skiving; can't you see I'm emailing?'), laptops ('Fragfest? All-out Hover Tank war? Certainly not; it's a 3D graphic representation of next-year's projected margins'), or any kind of spreadsheet (make sure you can bring up an elaborate diagrammatic representation with a triumphant punch of the button).

27. Blagging that pay rise

While some people seem to have the knack of demanding (and getting) pay rises, the rest of us are left pining hopefully for a beneficent boss to smile on us. Well wait no more.

You haven't had a raise in ages. Problem is the economy is stagnant (isn't it always?) and your boss thinks you're worthless (which, if we're painfully honest, may be true). No matter, a good blagger never lets little things like worthiness get in the way of getting the reward. A good blagger looks beyond the immediate and considers the long term – a lifetime of getting away with it rather than snapping after trifles.

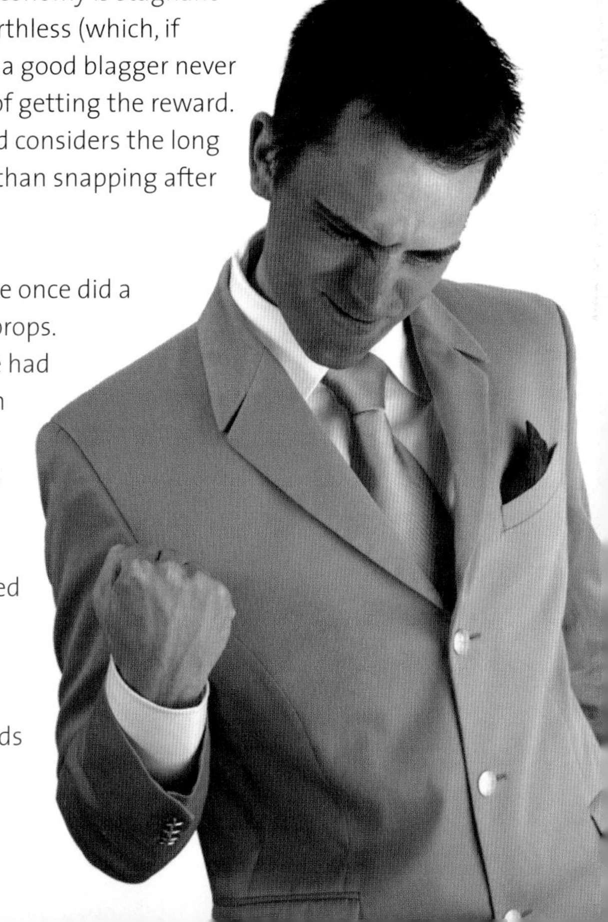

An assistant stage manager working in a theatre once did a bunk with the £100 she had been given to buy props. 'What a mug,' said a more seasoned ASM. 'If she had waited a bit longer she could have gone off with five times that.' So it is in business. It's only the people with no vision who fiddle their expenses for a couple of pints in the pub, or charge for a first-class train fare and sit in second. This is short-sighted in many ways. After all, do you need to impress anybody who sits in standard class?

Keep the big picture in view. Particularly at the start of your career, bear in mind that the rewards

of getting to the top are very substantial. Don't whinge about your early salary. Tell yourself that you are investing for the future. Agree to small or no rises and even no promotions for the first couple of years, then go for the big hike when you have something to argue with. You might be better off doing an extra few months at 20k a year rather than causing grief by bellyaching. The eventual return could be well worth it.

When you are going into a new job make sure that they really want you to join them, and preferably have told other contenders that the job is not theirs, before negotiating the salary. Asking earlier has two disadvantages. First, you may discover that there is a big gap between their expectations and yours. At that time you are negotiating from a position of weakness, since they have not yet decided if they want you. Second, it makes you look a bit petty if the salary is the only reason you're taking the job.

...you can ask for more money at any time.

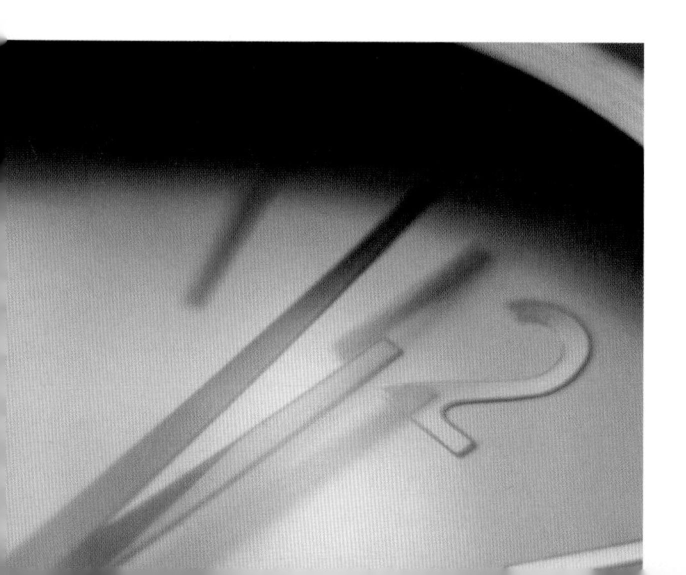

Whatever anyone tells you, you can ask for more money at any time. The key here is timing: ask when your value to the organisation appears very high. Do it when you have just brought off a big deal, or organised the district conference or made a useful suggestion for change. Focus on what you have done and what you will do in the future. Use simple techniques of negotiation like saying 'It's only £10 a week' rather than '... £520 a year'.

The same timing works when you're looking for a promotion. Think, act and look as though you are already in the new job. Seek out, and go after, vacancies. The manager of a small sales team in Scotland heard that the manager of a large team in a higher job category had been promoted. As soon as he heard this he telephoned his boss, whom he knew, and asked for the vacant job. We suspect the boss was simply saving the time and stress of interviewing when he agreed but so what? Job done

Here's an idea for you

Use recruitment agencies, the Internet and the HR department to work out the top and bottom ends of the sort of salary someone in your position gets. For a rough idea start by taking the salary survey at PayWizard (www.paywizard.org/). Now work out why you deserve to be in the top 25% of the band. When you have a good case, take it to your boss. If you are already in the top quartile, look for a promotion.

28. Jumping job when you've been rumbled

Here's how to get another job with a fat-cat salary when in your current job you've done nothing, nada, nix, not a sausage, and until now you've got away with it.

You've got away with it for two years. You're a legend at work; people talk about your continuous inactivity with awe. You've bumped up your 'working at home' days to two and a half a week and you've got a team that covers for you. But, you've been sussed. Your boss has discovered, or more likely been briefed, that you are what you actually are – a complete waste of space. It's time to move on.

We need to make another assumption here: it's much easier to move on in the same organisation than a new one. Where you are, you already know the levers to pull and the buttons to press to avoid work and, more importantly, avoid trouble. It's just not the time to relearn all of that in another place. No, you've got to move on in the same organisation. But you've got to get a new job against the background that the boss you've got right now thinks you're a skiver. And as sure as eggs are eggs, any potential new manager will ask your current boss for his or her opinion of you. However, this is much less of a problem than it seems.

Firing someone is very hard work...

It may surprise you, but your biggest allies in this enforced change of job are the people in the human resources department. 'But', we hear you gasp, 'they're the people who measure productivity, who check progress against objectives and generally are trained to spot skill gaps and non-jobs.' Correct, but they're also the people who make absolutely sure that managers adhere rigidly to dismissal and other personnel processes. That's why they're your best friends right now. Firing someone is very hard work and no managers want to go through the whole bureaucratic rigmarole if they don't have to, and that includes your boss. Think about it from your boss's point of view. The personnel department will dig for evidence. They'll find and brandish your last appraisal where the person who's trying to fire you said such nice things about you and your dedication to the organisation and hard work. They'll make your boss fill in forms, make statements and struggle through a long series of verbal warnings, written warnings, having witnesses at the meetings, offering you the chance to have a witness at the meetings and so forth. No one wants to do this; it's like swimming in treacle or kicking a sponge. Most people will do anything not to have to do it.

You need a reference

OK, you've searched the house magazine and found a new job that's suitable. It's a bit more money (nobody believes that anyone voluntarily moves sideways) but it's not so much that it would make your old boss jealous or even hopping mad. You've gone to the interviews and knocked their socks off. There's only one small cloud on the horizon – the new people are bound to talk to your boss. Answer: get your retaliation in first.

Talk to your boss. You have two objectives. First, help him or her to understand that you're not likely to give up easily if they try to sink you. Make it quite clear that you're not going to go quietly. This one is going to end in court and they're going to have to explain to a lot of people why they didn't realise that you've done absolutely bugger all for two whole years. Now find some positives. Why is the new job more suitable for your talents? Give them ammunition to fire that makes them enthusiastic about your ability and willingness to do the new job without saying anything at all about how you've done the old one. Remember: they're only looking for reasons to advance your case; they've already decided to avoid the pain of sacking you. Think about this reference business before you choose your new manager. Anyone your boss hates is a good candidate. 'Not only have I got rid of Ken, but he's gone to Roger. That should slow him down a bit.' Anyone your boss doesn't know can also be the right person: 'Well, it's no skin off my nose.

Here's an idea for you

Never treat an appraisal as an ego-trip. An appraisal is an important document to be used in evidence as you pursue your route to the top without actually doing anything. Think about the wording with the HR department in mind. All you need is to make sure it says that you've done what you were expected to do and that you're a loyal servant of the organisation. Those are the two things an employment tribunal are looking for.

29. Working by the pool

OK, maybe not by the pool, but at least earn your salary from your kitchen. Other people work from home, so why not you?

For an ever-growing chunk of the population, working from home isn't a euphemism for skiving; it's a way of life. They've cut out that hour-long commute, the grumpy boss hovering over your shoulder, office dress policy, and sandwiches at the keyboard for lunch.

For a start if you have kids under the age of six (or eighteen if they have a disability) and you have been working for a company for 26 weeks or more then you have the automatic right to apply to work flexibly. The idea is that you then have more time to spend taking care of your kids, but that could mean many things: for example, you could be applying to start work later so as to be able to take the kids to school, or to start earlier and finish earlier so as to be there to pick them up after school. It could also mean working at home a certain number of days a week.

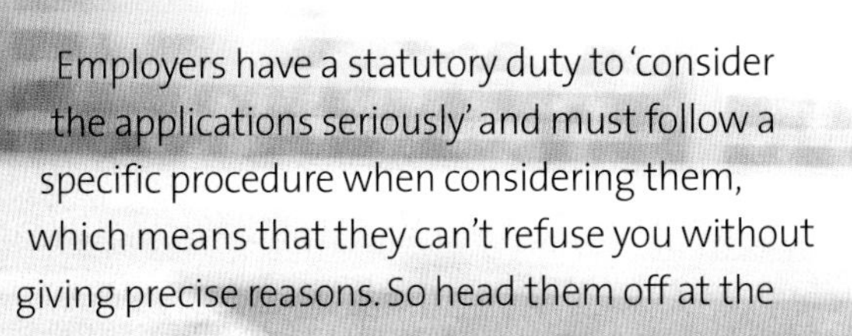

Employers have a statutory duty to 'consider the applications seriously' and must follow a specific procedure when considering them, which means that they can't refuse you without giving precise reasons. So head them off at the

Here's an idea for you

As part of the flexible working legislation you have the right to take a colleague with you when meeting the boss to discuss your proposal. So instead of reinventing the wheel seek out others in the company who have successfully applied for flexible working and get them on your side. A little flattery goes a long way and, after all, you are saying 'I want to be like you'. They in turn have already got good arguments for their (your) case: they can hardly sit there and admit that it doesn't work and all they do is slack off on company time.

pass by sitting down and putting together a killer application that can't be refused. What you will need to think about is the benefit to the company, not to you. Try to:

- Explain how you will make up exactly the same time so the company isn't losing anything.
- Point out that you will be more motivated and happy with your new timetable, and therefore more productive.
- Show that the company may stand to make savings in the office environment (perhaps they could do away with your desk or give your office workstation to someone else).
- Demonstrate that you have the appropriate technology and abilities to do your job from home (this may mean researching Voice over Internet Protocol (VoIP) telephony, for example, to handle phone diversions at no extra cost).
- Consider means of monitoring your performance that can be used to prove you are reaching agreed levels and so back up your claim to be more productive with the new timetable.

Your boss has 28 days from receiving the request to arrange a meeting with you and explore your proposal in depth. Fourteen days after that, the employer must write to you to either agree the new pattern and a start date or else provide clear business grounds as to why your proposal is unworkable. If that's the case, the letter also has to set out the appeal procedure for you to contest the decision. For more details take a look at the DTI website (www.dti.gov.uk).

When you're putting together your proposal you should consider how much experience your company already has of flexible working. Bear in mind that you may be seen as setting a precedent and so you are effectively establishing the benefits of flexible working in general to a company that may not yet be convinced about it. In that case, make doubly sure that you have the facts and figures at your fingertips and can explain how they would affect the company.

An interesting stat to bear in mind is that, according to the Equal Opportunities Commission, 80% of women return to work within 17 months of childbirth, but only 47% return to the same employer. By contrast, employers who offer flexible working patterns have return rates of 90%, saving the business replacement costs and retaining valuable skills and experience.

Finally, very few companies study their own productivity levels, and even fewer publish their findings. BT does both and found that home workers were actually 31% more efficient than their office counterparts. The happy worker, it seems, really is a more productive worker.

30. Winging a meeting

There's a good reason why we don't prepare for meetings: we don't have time. Seriously. Don't bother.

The Wharton Center for Applied Research recently found that the average senior executive spends 23 hours a week in meetings, and the more senior you are the worse it gets. If we prepared for meetings properly, there wouldn't be enough time left in the day to hold them. And if we did all the preparation and called all the people we should have done, chances are we would have solved the problem already, rendering the meeting even more useless than it already is.

Yet convention demands that when attending a meeting you look like you have put in some work, especially if you called it. If you are in charge, the most important thing about running a meeting is to create a detailed agenda. Don't worry: we didn't say a new agenda, just a detailed one. Keep a standard agenda template: comments from last meeting, unresolved issues, input from departments /working groups/key contributors, suggestions for next steps, any other business and date of next meeting. Then all you have to do is add the correct date, the title of the meeting and the names of people who you want to speak against each item. This name is never you. The other attendees will be so busy looking for their initials that they won't spot that it is the same agenda as last time.

Here's an idea for you

If you want to arrive late and/or leave early, keep one of those small suitcases with wheels on it and bring it to the meeting. Quietly park it in plain view. A late arrival means you just got off a plane or train. An early departure means that you really have to get to the airport or station right away. Your very presence will seem like you're doing everyone a favour.

Always allocate precise times to each item on the agenda, but make no effort to enforce these times.

The easiest way to control a meeting without contributing is to emphasise that you are listening. Remember, listening is good, because listening means not doing. If your agenda looks too short, invite someone, preferably on a mobile phone, to conference call in to the meeting. Connecting and reconnecting will swallow at least 45 minutes of the available time, and you can always shout 'What do you think, Derek?' down the line if you're in a tight spot.

If you are not running the meeting, but expect to be named on the list of people who will contribute content, the important thing is to convince everyone that you have a lot to say while saying as little as possible. Bring a long typed list (any typed list will do as long as it consists of at least ten points) to every meeting. Don't let anyone else see the detail on it. When

it's your turn, pick it up and scan carefully. Hearts will sink until you check your watch, glance at the agenda, and say: 'In the interests of time, I'll skip most of this, and just cover a few essential points.' Your diligence, humility and ability to prioritise will attract admiration from people who don't know that you are holding your shopping list.

In any meeting designed to decide something, there will usually be The Expert, the one person who knows what he or she is talking about. It would have been much better for everyone if The Expert had been allowed to get on with making the decision alone, but it's important to have a meeting so that you can contribute by agreeing with everything he or she says, and maybe steal some of the credit as a result. Accomplish this by identifying that meeting's Expert, preferably on the way in to the meeting, and engage in friendly banter, which might reveal what point of view The Expert holds. If possible sit opposite The Expert – this allows you to exchange knowing looks, raised eyebrows and vigorous nods on cue. The Expert's aura of capability will extend to you. If it's time for a comment, try 'As [insert name of Expert] says...' or 'I agree with...' Don't do this too often, though: everyone hates a kiss-ass, and if you're too vocal, you will be given things to do, which isn't the idea at all.

...if you're too vocal, you will be given things to do...

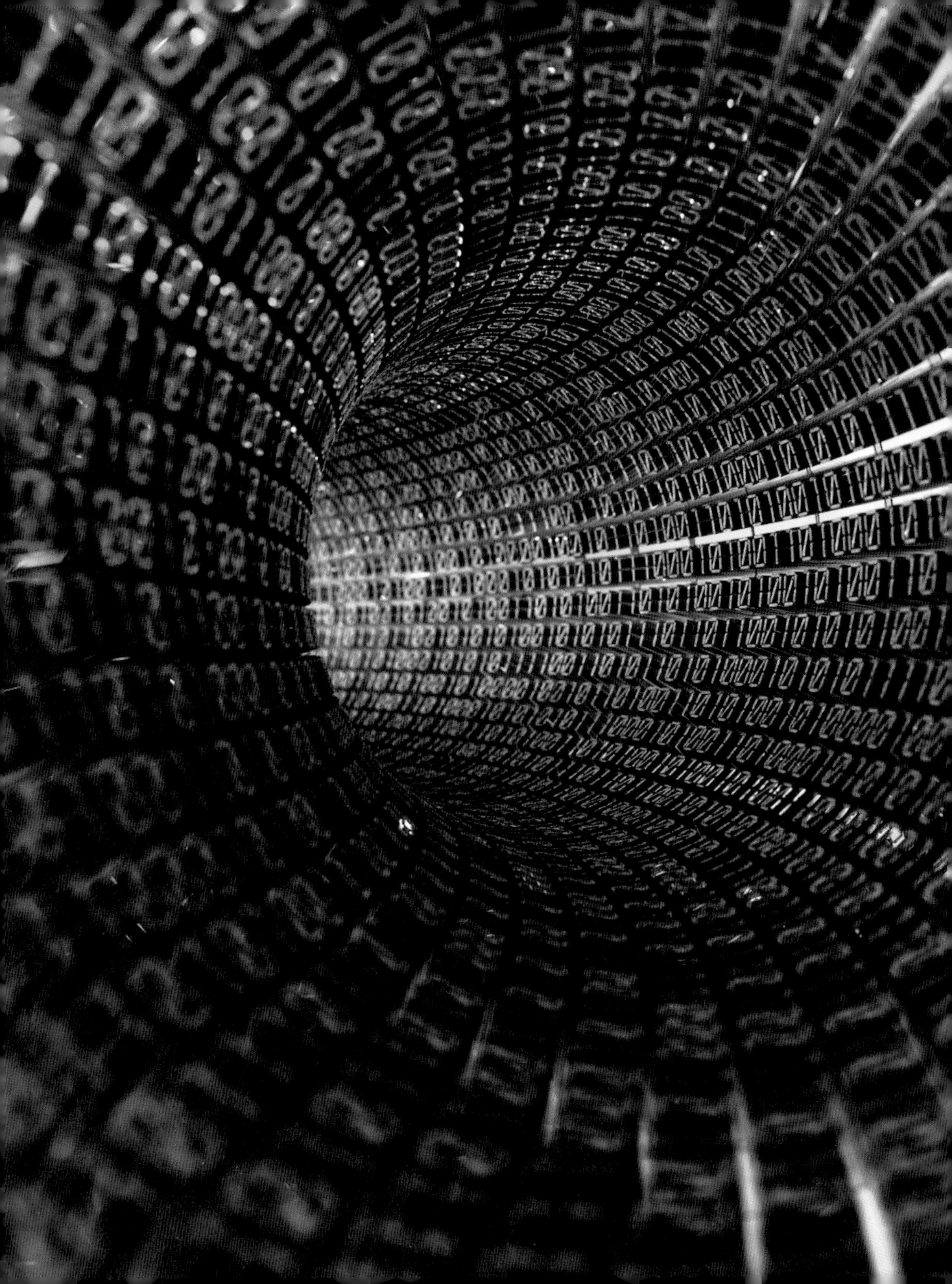

31. Stealth surfing

Your computer logs everything you do. When you're online, other computers are busy logging everywhere you go. If you'd rather surf in stealth, you must learn to become invisible.

Many people are surprised to learn that when we're on the Internet, we're never 100% anonymous – if the powers that be really want to find where you've been then they will. What you can do, though, is make it very hard indeed for family, friends and, perhaps most importantly, your employers to know where your tastes lie in the wonderful world of webbery. There are many levels on which you can be rumbled so let's start with the basic ones and move on up.

With your home/work machine you might think that closing down the browser means the end of your session but you'd be horrified what gets left behind. Internet browsers have a 'history' function which is basically a breadcrumb trail of everywhere you've been. Bad news. Bin it. The way to do that is to go to your browser and find the Tools menu. There you should find Options including both History (where you went) and Cache (files that have been stored to your hard disk while you were there) both of them being dead give-aways for where you've been and what you've been doing. Clear them both (with the 'clear' button) and set both to zero unless you want to leave a blatant record of what you're up to.

Don't bookmark a page you don't want others to find (you'd be surprised how many do). Check you didn't bookmark a page (for example, a chat room) in a previous existence when you had nothing to hide. While you're at it, ensure 'auto-complete' is off so that someone who accidentally starts typing another address or email address doesn't suddenly have the whole thing completed for them, exposing your secret penchants in the process.

Take the time to download some clean-up software such as Perfect Privacy, Eraser, Complete Cleanup, etc. There are many varieties of these, often free to try, which automatically wipe away the bits and bobs that filter down to your machine while you're online.

If that largely takes care of cleaning up your machine, there's always the issue of websites themselves knowing who you are and where you are coming from/going to. As far as the Net is concerned, you are (or rather your computer connection is) just a number but there are things at work out there (software trackers and marketing companies, for the main part) trying to join up the dots and identify us. At the very least, your Internet provider will know where you've been and if you access the web via a proxy server at work then so will your employer. To get around that you would need a cloak of invisibility. Fortunately they exist.

The usual approach is to surf via what's called an anonymous proxy. You don't go straight to the site you want; instead you go via a site which itself takes care of scrambling your identity so that the site can't see who you are. Of course the anonymous proxy could trace you if it had to (or if the police asked) but it's in their interest not to unless forced so that will usually hide you pretty well. The best known is Anonymizer (www.anonymizer.com) but there's a wide variety of alternative proxy servers and encryption solutions out there just waiting to turn you into the invisible man.

A word of warning. If you're surfing from work and your employer is pretty paranoid then bear in mind that they may have keylogging software that records what everyone is doing and will spot your activity even if unsure where you're going. There are anti-keylogging products, but the best thing is to ask a friend in the IT department what's in place and what it can and can't log.

For a useful list of tools that can hide you online try the Electronic Privacy Information Centre at www.epic.org/privacy/tools.html.

...you need a cloak of invisibility.

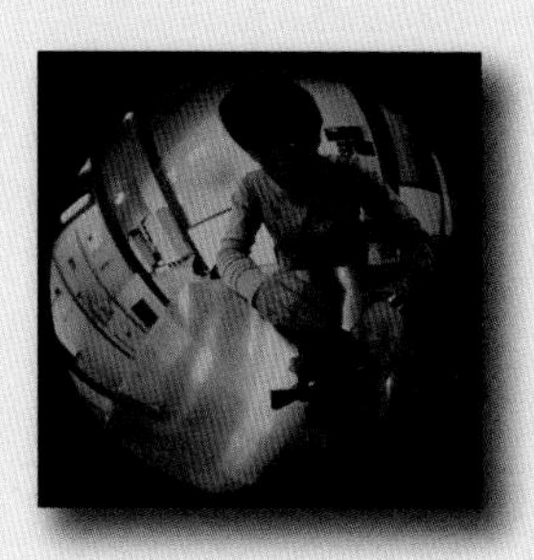

Here's an idea for you

One way of keeping your work machine clean is to use a USB memory key loaded with clean-up software and your own secure browser. When you want to surf the web, ignore the browser installed on the machine and instead plug in the memory key and launch your own browser from there. There are numerous commercially available memory key/browser combos available so that while you use your work machine, you shouldn't end up leaving traces on it. Bear in mind, though, that even this will still be detected if the system has keylogging/spy software so find out what's watching you first.

32. Go on, give them a shock

As part of your campaign to gain high exposure to senior people, take any opportunity you can to introduce new information into the organisation.

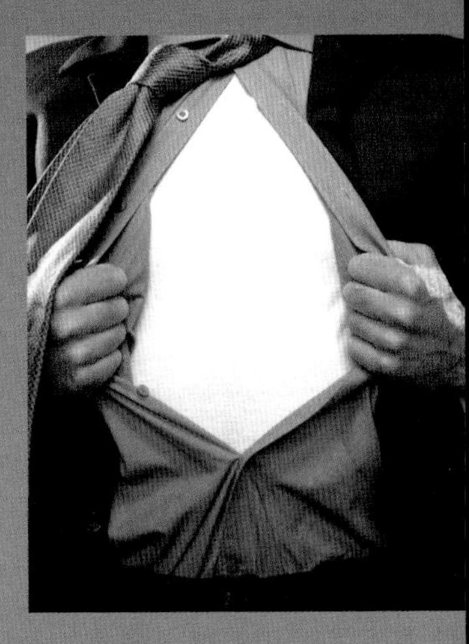

Look at your organisation as though you were the owner. Left to itself a company ossifies. All organisations need alert managers to tell them how the world in which they are operating is changing. And it is difficult to be sure what changes in the environment will have an impact on your particular organisation. This makes the gathering and proclaiming of new facts or statistics a fertile ground for standing out in the crowd. The aim here is to draw the attention of management to new information that might have a long-term impact. This is an area for lateral thinking. Remember, we are talking about the long term – you should be long gone by the time your predictions face a reality check.

Brilliant entrepreneurs do this stuff really well. They take, for example, something a customer said to them the other day, a project they just approved in research and development, something their teenage son said at breakfast together with a headline in today's paper and discover an insight. That's what you are trying to do here, develop the way of thinking that entrepreneurs use to plan the way ahead.

Make sure you set aside at least fifteen minutes of every day to read relevant published material; you will find this invaluable in presenting yourself. Reading technical papers, or even just the dailies, will help you to start to detect new and useful facts at an early stage. A rich vein for this type of information is the technical section. Technological change over the last ten years has rendered hundreds of traditional skills unnecessary. When, for example, did you last see someone literally cutting and pasting a newsletter?

Look for trends, sociological and other

Send notes to appropriate people quoting sources of information such as the Harvard Gazette that no one is likely to have read. The conclusion that you draw from the information must give senior managers food for thought. You must lead them to some clear conclusions showing problems, preferably catastrophic ones, or opportunities, preferably big ones, in the future. The area of demographics is another dead cert. Grey-people buying power, the growth of old retired people, the death rate in Russia and so on. I advocate strongly the use of real facts in this regard, but if you have to make them up make sure it is not remotely possible to challenge them.

If all else fails there is always regulation and health and safety. Find out the trends here and predict the impact on your organisation.

Gather new facts and statistics as often as seems sensible given that you are also over-performing in your day-to-day function, and you will almost certainly at some point do your organisation a big favour. It would have ossified in that area if you hadn't warned it: organisations don't spot trends. Sometimes, if the coming event is catastrophic, what you say will give them the most tremendous shock.

Health warning: Do not pull the facts and statistics stunt too often. Some people send off two notes a week. This is a mistake. You are trying to build a reputation as a person with their finger on the pulse, not as a crashing bore.

Here's an idea for you

Look for external sources of information that senior managers will find useful. Customers and competitors are very fertile ground. Spend a bit of time today looking at information about a competitor. If you are financially inclined, compare your competitor's annual report with yours and look for major discrepancies. Now see if you can get your boss interested in going further into it.

33. Relax your way to success

How to have a holiday at your desk

Imbue the old nine-to-five with a certain glamour and you'll be amazed at how much tension seeps out of your life.

You'll be raising your standards and that means lowering your stress levels.

Forty years has taught me that there are two ways to have a perfect day. One is in the grand tradition of the Lou Reed song. You hang out for a whole day with someone you really, really love who is loving you right back – or at least tolerating you. You don't have to do anything because just being with the beloved is so blissful it blocks out the boring little problems that usually stress you out. If you manage twenty days like this in your whole life time, you're doing pretty well.

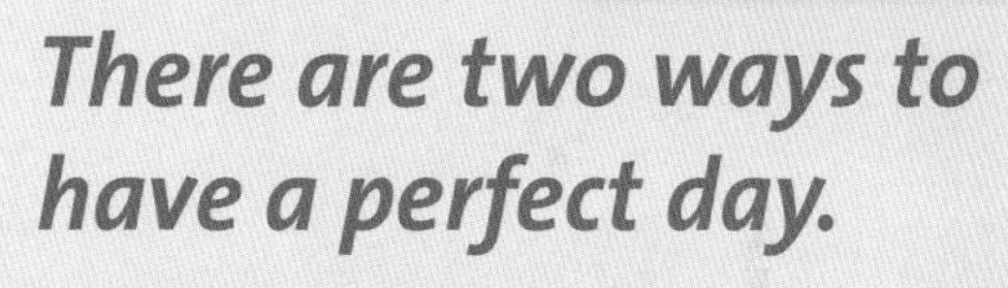

And then there's the second way. You build a perfect day for yourself and by adding grace and glamour to your life, you remove stress. It takes a little thought. But it is more reliable than true love. You can have a holiday of the 'mind' on even the most mundane day.

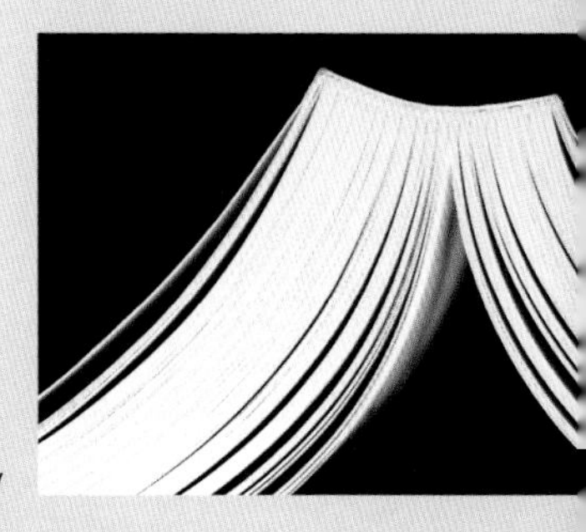

Reboot your commute

Give your journey to work an overhaul. Set yourself targets. Instead of a drag, see it as a purposeful part of your day. If it involves walking, buy

a pedometer. Learn a language. Use the time to repeat your mantras for the day. Be creative: write a page of free-hand prose on the journey in (not if you drive of course!). Start working up the characters for your novel. It's a terrific time to practice mindfulness, which can deliver the benefits of meditation. The list is endless.

Boost your environment

Your starter question: what five changes would make your work environment more pleasant. Here's mine. Getting rid of piles of papers and magazines that need to be filed. Investing in a china cup and no more sharing the office's grubby, chipped ones. Cheering up my desk with a bunch of pink tulips. Cleaning my keyboard – so filthy it's a health hazard. Turning down the ringtone volume on my phone. Everyday find some way to make your surroundings more pleasant.

Beat the mid-afternoon slump

When you feel the slump kicking in, stop working and get away from your workstation if you can. Go for a short walk in the sunshine, or take a nap. If you can't, try this: palm your eyes in your hand for a few minutes and visualise a calm and beautiful place. See this in as much detail as possible.

The journey home

This needs a different mood from the journey to work. If you listen to music, make it different from the tunes you play in the morning – slower, deeper. Small stuff like that really helps to emphasise that this is your transition period. Have a project that you work on at this time (planning your holiday is good). And if you read, keep the tone light. If in the morning you read French verbs or the novels of Dostoyevsky, read P.G. Wodehouse on the way home.

Spread love

When you pass someone in distress send them 'serenity' or 'calm' as a thought. Spread good and happy thoughts wherever you go. Smile. Be gracious. Be kind, compassionate, a force for good.

Not every day can be a high day or holiday, but changing your mindset, looking for grace and sheer fun in previous black holes of misery turns you into a force for light and transforms your day-to-day grind – it's the art of living lightly and it gets easier the more you look for opportunities to practise your skill.

Here's an idea for you

Clothes can play a huge part in improving the quality of our life. Every morning choose one thing that makes you feel good about yourself – a designer tie, stylish cufflinks, your favourite socks – whatever. Next time you're shopping buy clothes that help you radiate confidence.

34. How to love the job you've got

Sometimes you can't have the one you want. So you have to love the one you've got.

One in four of us wants to leave our jobs. We can't all do it at once, so here's how to cope until your personal Great Escape.

The bottom line

Hate your job? It's probably for three reasons – you hate the work (it's monotonous or stressful), you hate the environment, including your colleagues, or something else has happened in your life that makes work seem meaningless and you're ready for a lifestyle change. Or it could be that you're in denial. I'm going to come over a bit mystical here, because I firmly believe that sometimes we hate our job because we can't be bothered to address what's really stressing us out in our lives. Our energy is focused elsewhere and until we sort out whatever drama or sadness is soaking up our concentration, we're not likely to find the dream job anytime soon. So the advice here is not about refocusing your CV – there are

...always take an hour to relax at lunch.

plenty of other places where you can read up on that. But it will help you relieve stress in the short term and make you feel better about yourself in the long term. And that hopefully will help you raise your energy enough to eventually find another job.

Love your surroundings ...

... Just as much as you can. If your workplace is grim and drear, you are not going to feel good. Clear your desk. Sort out clutter. Personalise your work space with objects of beauty and grace. Pin up photos of beautiful vistas you've visited or would like to visit. (It's a bit less personal than family pix.) But whatever you choose to put on your desk, change the visuals every couple of weeks, otherwise your brain stops registering them.

Love your lunchbreaks

A lunch break shouldn't be a scramble for bad food and a desultory walk round a shopping mall. Spend time planning. Every lunch hour should involve movement, fresh air, delicious healthy food and at least one work of art. Works of art are easily available for your perusal (art galleries, department stores) and easily transportable (books, CDs). Always, always take an hour to relax at lunch.

Love your colleagues

Tough one. These could well be the reason you hate your job in the first place. If there are people who specifically annoy you, then find a way to deal with them. Your local bookshop is full of manuals that will teach you how. Allow yourself no more than five minutes a day unloading your woes about work colleagues to a trusted friend or partner – not anyone you work with. This is not goody-goody – it's self-preservation. The more you unload your negativity all over the place, the more you are talking yourself into a hole of unhappiness and stress.

Here's an idea for you

Boost work morale in a stressful workplace by starting group traditions beyond getting drunk on Friday night and moaning. Go out for a Chinese on pay day or book an awayday at a spa or have a whip-round every birthday and celebrate with champagne and cake.

Love yourself

Turn up. Work hard. Do better. Lots of people who are unhappy with their work kid themselves that they are working really hard, when in fact their work is shoddy and second-rate. If you're not up to speed, improve your knowledge base and skills. If your work is lazy, look at everything you produce or every service you offer and ask yourself how you can make it special, imbue it with your uniqueness, breathe creativity and a little bit of love into it. Doing every task diligently and with positivity will vastly increase your self-esteem.

Love your dreams

Most of us couldn't have got through school without the ability to drift away on a pleasant reverie of future plans. For five minutes in every hour allow yourself to dream. Read through job pages that aren't related to your present job. You may see a position or course that fires your imagination in a completely new direction.

35. Lead with style

The ultimate test of leadership is the top job. As you progress in that direction you need the people above you and the people below you to admire the way you go about leading your team.

Good senior managers can smell a well-motivated, happy team from a mile off. The team members exude confidence. They work hard and make sacrifices.

They display pride in their work and in their membership of what they honestly believe is the best bit of the organisation. Not only that, but everyone, including Human Resources, will know that people are queuing up to get into that team. How do you create this aura?

Some say leaders are born and cannot be created, and it's true that your basic ability to get on with people is, to some extent, your starting point for being a leader. But there are a number of leadership techniques that develop your natural ability to make things happen. Think about motivation – leadership is the skill of persuading people to co-operate willingly to achieve results. The 'willingly'is key: you cannot force motivation on people; they have to want to do a good job. Motivation occurs when people feel that they're able to make their very best contribution.

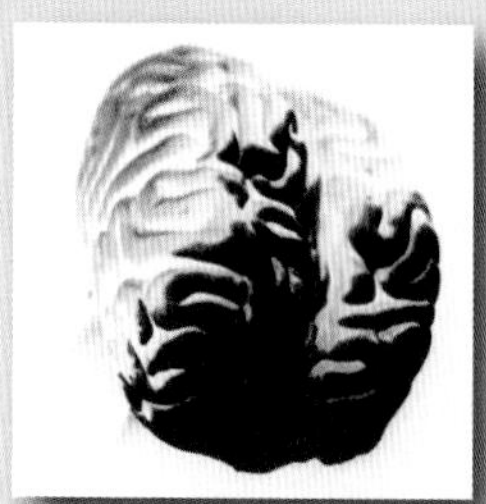

Do you tell 'em or sell 'em?

Some people talk about 'push and pull' management styles. Push is the 'do what you are told' or autocratic method; pull is the consulting, democratic way of leading people. You need a combination of the two for different people and in different situations.

Mike Brearley, sometime captain of the England cricket team, was reckoned to have 'a degree in people'. Here's an example told by Bob Willis, a fast bowler in Brearley's side. Willis was involved in Brearley's occasional winding up of the swashbuckling Ian Botham. When he felt that he needed to ginger Botham up, Brearley would signal to Willis, to take a message to Botham: 'Mike says that you're bowling like a girl.' Pity the poor batsman who faced the next ball from a seething Botham. Willis concluded this story by saying that if the captain had used the same words with him it would have destroyed his confidence and had the opposite effect. Useful things, degrees in people.

So, your team leadership style can range from giving simple directives to group discussion and consensus. If you tend too much towards giving directions you will, among other things, stifle the creativity of the team. That in turn reduces the number of times you will be able to take a good new idea to your boss. There is almost nothing that boosts a career more than being the first to make an innovative idea work and having it taken up by the rest of the company. Everybody will want to talk to you about it.

Here's an idea for you
Look at the risk of any plan or project you are proposing. Does it fit the risk profile of your division or organisation?

Finally

Always remember that people work for money but will do a bit extra for recognition, praise and reward. If you think someone is doing a good job don't forget to tell them. Show appreciation often. Don't wait for the end of a task to say 'thanks'. It is often a good idea to thank someone in the middle of a project for getting on with it without having to involve you.

So, show a genuine interest in other people, communicate well and pick the right style at the right time and you will probably become a born leader and smell beautiful to senior managers.

Show appreciation often.

Elsevier EMT 1.5913.3 ... 872
EmergMktFlt EFL 1.6515.3 ... 367
EmergMkt II EDF .16e 1.3 ... 53
EmergMktInfr EMG 1.6513.1 ... 73
EMD

36. A triple-whammy career boost

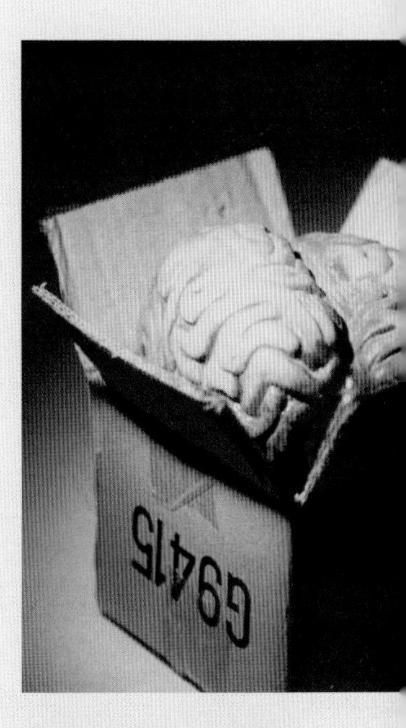

Taking an innovative idea to a customer and helping him implement it has three positive impacts in career terms. It gives you high-level exposure as loads of the customer's managers take responsibility for the initiative. It sells you and your products and services to your customer. It gives an opportunity for your lot to get on the bandwagon too.

Anticipating a customer's needs can pay all sorts of dividends

A few years ago a major book retailer was planning a summer campaign to sell business books at airports and railway stations. The marketing strategy was to attract business people to take a business book on holiday with them. A publisher's saleswoman, who had an excellent relationship with her client, came up with an innovative idea. She suggested the retailer commissioned a new book, not too serious but nevertheless a business book, to attract people into the business section. The retailer loved it.

The publisher assembled all the main ingredients. It was to be a 7 x 7 inch book so that it fitted on the end shelves in the bookshops facing you as you enter the store. The book was designed to look like an easy read with a large typeface and plenty of white space on the page. Because they'd fixed the size and font they knew how many

Here's an idea for you

Right, thinking caps on. Look closely at what your customer is trying to achieve. Look at what their competitors are doing. Study their trade press. Talk to other people in your organisation who provide similar products and services to their customers. Use the internet. From that research, come up with an innovative idea to take to the customer.

words would be in the book, around 50,000, and therefore what it would cost and how much they could charge – a straight tenner. Not £9.99 but a clean deal at the checkout. It's yours for ten pounds, one note.

The retailer's middle management then had to sell the idea to top management. Most book retailing doesn't involve wads of money up front, but this project required real investment. The deal was that the retailer would have exclusive rights to sell the first print run of the book, and the next two in a series, but without the normal sale or return deal. If the book didn't sell, it stayed in their warehouse; it did not go back to the publisher – a real benefit for the supplier.

A manager drove the project through the return on investment process that the company used, and after some time and a few glitches the budget was agreed and the project given the go ahead. There were now seven weeks to go before the book had to be on the shelves.

The saleswoman had cleverly spotted two types of need here – the things the organisation needed to do in order to meet its objectives, and the things that managers need in order to advance their careers, or give them an easy life, or do whatever turns them on. In the case of this book the needs neatly coincided. The organisation needed a book that would attract people into the business section, looked readable as a holiday book but could still be put on expenses. Middle managers were looking for a bit of creative thinking that would ensure that they would sell more business books that summer and that they could boast about to their bosses, all the way up the line.

The triple-whammy benefit picture

The publisher was laughing all the way to the bank, since it is not often that they get a guaranteed sure-fire winner, and the book retailer was busy rewarding and promoting the three or four people who claimed, modestly, to be responsible for the innovative idea, career benefit one. The publisher made a tidy profit, career benefit two, and there was a huge party with senior management from both organisations coming together to celebrate, career benefit three. (I got involved because they asked me to write the book in seven weeks. And that benefited my career too! Thank you Mark.)

37. Money, status, fun and power

How to get what you want

What do you want from your brilliant career? It's probably a mix of money, status, fun and finally power or influence. Let's look at the last of these, and find a way you can get agreement quickly to any proposal, big or small. This method is quick to prepare and must be reuseable.

Show them how to make the decision

Most managers are familiar with showing the benefits of a proposal to an audience. 'What's in it for them?' 'What does it actually do for the bottom line?' Well, we've had this dinged into us enough times during various training courses. And it's true. You are more likely to be convincing if you spell out the benefits of your proposition from the recipient's point of view rather than take the risk of allowing them to do it, or not do it, for themselves.

How about showing people 'how' to make the decision? This takes user-friendly propositions to the next level by adding another topic. So far we are all convinced that you present a proposal like this:

- Problem or opportunity
- Your proposed solution
- Benefits to the audience of the proposed solution

I want to add another element between the presentation of the problem and your solution – let's call it the basis of decision. Here are a few of examples of the practical bases of decision suggested by a seller of insurance policies to opticians:

- The package should include all principal business needs in one policy.
- The administrators of the scheme must have a lot of experience in your type of business.
- The insurance cover must be tailored to your business without losing its cost competitiveness.
- The underwriters must be first-rank UK-based companies.

Now, the salesperson could have promoted exactly the same ideas by banging on about the product she's selling. 'My product includes all the principal business needs in one policy. The administrators of my scheme have a lot of experience in your type of business.' And so on. There are two reasons why using the basis of decision approach gets better results faster in terms of persuading people that you have the right solution. The first is that it sees things from their point of view. (You often, for example, introduce the basis of decision with words like 'I understand you are looking for a solution that ...' or 'Seen from your point of view you need a solution that .... ')

The second benefit is that you can ask if the audience agrees with the basis of decision. If you've simply dumped on them a list of product features you can't say 'Isn't that right?' because they will just say that they don't know. If they give you a positive response to your proposed basis of decision you've more or less cracked it. Just tell them that's what your solution does.

It doesn't always work

I was selling a computer to an educational establishment. They had very little money and I showed them how, if they bought a second-hand machine, they could have much more power and functionality. I took my boss's boss into a meeting where I was hoping to close the business. I went through the basis of decision. I asked them if they agreed that I'd got it right and they did, whole-heartedly. 'Well,' said my boss's boss, 'that more or less describes our solution, so are you going to buy from us?' There was a short pause before the chairman said that there was one more thing – they didn't want to buy anything second-hand. Mmm, I'd missed that.

Finally

Like many effective techniques, using the basis of decision to get your own way is very simple. It's common sense, but it's not common practice. So it's good for your career and it gets results fast!

Here's an idea for you

Take an idea you are trying to persuade your boss or your team to accept. Write down the features of your solution and then turn them into a basis of decision. Some will be dead easy because they truly have merit when seen from the audience's point of view. Some will be difficult, probably won't pass the 'so what's in it for me test' and should be discarded.

38. Back the right horse

You need to get noticed. Identify who is important to your progress, and get to them. Sometimes that will mean bypassing a human blockage – perhaps your own boss, or some obstructive gatekeeper who is there to keep you away from the decision maker. Here are some tactics to leap such hurdles.

Suppose, for example, that your job is to supply computer and telecommunications solutions to the finance department of your company.

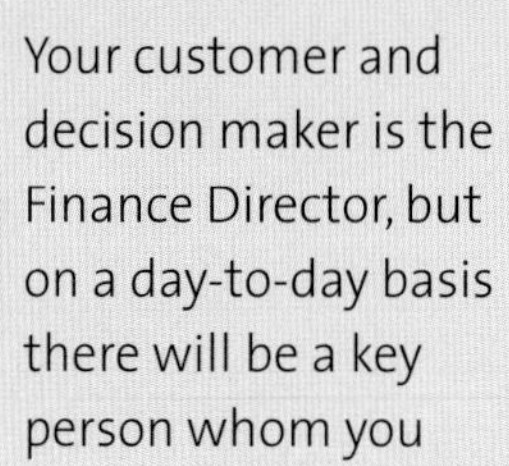

...they're probably scared of a brilliant careerist like you.

Your customer and decision maker is the Finance Director, but on a day-to-day basis there will be a key person whom you meet regularly and with whom you form plans for future approval by the Finance Director. Such people can usually be divided into three categories – the Good, the Bad and the Ugly.

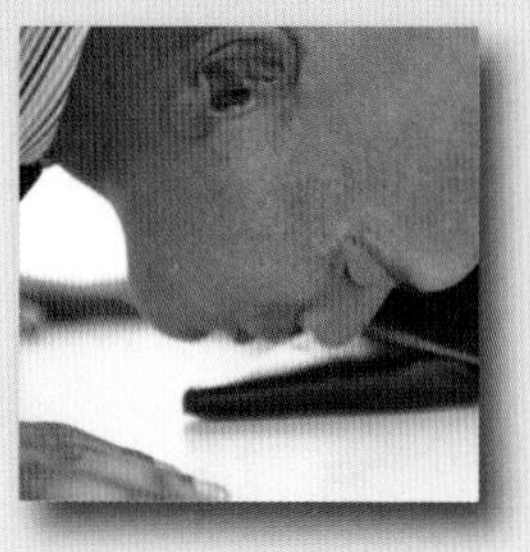

The Good are terrific to work with. They understand their business and they are happy to tell you all about it, so that you can come up with the best possible plan together. Cultivate such people. Latch on to their coat tails. Buy them lunch. Feign interest when they show you pictures of their family. Help them to enhance their reputations and they will help you enhance yours. They will probably be quite happy for you to talk to the ultimate decision maker should you need to, but they'll do it with you as part of the team.

The Bad are often bad because they are scared. They're scared of their boss, they're scared of making mistakes and they're probably scared of a brilliant careerist like you. They probably don't know enough about their business to really brief you on what it is they want and will probably bar you from seeing the decision maker until you have earned their trust. That is the vital element of dealing with the Bad – you have to gain their trust.

It should be quite easy for a cool careerist like you to do this. Achieve some good, high-profile results that end up on the Finance Director's desk, and make sure Mr Bad gets all the credit. But do this genuinely. If you have to, you can dump on him later by showing that it has been you and your team all along that got the results, but life is easier if you can avoid having to do this.

At the point when he trusts you, Mr Bad should let you meet his boss. There is a problem if he won't. Access to his Director is vital if you are to carry out your role. So, like it or not, you have to get to them. Remember, 'it is much easier to ask for forgiveness than to ask for permission.' Once you have created a relationship with his boss, Mr Bad will never be in such a strong position again to get in your way.

Here's an idea for you

Never ask Mr Bad for permission to go and see the decision maker. If he refuses (which he probably will), you're then in an impossible situation. If you go behind his back, then you're heading for a confrontation and the relationship will be ruined for good. No – do it first and beg forgiveness later.

Now for Mr Ugly. Mr Ugly is mean. He doesn't trust you, he doesn't trust his boss, he doesn't trust anyone. Quite often such people are bullies. You can't really play along with them if they are not allowing you to do the best you can for your customer; so you have to grasp the nettle and probably cause a major stink. Funnily enough, the way to deal with them is to cause them some fear, uncertainty and doubt.

Dealing with Mr Ugly

One of my salespeople had a Mr Ugly to contend with. I had to go in to see him and explain very logically that if my salesperson could not see the boss I would have to go in myself. I then displayed knowledge of what this bloke's competitors were doing and showed him that he was losing ground by not investing enough with us. I kept him just short of blowing his top and his uncertainty made him a bit easier to deal with. Unfortunately, however, he would not keep up with technological change and buy a 2960 B from us.

He would not even talk about it. The time had come to take a big risk. We made an appointment to go and see the Director, his boss, and we specifically asked that the meeting be with him on his own. As we had hoped, the Director knew there was something wrong in that part of his business and agreed, albeit with at least a show of reluctance. We were pretty nervous; this was a major knifing job on a fairly senior person in a big customer. The Director's opening was 'Now just before we get to the intriguing question of why you wanted to see me without Rob, I thought I better let you know that he has just recommended that we buy a 2960 B.'

R-935

39. Don’t live your life by accident

We do have a choice about how we live our lives. For example, we can choose to focus on work. Alternatively, we can place a higher priority on family and leisure. Whatever our choice, how do we get the balance just right?

Here’s a way of establishing whether you have the balance you want or whether you need to make some changes.

Check the current situation

There are 168 hours in a week, and you probably spend around 56 of them in bed. So, this leaves 112 hours for living in. Draw a table comprising three columns and three rows, resulting in nine square boxes. In each box write down an activity or area of your life where you currently spend your time, such as Friends, Relationships, Family, Alone Time, Work, Spirituality, Vision, Personal Growth, Health, Hobbies, Leisure, Creativity. If you need more squares just add them. Also include areas that you wish to get involved in, such as Fitness or Travel.

Here’s an idea for you

Create an action plan. All too often we talk about wanting to get fitter, visit friends or take up a new hobby, but another year passes and we never seem to get around to it. Head up columns with the areas you wish to work on, then create two rows for listing exactly how you intend to go about the change and when you intend to achieve this by. Also include a ‘completed’ box. The key is to break the path to success down into small, realistic and achievable steps.

Now add the number of hours in a typical week that you spend in each of these areas. Then convert these numbers into a percentage of 112 and write the percentages into the appropriate boxes.

That's your starting point. You may wish to ask your partner or a work colleague to take a look at what you've written to make sure that you're not indulging in any wishful thinking. If the percentages are just as you'd like them to be, then well done – there's no need for you to continue with the rest of this idea.

One person who did this exercise decided that he was spending too many hours watching television and too many hours working. The area that suffered as a result was his box marked Wife and Family. Following this realisation he resolved to refrain from watching TV between Monday and Thursday. He also committed to telling his boss that he was only going to work late three evenings a week and that he was leaving each Wednesday and Friday at five o'clock. He decided to ask for support from his team at work and to sit down with them to look at their work–life balance and to ask them what he could do to help them get their ideal balance.
He planned to take his wife out for dinner once a month and decided he would tell his two sons that every other weekend they could have half a day of his time to do anything they wanted to do, provided it didn't cost more than a couple of DVDs. His commitment to action made this exercise really work for him and his family.

Plan the future situation

Now look at your own table and decide on the areas where you want to make adjustments. Remember that you'll need to counterbalance each area where you wish to raise the percentage. And resolve to get started on any activities that you've added that you currently don't do. Now translate the percentages into hours and see whether you think you have a feasible plan.

40. Think your way out of conflict

Conflict can be good for us (as long as it's resolved quickly) and it can lead to better quality solutions to our problems. Unresolved conflict is the killer.

Back in prehistoric times, when our ancestors were preoccupied with survival rather than the daily Sudoku puzzle, they dealt with physical threat by either facing squarely up to it or by disappearing sharpish from the danger spot.

Fight or flight? Choosing the right option was literally a matter of life or death.

This is not just a matter of historical interest. Many psychologists believe that the human race is still hardwired to respond to danger in one of these two ways.

Nowadays, the source of the threat is more likely to be our boss than a hairy mammoth (not always

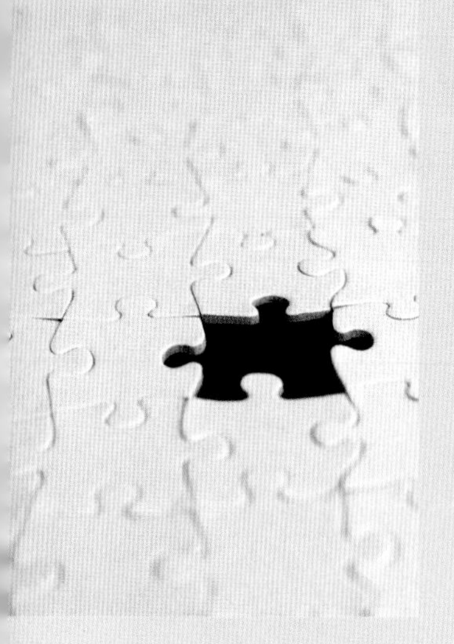

a lot of difference between the two, I accept), and the nature of the threat is more likely to be mental rather than physical. But whether it's a fist heading in our direction or a 'dangerous' idea, we are still likely to encounter biochemical changes in our body or our brain that our Neolithic ancestors would recognise.

The trouble is that the world has moved on, and effective problem solving in the twenty-first century requires a more sophisticated set of options. It was Georg Wilhelm Friedrich Hegel, the nineteenth-century German philosopher, who came up with the notion of a 'synthesis of opposites', the idea that a thesis could be juxtaposed with its opposite number (or antithesis) to generate synthesis, a new configuration that both includes and rises above the foundational elements. This phenomenon is known as a 'Hegelian dialectic'.

Here's an idea for you

When you next find yourself having a disagreement, try summarising what the other person is saying from time to time. This will help to clarify the issue and demonstrates that you are listening and trying to understand, and suggests that you are genuinely keen to find a resolution.

If we apply the Hegelian dialectic to the thesis of 'fight' versus the antithesis of 'flight', it is possible to achieve a synthesis – let's call it 'confront and problem solve'.

It's not a common approach – research shows that European organisations manage conflict by smoothing over and avoiding it 50 per cent of the time, aggressively confronting it 30 per cent of the time and constructively confronting it only 20 per cent of the time. But look beyond the Western mindset and we find that the Japanese, for example, have achieved much of their industrial success over the years by embracing the principle of synthesis.

Richard Pascale, writer, consultant and a member of the Stanford faculty for over twenty years, is a firm advocate of the need to move beyond thinking in absolute categories (like right or wrong and black or white), to thinking that can reconcile opposites. Pascale calls this transition the move from 'either/or' to 'both/and'.

So how can we harness constructive conflict in practice?

A Harvard Business Review article by Kathleen Eisenhardt, Jean Kahwajy and L.J. Bourgeois III suggests five ways to achieve this in a work context:

- Assemble a team with diverse ages, backgrounds and industry experience.
- Meet frequently to build familiarity and mutual confidence.
- Encourage team members to assume roles outside of their obvious functional responsibilities, and so discourage 'turf war' thinking.
- Apply multiple perspectives – role playing, putting yourself in your competitor's shoes, etc. This can enable a fresh view of the problem.
- Actively and overtly manage conflict. Ensure that consensus is real and not just an indication of disengagement.

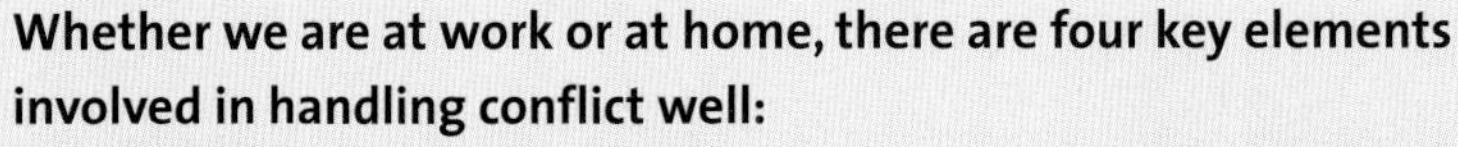

Whether we are at work or at home, there are four key elements involved in handling conflict well:

- Develop a commonly agreed goal. Once all parties have agreed what the overall objective is, it becomes a lot easier to frame decisions as collaborations.
- As far as possible, depersonalise the conversation. If the discussion becomes characterised in terms of doing something Linda's way or Barbara's way, things can rapidly descend into a battle of personalities. So aim to debate on the basis of facts.
- Develop multiple alternatives. Research shows that the more choices there are on offer, the less likely unconstructive argument is to break out.
- Keep a sense of humour. Humour has a powerful positive effect on people's moods. When the discussion is kept playful and light, people listen more and are generally less defensive.

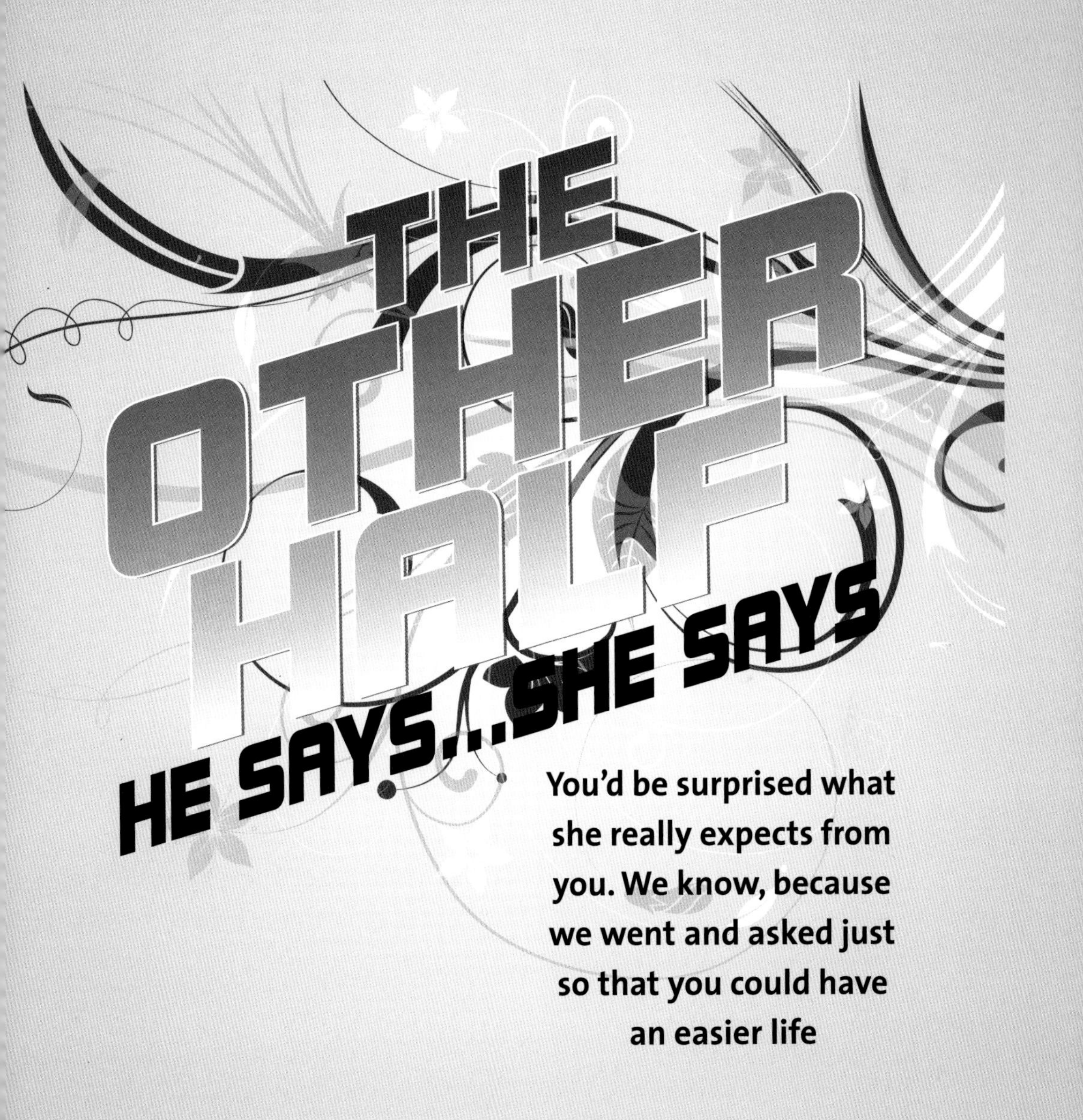

THE OTHER HALF

HE SAYS...SHE SAYS

You'd be surprised what she really expects from you. We know, because we went and asked just so that you could have an easier life

Commander

When it comes to seduction technique how do you measure up?

The formula for the perfect date involves:

1. A surprise trip to Paris, champagne, a suite at the Ritz

2. A film, a great meal, an invitation to coffee afterwards

3. Nakedness and beer. In either order.

The answer to 'does my bum look big in this?' is:

1. Are you kidding? You could wrap yourself in a tent and you'd still look like Scarlett Johansson on her wedding day.

2. Honey I love you just the way you are.

3. Yes. Ow.

She turns to you and asks how you see 'our' future; do you:

1. Hold her in a strong but tender embrace, look intently into her face and say that for you she is the future.

2. Try manfully to suppress panic visions of children and a mother in law

3. Reply with something witty and charming, just as soon as you can remember her damn name.

nd or... Mr Bean

Mainly 1s: Smooth, very smooth, in fact just a little too smooth. You might think you've got this thing cracked but you could do with reading what the ladies have to say about romance.

Mainly 2s: Well you're honest, but probably also honest enough to realise that you're just not quite as successful with women as that other guy. You know the one.

Mainly 3s: You're still living with your mum aren't you?

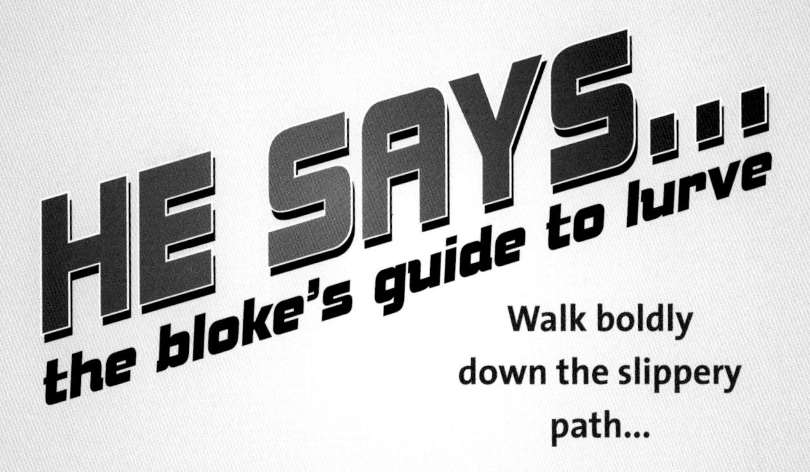

Walk boldly
down the slippery
path...

41. Bloomin' marvellous

If you need something to push the buds of your relationship into bloom, we've got just the thing. Want your love life to blossom? Say it with flowers.

Whatever your sentiment – striking, sensual, sanguine or sexy – there's a stem out there that will say it for you. Smell is our most powerful sense, arousing all sorts of memories and primal urges.

You can't go wrong with roses. Velvety crimson petals exuding the heady smell of rose. Reeks of seduction, doesn't it? Orchids, jasmine and lilies are also renowned for aphrodisiac scents. But wilted daffodils, suffocating in their cellophane wrap, are best left on the petrol station forecourt. Flowers ought to be bought from markets, or plucked from your own garden.

Lots of people make the mistake of thinking flowers are just for women. But a shallow bowl of succulents can look macho in most homes and workplaces. Their round, sensual shapes survive weekend drought.

Why don't you fill some empty glass jars with cut flowers? You can use coffee jars, cooking sauce containers or jam jars. Soak off the label, fill it with water and bung in some blooms. If you cram the flowers in tight, it doesn't matter what you use. Daffodils, tulips, peonies. They don't have to be shop bought. Even daisies and buttercups look fantastic. Either distribute the jars randomly around your home or group them in threes in the dining room, mantelpiece or bedside table.

While you're at it, is there any way you can personalise your floral gift? Jan is a chemist. Previous boyfriends had been put off by her long hours in the lab. Her boyfriend Clive grew a pot of gerberas on his window sill and then put twelve single stems into water-filled test tubes in a test tube rack. She was pleasantly surprised, but also understood the subtext: 'I understand your job is important and I support you.' Jonathon gave his partner Ruth a terracotta pot of sprouting sunflower seeds. On the pot he wrote 'My love for you keeps growing.' Corny, but it worked. James's wife was feeling miserable and unattractive after chemotherapy. She was delighted with his present: a Venus fly trap with a little note, 'You're still a great catch.'

To be really flash with flowers, you need to be *au fait* with the hand-tied bouquet. It is a bit tricky at first, but you don't need sixteen weeks of advanced floristry evening classes to get the hang of it. Just follow these six steps. It's worth the effort:

Here's an idea for you

If you've left it too late and all you can find is a wilted bunch at the twenty-four-hour shop, shame on you. But, hey, all is not lost: take everything out of the wrapper and remove any ties. Pick out all the droopers and bin them. Cut off any brown or gunky bits from the remaining flowers. Now put them in a bucket of fizzy mineral water, or still water with soluble aspirin. Empty your fridge and shove the bucket in for about half an hour. If you've time, see if you can do a hand-tied bouquet; otherwise, just re-wrap. By the time you hand it to your beloved, it should look stunning!

- Put the stems in a bowl of water and, using a sharp kitchen knife, remove all the side-shoots and leaves that will be underwater when the bouquet is in its vase.
- Choose one striking flower and hold it upright in your left hand (or right hand, if you are left-handed).
- Add a few flowers. Make sure that the flower head is to the left and the stem is to the right. As you add flowers, twist the flowers a quarter of a turn.
- Carry on adding flowers a few at a time and twisting. Twisting makes a spiral stem so the flowers stand upright.
- When you have run out of flowers, tie with ribbon at the place where you were holding them in your left (or right) hand.
- Wrap more ribbon round the stem if you want to. You can use raffia, wire or twine instead of ribbon.

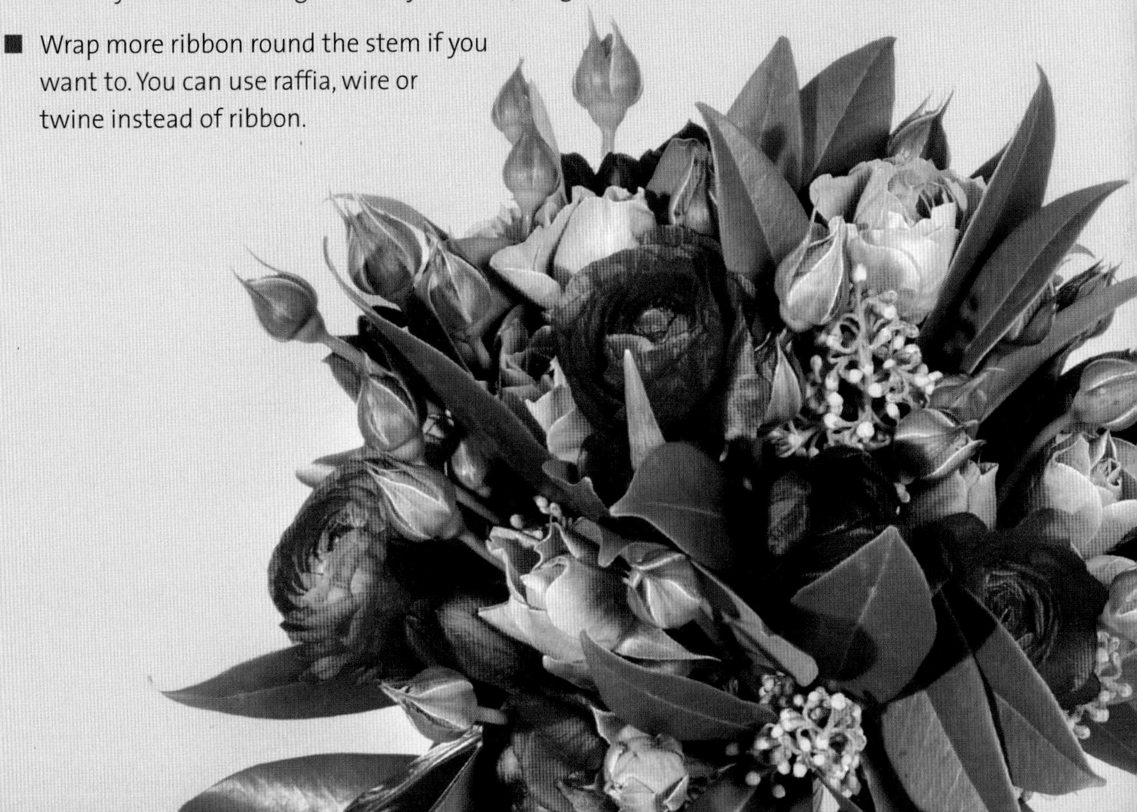

42. It's in the kiss

If you believe a kiss is just a kiss, you've been conned. It's such an intimate act that prostitutes never let clients kiss them (allegedly). Want to recapture the closeness? Pucker up.

Every teenager knows kisses are an end in themselves, not just a preliminary to sex. There's mileage in them there lips.

Lucky lips

We tend to be conscientious when it comes to countering smelly breath, reaching for mints or sprigs of parsley if we've eaten onions or garlic, but how many of us pay as much attention to the state of our lips? Call us sexist, but women tend to be better at looking after their lips than men (which may be why they're called chaps). So guys, if you're tempted to skip this section, stay a while. Chapped, rough or scratchy lips are a major turn off. Instead, think silky, supple lips, ready to take you wherever you want to go. Women get it wrong too, by overcompensating with lots of lipstick. It may be a good look for performers, but not for performance kissing. A daily slick of balm or flavoured gloss should keep your lips in perfect kissing condition. But avoid applying it just before going into action – slippery lips make sloppy kissers. If your lips are very chapped, try exfoliating them gently by covering them in balm and rubbing softly with a toothbrush. Now down to business. In books, kisses are often described as greedy or hungry, as if one person is eating the other. By all means nibble, but never swallow.

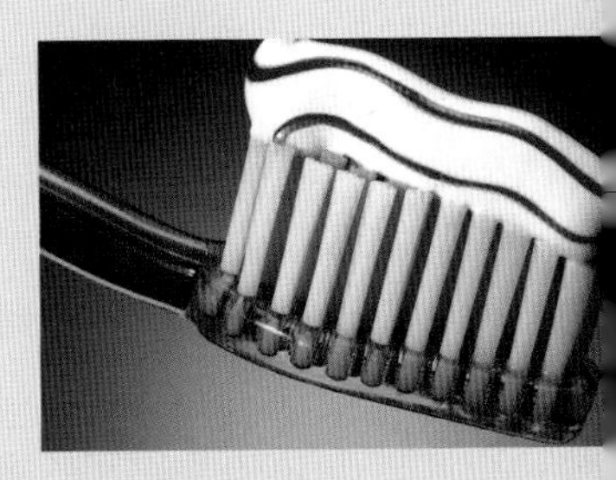

Here's an idea for you
Set aside at least fifteen minutes and have a no-tongues kissing session that doesn't lead anywhere else. Rub your lips together, kiss the corners of her mouth to make your partner smile and enjoy all the new and forgotten sensations.

When you kiss, think about how you move your lips. Let them dance a little, playing with different degrees of friction and tension. Nibble, squeeze or trap your partner's bottom lip or tongue. Mess about and have fun.

French kissing

We know you've had a few tongue tussles and we're not out to teach you any basics. But if you don't mind, we'd like to pull you over for a speed check. Slow and romantic or fast and passionate, the speed of a kiss tells you a lot about the kisser's intentions. As a general rule, we suggest warming up and starting slow. Changing speed mid-kiss should be like changing gear, smoothly and at appropriate times. Try not to clunk or over-rev. Of course, sometimes we all like the thrill of going from 0 to 60 in three seconds, but not when we've just woken up.

Millionaire's kisses

Add glamour, style and fizz to a humble kiss. Take a sip of champagne, hold it in your mouth and kiss your partner. Chilled bubbles on your lips and tongue introduces an extra dimension.
For a less bling-bling version, try a frozen cocktail with a fizzy mixer.

Kissing in the back row

One reason kissing is so popular with teenagers and older illicit lovers is the danger involved. The heady excitement that

...we suggest warming up and starting slow.

comes with the fear of being caught. Committed couples often get to a stage when this pleasure is lost and physical intimacy is taken for granted. Why not recreate early tension by having furtive kissing sessions in semi-public places, like lifts and cinemas?

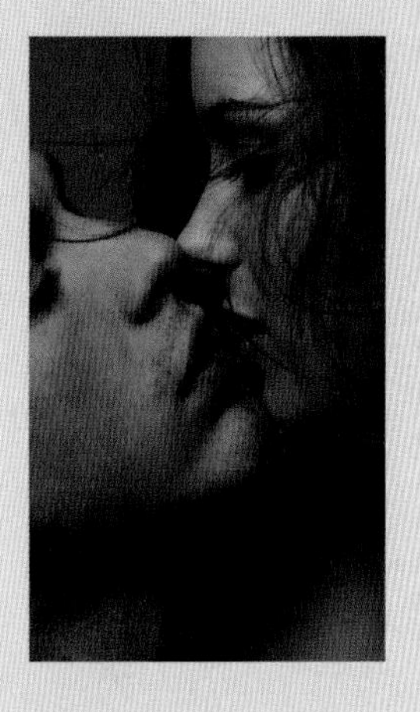

Kiss and tell

Kissing's not just for lips. Rediscover your partner's body. You know about the importance of kissing places like the insides of elbows, between the shoulder blades and the backs of knees; to discover your partner's secret kiss-spots, you'll just have to ask and hope they kiss and tell.

43. Cheap thrills

Relationship repair often means spending big bucks. Everyone knows going out keeps relationships fun, but you don't have to blow a fortune to blow the cobwebs out of your affair.

Showing your partner she means the world to you doesn't need to cost the earth. Once you know how, it's easy to show your lover a good time without busting your budget.

Free for all

There may be no such thing as a free lunch, but many re-energising fun days and flirty nights are free. When was the last time you held hands and went walking at sunset or in the morning? Or played hide and seek? Or truth or dare? Or sardines? Time to make a list of things you've always wanted to know about your other half but never dared ask: think up some steamy forfeits and enjoy a night in with a difference. For an adrenaline surge, take your partner for a spin in her fantasy car. Glam up, visit a swanky showroom and ask for a test drive. Once you've got a taste of the highlife, you might like to try the outing we call Penthouse Sweet. Dress like millionaires, adopt assumed names and make appointments with out-of-town estate agents to see dream properties in exclusive areas. Upmarket viewers are often provided with complimentary champagne...

Drama Queens (and Kings)

Want to add some drama to your relationship but can't afford a babysitter and dinner on top of top-price theatre tickets? Matinees are often half price. If evenings are your only option, university drama

Here's an idea for you

The key to lasting love may be on your doorstep. Play hometown tourists. Raid your nearest tourist office for free maps and leaflets about local attractions. Get out there to see your neighbourhood and each other in a better light.

departments often put on cut-price performances for the public. If you get tired of just watching you may even want to join a local amateur dramatic group and join in the action.

Get crafty

Many artists and crafts people have open days and other free events in their studios. Find out through local arts schools, libraries or craft councils. Learn a new skill or have creative evenings in: from painting to creative gardening find something to do together.

Lessons in love

Swap skills. Teach her how to change a tyre and get her to show you how to waltz. The student–teacher dynamic is powerful and guaranteed to add oomph to your love life.

Ten cheap and cheerful dates

- Have an art house or blockbuster home cinema night. Rent the first film you watched together, make mountains of microwave popcorn and turn your sofa into the back row.
- Hire a tandem and explore. Life is sweet when you're on the seat of a bicycle made for two. Add panache with an inexpensive cheese, bread and wine picnic.
- Eat at home but go out afterwards for dessert and coffee in a swanky restaurant. Share an ice cream sundae and let her have the whole wafer.
- Rendezvous in an exclusive hotel. You don't need to book a room, just put on your finery and people watch in the foyer. Drinks may be pricey, so just buy one and enjoy complimentary nibbles.

- Drive down memory lane. Window tour places that have special memories: where you went on your first date, had your first kiss, proposed, your favourite restaurant or view, wherever makes your hearts beat faster.
- Hunt down her favourite author and surprise her with a visit to a book signing. Bookshops advertise forthcoming events, but to find out what her author has planned, contact the publisher directly.
- Serve your partner breakfast in bed with a themed twist. For a French breakfast, put on some accordion music and serve hot coffee and pain au chocolat. French waiter's outfit and moustache optional. French kisses, on the other hand, are just a serving suggestion.
- Put stars in her eyes. Rent a book on astronomy from your local library, pitch a tent in the garden and teach her about stargazing.

- Grab some culture. Many museums, art galleries and exhibitions are free. It also pays to hunt out smaller, specialist places as they're often more intimate.
- Drop in on an open mic night at a comedy club. As this is where new acts cut their teeth, you won't see any famous faces, but what a thrill to see someone before they were famous.

44. Burning the evidence

Modern communications gadgets may offer convenience but they also compromise our privacy. Here's what to do to stop others blundering into your private life via the latest devices in your home.

Once upon a time, if you were communicating with someone and preferred to keep it quiet, all you had to do was burn the letter after you'd read it. In this day of mobile phones, email and instant messaging that's become a whole lot more complex.

When the French government first discussed British Telecom's idea of the 1471 code (the number you punch into your phone to see who the last caller was), the debate quickly turned to the subject of wives and mistresses. It was argued that when (not 'if' – this is France, remember) the mistress called, the wife would only need to enter the 'last-caller code' to discover the offending number, even if the mistress had immediately hung up. The debate actually held up the introduction of this facility across the country. As it happens, these worries weren't completely unfounded because 'last call received' is probably second only to unerased text messages and emails as the greatest give-away of our time. So get smart.

Here's an idea for you

So, you're too smart to use email, preferring instead to use instant messaging (IM) because that leaves no trace, right? Ahem. Leaving aside the fact that the messaging provider archives the messages, the default of most systems is to archive your message history for the session until you sign out. So make sure you sign out, and make sure nothing is saved after that by going to the Preferences menu and choosing Archive options. Be sure too that whoever you IM with does the same otherwise they may be saving your communications without knowing it.

We'd like to think you're an honest person but even us honest ones sometimes need discretion in our communications. The Manly Man team recommendation is twofold. One, where possible ensure that discrete calls are made from the other person to you and that they always dial the 'number withheld' code (141) before calling. Two, get a second mobile. Inform everyone that it is a work-only phone and that work policy means you have to have a pin code number on it (common company practice these days). Only use that phone. Whatever you do, always manually delete your call records and both incoming and outgoing texts. Not all phones save outgoing messages but it's guaranteed that if you've sent something dodgy then yours will. So, never forget. The other thing is that none of this is worth a damn if you don't keep a tight hold on your phone bill, so make sure that it's delivered to a safe address and destroy or hide as necessary.

With computers, people tend to forget that the darned things actually monitor every single thing you do and keep a record of it. 'No problem,' we hear you say, 'I delete everything even remotely naughty'. Yeah, right. This is why that's not enough.

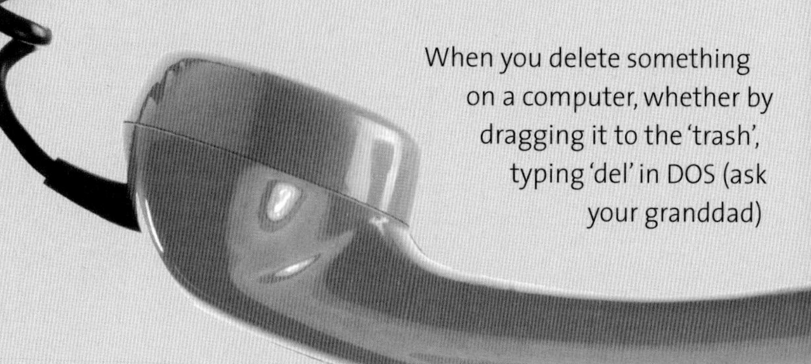

When you delete something on a computer, whether by dragging it to the 'trash', typing 'del' in DOS (ask your granddad)

or selecting and 'deleting' in your mail program then you might think 'job done' but that's not how it works. The computer doesn't actually delete the files (nope, not even when you click 'empty recycle bin'), instead it marks up the disk space they sit on as being free for use should something else want to be saved there. You can't be sure it's gone until you delete completely then use the 'compact all folders' command in Outlook or whatever mail command you had. To be completely sure, then defragment your hard drive. If using Windows go to Start, Programs, Accessories, System Tools and there you'll find Disk Defragmenter and Cleanup utilities.

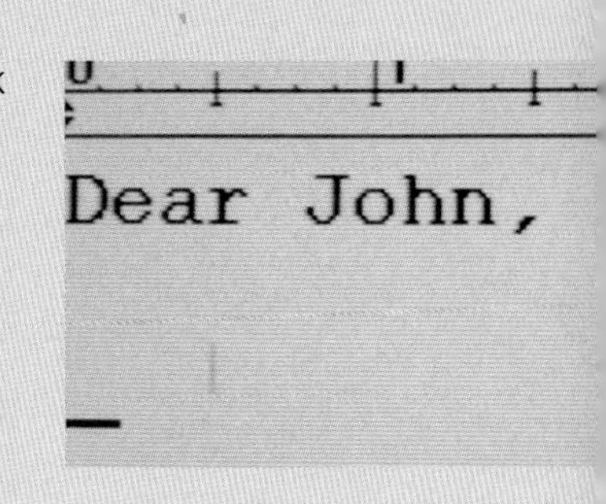

When you send a message, a copy of it is added to the 'sent' folder. When you delete that message, a copy will be made in a 'trash' folder so check that the message and its many copies are all gone. If you think you're up against someone who understands how to undelete and recover damaged files (your teenage kids perhaps) then rename a new file with the same name as the old one (including the suffix after the '.') and copy it to the same folder or directory that held the incriminating evidence.

...most people who get caught out do so because they are simply careless.

Remember too that most people who get caught out do so because they are simply careless. If there's someone you don't want to be seen communicating with then don't use an electronic address book. Similarly don't ever save their number in your phone. After all, no self-respecting spy would ever write down his or her contacts. If you're opting for discretion then it's time for you to go into James Bond/Mata Hari mode.

45. Making her happy
... after not-so-great sex

If you've just had sex and it was a bit of a flop, don't panic; there's still time to rescue the situation and have her purring for more.

If you can get away from the myth of genital sex being the most crucial part of a sexual encounter, there are endless ways to please your partner.

Some men approach sexual intimacy like porno stars constantly seeking good 'wood'. They worry about how hard they are and how long they can last, but in reality only around 30% of women actually climax as a result of penetrative sex. That leaves plenty of room for sexual play where you're only limited by your imagination.

If you came a little quickly and she's still excited, instead of worrying about your performance, concentrate on getting her to climax. Ask her what feels good or, if she's shy, get her to push your head/hand/sex toy in the right direction. One of the easiest things

Here's an idea for you

If you feel unsure about how to skilfully manipulate her clitoris and vulva area, try anal play instead. As well as being more straightforward, pleasuring an alternative erogenous zone can accentuate stimulation elsewhere. You can try massaging the anus with your fingers and/or tongue. If she likes it you'll soon find out! If you are not fluid-bonded you can use a dental dam over the area. She may prefer you to concentrate just on her anus, or tease her there in combination with vaginal stimulation. Go for it!

...doggy style is a great way to receive oral sex...

to do is to slide down and play with her throbbing vagina and clitoris with your lips or fingers. The feel of a soft tongue on her already sensitised clitoris and vulva can feel especially good after she's already been penetrated. Dr Ian Kerner suggests in *She Comes First: The Thinking Man's Guide to Pleasuring a Woman* that oral sex, rather than being an optional element of foreplay, is actually 'coreplay' and that men can become better lovers simply by giving more oral sex.

Rather than diving straight into action, try teasing her first by licking her legs, thighs and belly so she'll be more excited when you actually get down to business. Get her to put her hand on your head and to guide you to the right spot. Some women prefer clitoral stimulation, but others have more sensation on the labia lips, or just inside the vagina. Let her guide you with her hands or voice. Cunnilingus is an art in itself and there are many variations of tongue movements. You can try moving your tongue in small circles, clockwise or anticlockwise, up and down, from left to right as well as varying the speed. Some women like the sensation of your lips on their vaginas as well as your tongue. Experiment with different techniques, paying attention to her physical responses, and encourage her to indicate her preferences.

Some women find cunnilingus more stimulating in different positions. For instance, doggy style is a great way to receive oral sex because the vagina is naturally more open. Improve the missionary position by putting a few pillows under her buttocks. When you raise the area you also increase blood flow. You can also try kneeling down at the foot of the bed/sofa/chair – often it's easier to practise cunnilingus when you approach her genitals from a lower position.

If she likes penetration and finds it easier to climax this way, then don't be afraid to use sex toys. The advantage of these is that you can buy the shape/size/material that works best for her. Sex toy play doesn't have to be about penetration, it could be that just the thrill of a buzzing vibrator or a partial insertion of a dildo is enough. Use lube with sex toys and be gentle at first; when she wants it plunged in to the hilt, she'll let you know.

If you have a shy partner, get her to sit on your lap with her back to you and encourage her to play with herself while you massage her legs and breasts. This position should reassure her enough to be able to let go and climax.

Finally, don't forget after-play, the caressing and touching that makes the come-down just as good as going up.

46. Of course I didn't forget, darling

Do not be fooled into thinking that perfect performance during the other 99.7% of the year can help you if you forget that one special day and you don't know how to get away with it.

There are three important days in the Official Relationship Calendar: your partner's birthday, your anniversary and Valentine's Day. Should be easy to remember, huh? But we know it's not.

Valentine's Day

St Valentine himself wouldn't associate this day with happy thoughts. Having been arrested for illegally marrying couples during the reign of Roman Emperor Claudius II, on 14 February he was beaten to death with clubs and his head was cut off and put on a spike. Those of us who have forgotten St. Valentine's Day will know how he must have felt.

If you somehow miss the prompts that 14 February is approaching – for example, by spending the first six weeks of the year in a remote cave – the sudden realisation that you are expected to be calculatedly romantic for the day can be a nasty shock. The first five minutes of this crisis are the most important. Never admit you have forgotten. Use a raised eyebrow and cheeky grin to suggest that you

have something huge planned meticulously for later in the day. If you have failed to convince, attempt some light-hearted tickling or banter to show how relaxed and carefree you are.

Only a very naïve partner will fall for this completely. It's a stalling tactic so you can get to the office, where you can't be watched like a hawk while you fix the problem. This involves the application of money in liberal doses. Your first call is always to the florist closest to her location, the one who will deliver a bunch of flowers for a delivery fee nudging three figures. Forget non-local florists. They don't need your kind of business today, and won't deliver until several days after your relationship has been terminated.

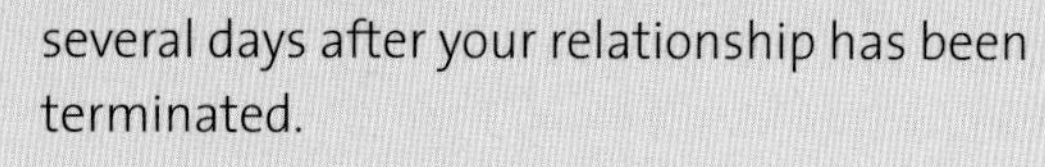

Never admit you have forgotten.

No matter how desperate you are, never, ever, buy flowers from a garage.

When booking a restaurant, don't start with the lovely little brasserie around the corner. It was booked solid eight months ago. You're going to have to aim for restaurants that you can't afford, because people like you who aren't idiots have booked all the affordable ones. Remember, you have set up the expectation that you have everything planned, so a tandoori 50 miles away is not good enough. Never go out without a reservation: four freezing hours of fruitlessly touring restaurants packed with smug couples is not a romantic date.

Anniversaries

Your anniversary is easier to plan at one hour's notice: unlike Valentine's Day, the rest of the male population isn't frantically doing the same thing as you are. However, anniversaries involve the vague expectation that you will do something romantic and intimate that doesn't involve underwear until much later. This can be confusing and stressful.

Birthdays

The most important thing when forgetting your partner's birthday is to realise you've forgotten on the day. There are some early clues to warn you that you may have forgotten: you will probably experience a moody silence; there will be lots of brightly coloured envelopes that are not addressed to you in the morning post; her relatives will call and sing happy birthday down the phone.

When the penny drops, act with speed and efficiency. For this, forward planning is the essence. You can start planning right now for the inevitable day when this happens to you. Keep an emergency greetings card in the house. When she said, 'I'd really like one of those for a present,' six months ago while you were watching TV or reading the Sunday colour supplement, you did write down what she was referring to, didn't you? Giving her something that has previously been mentioned in an offhand way (because that's why she brought it up) shows you have been planning this for months, and couldn't really have forgotten her birthday. Accept her apology with good grace, and immediately start the preparation for when you forget again next year. The key to long-term success is not to overestimate your ability to learn from experience.

Here's an idea for you

Go for a high-risk, high-reward scenario: cook something. To do this, you have to be able to use the cooker, and the meal has to be something that your partner actually likes, so try and remember what that is. Buy the book by the chef that she likes watching on TV, and pick something with not many ingredients that takes less than four hours. The beauty of cooking is that, short of actually poisoning your loved one, you're allowed to make mistakes. At least one component might well be inedible, but that's endearing. Start cooking before she arrives home. Wear an apron. Light a candle. Put on that CD of hers that she knows you hate.

47. Clawing your way back from fatal faux pas

There are many books about etiquette and how to avoid social gaffes written by people who are skilled in the subject. These books are not for you.

The problem with etiquette books is that they don't take account of the environmental factors involved. The people that write them have long ago achieved power over their own destiny and manners, while you have not. This is a fancy way to say that you're often drunk, trying to get drunk, or thinking that the only way to get through the following three-hour social situation is to get even more drunk.

This is a disadvantage. Your short- and long-term memory is impaired by the effects of alcohol, as is your judgement of situations. In combination, the two factors can have awkward consequences – such as simultaneously having sex with someone and forgetting her name. In case you were wondering, this example is a serious gaffe, especially if the person is a relative, a relative of your spouse, or the supermarket delivery girl.

Here's an idea for you

To avoid forgotten name embarrassment, use the 'buy one, get one free' tactic. You're standing with a good friend or partner (let's call her Deborah) and someone whose name you have forgotten approaches. Make a one-sided introduction. 'Hi! Great to see you again!' you say to the stranger, who is either your boss or the guy who collects the pint glasses – you can't quite remember – 'This is Deborah!' Hopefully, the boss/glass collector will give his or her name without a prompt. If not, you're stuffed.

All of the techniques below can be performed drunk. In fact, that's the only time most people could get away with any of them. The key is total commitment. Don't worry about practice: trust us, you'll get plenty of that.

The maiden aunt: This is strictly for when you have more social status than the person you are talking to. It has the advantage of honesty and can be used for any gaffe. It has the disadvantage that you will regularly cause offence, but if you've bought this book, that ship has probably sailed already. You stop talking, stare at the person as if they have just arrived on the planet at that moment and then say, loudly and firmly, 'You know, I've completely forgotten who you are' or 'I think that was your girlfriend I just goosed'. There is a limit on the number of times you use this on the same person.

The designated driver: Travel everywhere with a friend who is more charming and responsible than you. When you insult or offend someone, your chaperone is on hand to clear up the mess. This is an approach favoured by upper class British males, among whom it is known as 'marriage'.

The bon vivant: This one has the advantage that it can be used repeatedly throughout an evening. Whenever two people approach whose names and personal details you can't for the life of you remember, grab them warmly and shout 'My guys! Now I'm sure you two must have met before!' Do this confidently enough, and they will bask in your approval. You can thereafter say or do more or less what you like, because you are The Man. Take care that they aren't already good friends, or they may turn round and say, 'Yes, but who are you?' In which case, use the Cleese (see over).

All of these techniques can be performed drunk.

The Cleese: A panic measure, to be used only in extreme situations. Elaborately feign a distraction. This may involve attending to an untied shoelace (if possible, your own) or pretending to choke on a cocktail sausage. Fainting is usually too extreme and potentially hazardous.

The woolly: This is often employed in a family situation. For example, when you have children, you are so tired you can barely remember their names, never mind the names of all the babies that belong to the people who used to be your friends. Your friends, however, consider their children's names to be somewhat important, and would be offended if they knew you had forgotten. So on emails, cards and letters, use general forms of greeting if in doubt. 'The Smith family' is slightly formal. 'Ian and Deb and family' is better, but remember, if they only have one child, you've just given the game away. Using 'How are the little ones?' normally gets a response that 'Jemima is extraordinary, she's reading already, and Jason still has that twitch.' Forget the dull anecdotes (you'll hear them again), just write down the names. If you think this isn't true, just wait until Christmas and see how many of your cards are addressed to 'All at number 42'. They're all doing it.

(Pankow)
BERLIN

48. The perfect alibi

There will always be times in our lives when we are not actually where we say we are. It's a good job that teams of boffins have come up with the cutting edge in alibi technology.

Covering your tracks is essential when being pursued by something big, fierce and equipped with pointy teeth, like the other half, or your boss. Lying is the traditional response to this but to be really convincing you'll need an alibi and this is what modern technology was made for. Welcome to the era of the alibi agency.

You may remember the story of the pub that put its phone in a soundproof booth along with a mini-jukebox into which you'd drop your coin and be rewarded with the sound of typewriters or airport announcements while you phoned. The advance of technology means that this is now within the grasp of us all; indeed, probably literally in your pocket.

In Japan there is a camera phone alibi service that allows you to store a picture of yourself cunningly pasted over a suitable background (on the train, behind the desk, in the Oval Office etc.) and send it to people, as in 'There you go honey. Now do you believe I'm at work?!' A Romanian company called Simeda has done the same for sound files, allowing subscribers to select from traffic jams, train noises, heavy machinery, or even a dentist's surgery. These then

Here's an idea for you

Looking for a quick get out? Look no further than your phone. One mobile service in the States, for instance, set up a 'Rescue Ring' facility whereby you can have your phone called at a set time to get you out of a corner. The 'Escape-A-Date' service goes a step further and will phone you with a suitable excuse. Your escape mate tells you exactly what to say ('roommate locked out', 'summoned to meeting' etc.) and you just repeat it word for word. Or you could just get a mate to do the job for you – if you trust them that is.

play as background noise during the phone call to back up your story. If you're a chronic liar, it's even possible to assign a selected background track to play automatically when certain numbers call you. Of course, that still takes a certain amount of common sense – your telephonic persecutor may get suspicious after the twentieth time they call and find you're still on the train.

For the full service you're going to need an alibi agency. Alibi agencies offer a range of services from the simple to the complete life screen (bought by the year). Simple alibis might be as basic as an answering service that says you are where you said and promises to pass on the message. The Full Monty will actually make use of real companies and have real secretaries (who themselves don't know you're not a business partner) take the calls. It will also issue business cards and provide a variety of 'colleagues' to call, be seen with, etc.

Moscow-based company Alibi is run by alibi specialist Dmitri Petrov (thinking about it, probably not his real name) and offers a wide variety of convincing ruses. For example, someone who is running out of reasons for repeated absences can have a 'friend' turn up at the house loaded down with fishing gear to drive him off for the weekend. Or a wife looking to get away for a while with no questions asked might be sent a totally convincing looking summons for a court appearance or jury duty in a far away city. A phone number with the summons would be answered by the agency confirming in best bolshy bureaucratese that yes this is indeed the judicial system at work and no she can't get out of it.

Welcome to the era of the alibi agency.

Funnily enough, not all alibis are for the reason you were thinking of (oh yes you were). Alibi-Strohmann of Germany tells the story that one of the hardest alibis they ever had to provide was all about blindsiding a girlfriend for two months so that she had no idea her boyfriend was busy ... arranging their surprise marriage.

49. Lying – and not being caught

Lying isn't always a bad thing – we're all familiar with white lies, with business bluffing, and protecting people's feelings. As long as we don't get found out, no problem.

The Manly Man editorial team are confident that you only have other people's best interests at heart when you want to deceive and thrive. Instead of guilt, all we need concern ourselves with is not being rumbled. Bad liars get caught for a number of reasons but the most likely are: failing to deliver the lie convincingly; failing to do the necessary homework; and failing to prepare a fallback lie.

Failing to lie convincingly is a beginner's mistake and suggests that the liar is either totally unprepared, very nervous or cursed with a conscience like a plague of Jiminy Crickets. You'll have noticed that some people lie naturally and easily – otherwise we wouldn't have lawyers and politicians. The trick – as it so often is in getting away with things – is confidence. At the pathological end of the scale, these liars are utterly convincing because they actually believe their own lies.

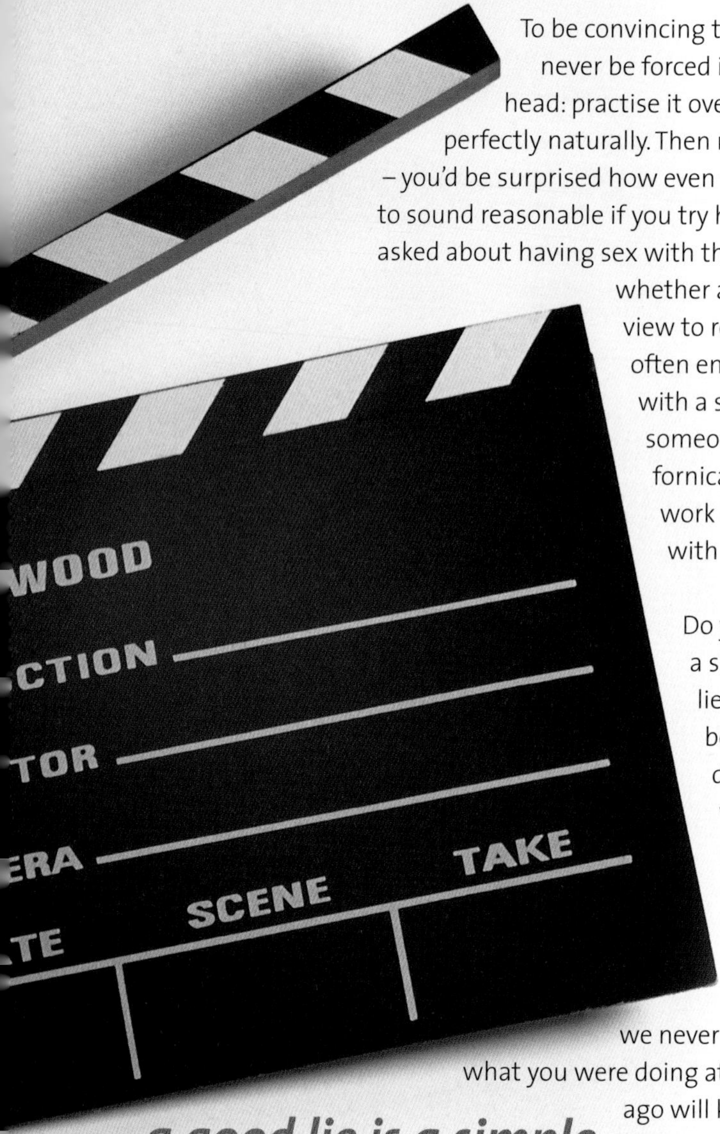

To be convincing there are a couple of musts. Firstly, never be forced into telling a lie off the top of your head: practise it over and over so that it comes out perfectly naturally. Then rationalise it until it seems reasonable – you'd be surprised how even the utterly implausible can be made to sound reasonable if you try hard enough. If you're likely to be asked about having sex with the HR director, question for yourself whether anything other than full sex with a view to reproduction really counts. Do this often enough and you too will be able to deny with a straight face that you had sex with someone even though you regularly fornicated like ferrets in a sack. (This won't work if that person has clothing stained with your bodily fluids by the way.)

Do your homework because a good lie is a simple lie, and the common everyday lie is often made more convincing by being decked out with some concrete details. Don't say you were in the pub with mates. Say you were in the Rat and Drainpipe with Bill and Ted. It's just that much more precise for the listener and so paints a more realistic scene. (The exception to this is that there are some things we never remember, so a policeman who asks what you were doing at 9.00 p.m. on Wednesday three years ago will know for sure you're lying if you come snapping back with names and locations.)

...a good lie is a simple lie...

Obviously there's no point delivering detail if it is going to melt away like mist as soon as the light of investigation is shone on it. Try to come up with details that can't be checked or, if they can, make sure they do tally. Try not to bring other people into the loop – asking Bill and Ted to provide an alibi for something is a highly risky strategy and greatly increases the chance of the lie being rumbled. Not just because Bill and Ted are themselves rubbish liars, but simply because with more than one person trotting out a made-up story inconsistencies are sure to start appearing.

This point is why you need to prepare a 'follow-up lie' (FUL). The FUL is kept in reserve for when your original porky pie is crumbling in front of your face. This requires good acting ability so you will need your FUL to be even better rehearsed than the original. A FUL requires careful delivery. It must be seen to be dragged physically from you, with all the pain and messiness of pulling teeth. Above all it must be cringingly embarrassing – which will immediately explain why you told the first lie. If, for example, your FUL is that you were seeing the doc about a really foul personal hygiene problem you will have explained lie one, discouraged further questions, and possibly gained sympathy all in one go. Result!

Here's an idea for you

Before you try it on other people, always practise telling your lie in front of a mirror. Watch your body language. Give-aways include raising your hands to your mouth, any nervous foot tapping or movements, folding your arms around your body, and confused gestures like shrugging as you say 'yes'. Practise the lie until your body shows no stress when you tell it. Say it often enough and you might even start to believe it wholeheartedly, at which point you are ready for the telling. To spot your weaknesses, practise a couple of totally random lies right now – you could start with something utterly implausible like 'I never inhaled'.

50. Breaking off a relationship

Dumping your partner is traumatic for sensitive souls, so we procrastinate. This usually means we do it in grim instalments.

With the right mind-set there's a better way.

At the minimum, dumping involves gruesome conversations during which tears mingle with you awkwardly mumbling 'sorry, sorry, sorry,' and staring at your feet for what seems like three years. At worst, it can lead to raised voices in the pub as you hiss 'Can't we talk about the thing with your brother/sister/grandmother later? It was New Year! I was on antibiotics!' People you never met stare at you thinking 'You bastard! How could you?!'

If you had known the break-up was going to be like this, you might not have got into the relationship in the first place. However, we're betting it won't stop you from being in the same situation a few months later. That's why it is vital to have some pain-free strategies for finishing a relationship cleanly and leaving unscathed, for everyone's sake. Actually, mostly for yours.

This is not unnatural or unethical. You used low cunning to get into the relationship in the first place, so why not use the same ability to get out of it? Think of it as a negative chat-up line.

Rule one (of one): get on with it. Don't listen to those people who advise taking the easy way out, either by just not returning calls and hoping that someone gets the hint or, even worse, going into hiding. That's just putting off the evil deed. And don't take the chicken's way out and ditch her by text message (not that this stopped 9% of us from dumping a partner by SMS this year – 20% among 15 to 24-year-olds). The danger is that you'll get into one of those interminable back-and-forth text exchanges that can last longer than the relationship. Email is worse. Your ex will forward the mail to everyone who knows you, and you'll never cop off with her friends ever again. Considering this is probably one of the reasons you wanted to break up to start with, that's poor thinking.

goodbye sex is a very, very bad idea

So, do it in person. There's only one location to do the deed: at her place. This means your ex can tell you to get out RIGHT NOW, which may be the first time in months that you've wholeheartedly agreed on what to do next.

Set yourself a time limit for discussion, measured in minutes, not days. Get right down to business, but avoid clichés. 'It's not you, it's me...' isn't fooling anyone. 'I love you, but I'm not in love with you,' 'I need some space,' and 'It's nobody's fault' are just twaddle, passing time until the sobbing/shouting/glass throwing starts. This is one of the few times in a relationship that it's okay to talk solely about yourself. If you say 'I hate the way you eat', your soon-to-be-ex can offer to change their eating habits. If you say, 'I wake up every morning hating you,' there's no obvious counter offer.

If the relationship is obviously boring and tetchy, you can attempt mutuality, as in 'We both know ...'. This wins you kudos for honesty, which can speed you through to the end credits. Your ex can also feel that she was as much the dumper as the dumpee, and can tell all your friends that it wasn't your idea, which is a small price to pay.

Finally, be generous. It's over, but let her know that some element of it has been fantastic. Emphasise that this fantasticness is now past tense. Don't carry this complimenting thing too far: goodbye sex is a very, very bad idea in all cases.

If all else fails try one or more of the following: move to Albania; grow a moustache and change your name; take out a restraining order; frame your ex for a serious crime; change your sexuality; change your sex.

Here's an idea for you

Don't set the whole dumping thing up over time by saying 'We need to talk', 'Let's get together sometime and see where we stand', that sort of thing. This isn't going to help get the whole thing done without recrimination. Always remember, speed and efficiency are best for both of you. Surgeons don't remove an appendix by spending two weeks prodding the area with a scalpel to see what happens.

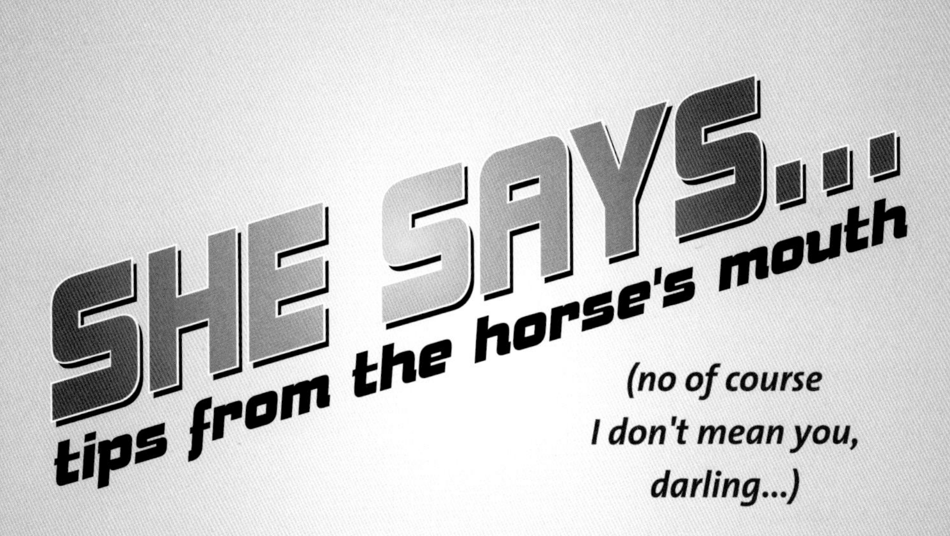

*(no of course
I don't mean you,
darling...)*

51. If I said you had a beautiful body......*

Chat up dos and don'ts

When blokes talk about lines to try on women you are guaranteed to hear the story of Dave. Dave is this mate, well more the mate of a mate (and absolutely never someone present) who has the whole pick up thing cracked. He just goes up to every woman in the party and says "hi, I'm Dave, do you fancy a f*?" Of course he gets shot down in flames nineteen times out of twenty but because he asks every single girl he meets the law of statistics means that he gets it more than any other bloke around the table. At this point every man present mulls for a minute and nods sagely at the wisdom of Dave.**

So here's the heads up. Dave doesn't exist. Dave is proof that men like rational concepts like statistical probability and secretly wish they applied to irrational things. Like women. If Dave did exist he would have to have a skin thicker than Superman's pet rhino and be happy living with the fact that he's never going to get a second chance with all the girls he tried his killer line on. Dave is precisely as likely to get laid as a builder whistling at anything walking past in a skirt.**

In fact when we asked our scientific sample of women what a good chat up line would be most of them immediately replied that any

* **Don't even think about it.**

** **Note to builders; it doesn't work, it never has, and it never will.**

line" will just sound corny. Which sounds reasonable, particularly when it comes to lines about angels, dreams, etc. but misses one significant point. Women don't always mean what they say any more than we do. Ask a woman how she would respond to a chat up line and she will sneer, or maybe laugh (which isn't such a bad thing) but equally there is no woman yet born who doesn't like being told she looks beautiful. Of course it helps if you can deliver that line with conviction and you're able to hold yourself upright without the help of furniture at this point.

Recently the boffins from Edinburgh University put this science to the test with a sample of 40 lines and two hundred subjects, from which top boffin Dr Christopher Bale concluded that. "The highest-rated lines were those reflecting the man's ability to take control of a situation, his wealth, education or culture, and spontaneous wit.

"You're the most beautiful woman I've ever seen, and that's not saying much for you."

Groucho Marx

A direct request for sex received a low score, but it was not the least effective gambit." Curiously the most successful line in the Edinburgh survey was "It's hot today isn't it? It's the best weather when you're training for the marathon." Presumably this combined the common ground of talking about the weather with the suggestion that the man delivering the line is a honed athlete. Or self-obsessed and sweaty depending on how you look at it.

Ones that certainly don't work are crass favourites, such as

'Hey beautiful – is there room in your purse for the keys to my Ferrari'
(suggests car obsession with the woman as accessory)

'Get your coat – you've pulled'
(aggressive – likely to elicit short sharp comeback)

'If I could rearrange the alphabet I would put you and I together'
(not only corny but what is she supposed to say to that?)

Better bets include the simple but blindingly effective "can I buy you a drink", and anything non corny but funny like "I have lost my phone number, can I have yours?".

Here's an idea for you

Try to avoid lines that ask for yes or no replies. There's a line of thought that says that the most important thing is to open the conversation and then you have the chance to show off your glittering wit/ compassion/ stinking richness. Oddly enough something like 'what's your favourite pizza topping' works because it's not offensive, usually gets a reply, and gives a starting point to find out about shared tastes.

52. First date dos and don'ts

First dates seem daunting but in reality there are a few simple rules that should see you through

1. When it comes to first dates you should act as if 1920s manners were still in place, and then be pleasantly surprised if it turns out your date has heard of the equality of the sexes.
This means that yes you pick her up in a car (if you have one – and only if it's presentable). Yes you do open doors for her, offer to take her coat, etc. Most of all yes, you're paying, and look happy about it. Of course if she insists on splitting the bill etc that's good but the best is to say 'let me get this one – you pay next time' because it leaves it open if she's only offering out of politeness. It suggests you'd like a next time, and it makes you sound both generous and easy going without being old-fashioned. Don't be passive – make decisions about where to go, what to do, what wine etc. but be sensitive to the fine line between being active and being domineering, which is a real turn off.

2. Make sure you've got something to talk about.
Going to a movie is both good and bad. If you spend two hours of a three hour date sitting in a darkened room ignoring each other that's bad. If you plan a film followed by coffee/drinks/meal then you've got something you can both talk about. Even if it's just how bad the film was.

Here's an idea for you
Films are good but for a real icebreaker try taking a class in something you'll both be bad enough to laugh about. Think ice skating, or roller blading and make sure neither of you has done it before, and your sense of humour is stronger than your manly pride. If it is, and you can show that you can laugh at yourself as you both take tumbles, then you're going to have made a good impression and have plenty to chuckle about as you then move on for coffee/ food/drinks.

3. Remember it's not just about you.
Of course you want to impress what a great guy you are but for heaven's sake make sure you say enough without going on about yourself. Listen to her. Let her take centre stage, don't try to top her stories.

4. You bought her dinner so now you expect sex?
Whoah there feller. Short cut to disaster. If you really want meaningless sex for a budget then go to a pro, don't insult the lady. You're not going to get laid tonight. At least not unless she tears your clothes off right there in the restaurant in which case, just possibly, you might be in luck.

5. It doesn't have to be the evening.
An evening date does add a little pressure. If you're a little shy or unsure try thinking about a lunchtime meeting, or an afternoon in the park. Art galleries are good if you know that's what you're both into, zoos are a fairly safe bet if you don't know much about each other.

6. Steady on the jiggle juice.
Nerves, sexual tension and booze make for a dangerous cocktail. More dates have been ruined by a drink too many than anything else so watch how much you drink, no matter how roaringly it's going.

7. She's the star, don't introduce cameos.
This is not the time to talk about your ex-girlfriend, or the other girls you fancy at the office. Even if it's just for tonight, the one across the table now represents the entire female sex so even if Jessica Alba happens to walk past naked your eyes should remain glued to your date.

"Nothing defines humans better than their willingness to do irrational things in the pursuit of phenomenally unlikely payoffs. This is the principle behind lotteries, dating, and religion." **Scott Adams**

53. Notice anything different?

NEWSFLASH: you're not perfect. Stop doing all those irritating things hat women hate. Yes, we mean you.

et's get the most irritating thing out of the way first. A female riend who has prominent breasts often has to give words of dvice to men who are talking to her.

I'm up here!' she says.

f you remember one thing from this hapter, eye contact makes a much better mpression than eye-to-cleavage contact. A more general principle is that when you re out with your girlfriend, ogling other women isn't going to make it a happy ccasion for her.

f you're still reeling from the information hat staring at women's breasts might be a problem for her, here's another evelation: that belching joke you do is getting old. The same goes for the farting. ust because it worked in your maths esson when you were 13 doesn't make it omedy gold among adult females

Here's an idea for you
If you're cohabiting, remember that the remote control belongs to both of you. If you love your girlfriend or wife, try giving her joint custody of it. If this is stressful for you, phase it in – for example, she gets control of the remote on Tuesdays and Thursdays, gradually leading to full equality when you can handle an evening in front of the TV without grabbing it off her. When you have the remote, you can also help by not doing that thing where you watch each channel for 10 seconds before flicking to the next. It was irritating when there were four channels; now there are 200, it is grounds for divorce.

If the lack of fart gags means you're forced to rely on conversation instead, you're not out of the woods. All-male conversational staples such as showing off your trivia knowledge, competitive bragging based around car ownership or sporting achievement don't work as well in mixed company. Instead of talking about yourself, what you know, what you have done and what you want to do next, try mixing in a few questions. After asking the question, wait and listen to the answer, rather than thinking about yourself until your female companion stops speaking so that you can say the next thing on your mind.

Having conversations in this way, involving the equal exchange of opinions, involves the possibility that you might have to concede that you were, perhaps, on some small point, wrong. These displays of vulnerability are more impressive for women than your dogged insistence on being correct. Because her expectations of you are low in this regard, you have a surprisingly large window of opportunity for admitting error. Saying, 'I'm sorry about last night. You were right, I was wrong. Tomatoes really are a fruit,' can repair all the damage you did when you stomped off to the pub in an instant.

Driving offers the most important opportunity to admit you are wrong. She might not have a great sense of direction; but she has the sense to admit it when she's lost and ask for directions. We do not.

You can remember who won the European cup in 1989 and the date of the first moon landing so why can't you remember your girlfriend's birthday, your wife's wedding anniversary, or Valentine's Day? Dates might not be a big thing to you, but if they are to her, you're trading a lifetime of resentment for the price of a diary. Write these things down, just once. Set up a reminder on your computer so you buy a card and present and book a restaurant before she has to start dropping hints.

"God gave us men a penis and a brain, but only enough blood to run one at a time." **Robin Williams**

Simple compliments really work, but you have to be able to give them at the right time and in the right words. If the woman in your life is making an effort, tell her she looks good without prompting. Making a joke by adding 'for once' drives her totally bananas, and not in a good way.

When she tells you that she is not your mother, that's not just information. It's meant to alter your behaviour in some way, for example by balling your own socks once in a while, or putting the cap back on the toothpaste. And while we're in the bathroom, put the loo seat down afterwards, and wipe up if you splash on it. 'It looks like it would be quite easy to aim that thing,' one of our sources tells us, 'but for some reason he manages to miss every time and leaves it as a sort of present for me.'

Finally, when you hear a phrase like: 'I'm going to get my hair coloured purple', or 'I'm going to try on my new bikini,' store the information for later. Then for once you can respond correctly to one of the most chilling questions a man can hear from his partner: 'notice anything different?'

54. You're wearing that?

We all have our favourite clothes. That t-shirt with the hilarious pun on the sportswear manufacturer. Those jeans with the ripped knees. Those really comfy (and really ripe) trainers. She hates them. With a passion.

There are bound to be items of your wardrobe that she doesn't like as much as you do but there are certain items that men think are fine and women universally despise. Present yourself in front of her in any of the cursed clothing items and you might as well wave a red rag to a bull. Likely suspects include:

Trophy T-shirts. Whether it's from the London marathon, the team shirt of a stag weekend, or the 'my mate went to Antananarivo and all I got...' then however much these shirts bring back good memories for you all they say to her is that you're harking back to something that isn't about the two of you. Unless she was there too in which case you can just get away with it if you pointedly mention that you like wearing it because it reminds you of her.

Any underwear with signs of wear/holes/stains. As soon as underwear starts to show its age it has to go, no matter how comfy, because it's better to bin the undies than risk being binned yourself. Because women know we're filthy beasts they like us to sport underwear that looks like it's just been sterilised. Anything less and they can't help but shudder and imagine what level of hygiene is going on inside the knickers in question.

Here's an idea for you
Love that item of clothing but know deep down that she doesn't? Then don't just stop wearing it – make sure you hide it or put it somewhere off limits if you want to save it for those special occasions when she's not around to object. Don't just leave it in the drawers because otherwise she'll have an excuse to throw it out; 'oh that thing, but darling you haven't worn that for year....'

Vests. You can't really win on this one. If you have a Calvin Klein model physique then you're going to look gay (fine if you are, not so hot if you're not) and if you don't sport a six pack then you're going to look like Homer Simpson (fine if you're attempting to bed Marge, not so hot otherwise)

Y-fronts. They were good enough for your grandpa so they're good enough for you, right? Wrong. Oh so wrong. Y-fronts are no more practical than boxers or briefs but come with the unique disadvantage of those distinctive lines on the front. As if your penis had its own parking place marked out for it. Not good.

Shirts tucked into underwear. Why? Did you dress in the dark?

T-shirts tucked into trousers. It's a t-shirt, so it's casual right? Let it hang casually outside the belt. And if you have a belly, a belt, and a t-shirt on the wrong side of the latter then you might as well start saving for an inflatable girlfriend.

Shirts tucked into Y-fronts. Why are you even reading this chapter? You don't have a girlfriend.

Speedos. No, not all swimwear, and some Speedo shorts are great but be realistic about your age and physique. Women have long noticed that there's a peculiar inverse logic to beachwear and men by which the younger and fitter the man, the longer the shorts (think surfers in board shorts) while the older and fatter the man, the skimpier the briefs. No Mediterranean beach front is complete without a tandoori-tan, beer bellied bloke in a pair of skimpy white briefs. Just for Pete's sake make sure it's not you.

Homer: *Look everyone! Now that I'm a teacher I've sewn patches on my elbows.*

Marge: *Homer that's supposed to be leather patches on a tweed jacket, not the other way around. You've ruined a perfectly good jacket.*

Homer: *Incorrect, Marge. Two perfectly good jackets!* **The Simpsons**

55. I've had a bad day

This is where you come in

Coming back at the end of the day should be a joyous reunion. So how come it's so often a flashpoint of tensions, sulking, and grumpiness?

You may have heard of all that *Men are from Mars, Women are from Venus* stuff which suggests that men respond to problems by 'retreating to their caves' when under stress until they have worked out an answer. Women on the other hand tend to respond to the stress by trying to draw nearer, leading to a conflict in which she is trying to approach just as he withdraws. Or something.

Well here's the heads up. If you want it to work out with her, and we're presuming you do, then you're going to have to make the effort to meet her half way. The idea of the man working and the woman staying at home is pretty much dead so that means coming home is just as likely to be both of you, or even just her, which changes the rules slightly.

Of course in an ideal world you buy flowers, light candles, pour a scented bath etc. and generally be just perfect. Unless you've been sitting on your bum in front of *Neighbours* all day, however, you probably don't have the energy, and besides if you start doing that nice stuff out of the blue I guarantee she'll presume you're having an affair.

Here's an idea for you

The moment of coming back is so potentially loaded as both of you are fully charged with the pressures of the day. So sidestep the flashpoint and change your routine so both of you get back, do something (take a bath, watch the news, open the mail) and then get back to each other a little later when you're a little more relaxed. Now is the time to ask how her day went. And listen.

Before the door opens

First up remember that this really is one of those cases where if you're not part of the solution you're part of the problem. If you are still all fired up with the day's niggles then you will not only do a poor job of trying to soothe away hers, but you will probably add to them. So start off by taking control of yourself. If you've arrived home then before opening the door stand upright, pull your shoulders back, and take a moment to compose yourself by breathing deeply, focusing purely on your breath and not on your work. Think for a moment about what has annoyed or upset you during the day so you know what is bugging you and aren't a seething mass of unfocused resentment.

If you're not part of the solution you're part of the problem.

If there is anything you really believe is her fault then think clearly about how you want to address it – concentrate on the desired outcome or solution, not on your

emotion. If you realise there is nothing that is her fault then get that absolutely straight before you walk in and grump at her for no good reason.

Once you're together

If you both have stressed lives then acknowledge that first. Simply saying that you've both had a bad day is a useful reminder that the problem is not each other but comes from outside the couple. Do talk about your respective days but don't make it some kind of competition where you have to cap each other. Chances are that things she found serious won't seem such a big deal to you and vice versa, so instead try to come together in a more 'us against the world' comparison of just how annoying and stressful the outside world can be.

Going the extra mile

Listening to the story of her day is probably the single biggest thing you can do but if you have the energy then making an effort will go a long way to making her happy and that means making you happy. You don't have to give her a full shiatsu massage (though that's not a bad idea). Just slip her shoes off and massage her feet for a minute. Or rub her shoulders. Or fix her a drink/coffee/snack.

56. If I lose that loving feeling...

You're looking for somewhere else to live

Congrats, you're shacked up together, your feet are under the table. Literally. Which is good because if they're on top of the table you could find yourself being shown the door.

Cohabiting is not the natural step people imagine it to be. Just because you're in lurve doesn't mean living together is a no-brainer and if you don't step carefully around the pitfalls you will be adding to her automatic mental catalogue of things that annoy her about you. Unreasonable? Of course, but also avoidable so better safe than sorry.

The Talk

It doesn't matter if you've been staying over at hers/she's been staying at yours for years the moment one or other of you is about to move in then the ground rules change. So sit down beforehand and have The Talk.

Here's an idea for you
Create a To Do board. It could be a white board, the fridge door, or a cork board but its purpose is as a reminder of all the stuff that hasn't been addressed. Unexpected bills and tasks go up on the board as a reminder that you have to make a joint decision about it rather than just getting put off because neither of you really sees the problem as their own.

The stuff you're going to have to sort out is basic things like who pays what bills. Do you split fifty fifty or is one of you the bigger earner and happy to pay a bigger share? Who's going to buy the shopping? Would a household kitty help? Speaking of which who takes care of the pets/walks the dog/feeds the goldfish/waters the plants? Are you expecting her to wash your clothes? Leaving aside whether or not that's reasonable in this day and age it's definitely a good idea to say so now rather than plunge in and have her find out the hard way. Think about what happens to the other person's furniture – which sofa gets to stay? What are you going to do with the rest of your stuff? Sell it? eBay works wonders for this sort of stuff. Store it? If you have to go to professional storage that's going to cost so take that into account. Bin it? And how are you going to transport it?

If all this sounds seriously unromantic it's because it is, but these issues aren't going to go away by themselves and if you don't address them up front they will rub and chafe at your relationship. Don't let money become a biggie. Consider a joint account for household expenses and a separate one for your self indulgence. That way when you blow a month's salary on computer games or fishing tackle she's less likely to resent it. Be wary of things that fall in between. You might think a plasma screen TV is a joint expense for the house, she might think it's just a boy's toy for watching footie. Discuss first, buy later.

If there are things you really hate – like her collection of cuddly toys (or yours) then get that out in the open right from the start. Ideally you would both have some private space which can act as a den for your magnificent collection of toy soldiers or a hideaway for her fake leopard skin furniture. In reality however, most of us barely have the space to swing a cat so you may have to agree on his and hers cupboards for the stuff that isn't fit for shared display.

"All marriages are happy. It's the living together afterward that causes all the trouble." **Raymond Hull,** *writer*

Hygiene is a biggie. In most households it's the man who's messier and most often we don't even really notice that. Having your sports kit strewn across the floor looks homely to us, but to her it may be marginally less charming. Have a chat about who does the basic chores of cleaning and consider a rota whereby you alternate who does what or divvy up different tasks so that yes, it really is your problem if there's a ring around the bath.

57. It's the thought that counts

Presents are a minefield so careful where you step

We've all bought people things because really we wanted them ourselves. The lingerie business makes a lot of money (and has a good old giggle) selling thongs to eternally hopeful blokes who will give them on birthdays and never see them again.

Underwear is a tough thing to get right and one that women don't really like so it's best avoided unless she has clearly indicated she wanted something and you checked her size against the stuff she really does wear.

Check your facts

Don't wing it when it comes to sizes.

Men typically have no idea what a size eight is and telling shop girls that 'she's kind of your size only with bigger breasts' is only going to get you in trouble. Do be careful not to take the size from those clothes she intends to get into next summer – only go on the basis of something she wore yesterday. Don't get caught studying her underwear labels, by the way, as this can very easily be misinterpreted.

Get help

When in doubt get some professional help. If you're buying anything where male judgement may not be up to the task (perfume, flowers, Meg Ryan movies) then find someone who knows. Don't just tell the florist you want some flowers, tell them what the occasion is and give them an idea of her character (adventurous? conservative? glamorous?). This doesn't work well with petrol stations, which is another very good reason not to shop at Shell if you don't want to spend the night in the spare room.

Step up a gear

Don't ever buy her something that you would be happy to give to your mum. Choccies and bath salts are the obvious examples. That said, women do like both the above so lift your game by thinking of the next step. Bath salts are so so, but buy her a voucher for a day in a spa (see above on getting help for this choice) and your thoughtfulness will be held out as an example to her female friends. Of course their boyfriends will then hate you.

When it comes to chocolate the rule of thumb is that if you can buy it in a supermarket then it just doesn't cut it. Chocolates should be either Belgian, or handmade, or both to really fit the bill and there are plenty of online chocolate specialists at hand to help you. Try www.chocolatetrading.co.uk.

"Homer, I've gone through seven years of receipts, and you've spent less on gifts for me than you have on temporary tattoos." **Marge Simpson**

Take notes

Her birthday only comes around once a year but all year long she will point at things in magazines and comment on stuff in shop windows. Pay particular attention to things she picks up in shops even though she doesn't buy them. Then when you get home make a note. You'll thank yourself when it comes up to the dreaded b-day.

Still stuck?

Try one of the online gift shops that specialise in oddball things. Iwantoneofthose.com is a good starting point, with gift ideas ranging from chocolate fountains to goats (she doesn't get the goat; some deserving villagers get to keep the goat).

Be selfless

You're not going to like this but sometimes the best present is you. Nope, not the way you're thinking, but giving up your time to do something you don't want to. Like going to a spa with her, or her kind of ideal weekend away, something she knows you don't really want to do. That way she not only gets her way, but sees that you're prepared to suffer just to be with her. Just don't sulk.

Here's an idea for you

If you truly want her to wear a thong or any item of underwear made of waterproof material and/or provided with holes in unusual places then give it to her on your birthday not hers. That way she's got to humour you at least once.

58. Keep it clean guys

You might think you're house-trained, but chances are she's not so sure

Cleanliness, as we all know, is next to impossible. Such is the perverse mentality of our twisted sisters, however, that a lack of cleanliness can very easily come just before being given the push.

Get a group of women together and ask what bugs them most about their men and you will be treated to a check list of cleaning issues like you wouldn't believe. We tried to get some feedback on the subject from our scientifically selected opinion group of the opposite sex and had to give up because once started on the subject they just wouldn't stop. So for a little harmony around the house just remember that washing up gloves aren't just for kinky sex. Here's a basic tick list.

Toilet training

You know the one about putting the loo seat back down so you shouldn't have to be told. For some reason women fix on this as proof positive of male thoughtlessness, so leaving the seat up is pretty much the same thing as wearing a T-Shirt saying 'yes I've completely taken you for granted, now where's my dinner'. Although that said I once lifted the seat in a house shared by five women to find a message taped to the underside saying 'thank god; a man in the house'.

I realise you're a gent so you're careful not to miss. But it seems we do sometimes, and oddly enough drop marks on the seat or on the floor

Here's an idea for you
If you're moving in then think about getting her a dishwasher as a present. Don't see it as an expense, see it as an automated white goods argument remover. Even if she knows exactly why you're doing it she's hardly going to say no.

don't seem to go down too well, so look out for it and if you drop, you deal with it. If you do happen to have had a couple of sherberts too many and you're relieving yourself in her place then swallow your macho pride and sit down. No one will know. This goes double for first dates. Be warned however; loos are just the beginning.

Minty freshness – all over the place

Nobody actually cites the toothpaste as the reason for divorce but any marriage counsellor can tell you that squeezing from the middle, and leaving the cap off rank right up there with hating her mother (and saying so) as one of the fastest ways to kill off all things connubial. Do yourself a favour, buy the stuff in one of those pump type tubes that squeeze it out for you and don't have a cap to lose.

Knickers

Another classic trap this. You think nothing of leaving yesterday's knickers casually draped over the chair because that's where they landed when you did that little flip kick you use to get them off. She doesn't see that. She sees a flashing billboard that says 'I think you are my mum and will willingly pick up and wash my soiled undies'. Even if that's exactly what you do think you must learn to love the laundry basket if you want her to do anything for you ever again.

Washing up

Always offer and always mean it.

Sock

See knickers but with one other little tip – take them off before your trousers. Very few men look good in just their socks and the rest of us just look like we've stopped making an effort. Which is the entry ramp to the slippery slope.

"Cleanliness becomes more important when godliness is unlikely"

P.J. O'Rourke

59. No thanks for the memories

Dealing with ex-partners

Keep your ex-partners out of this relationship because that's not the kind of threesome you want to find yourself in.

Exes are a fact of life, but unlike death and taxes they are not an inevitable one. As grown up as it may seem to stay in touch with your ex you are taking real risks with your current relationship if you do. While there's no point pretending they never existed, there is a lot to be said for leaving them firmly in the past.

Here are some rules to make you an ex-pert:

Never compare

Of course you would never be thoughtless enough to do a thing like that would you? You would never say 'she was much better than you at that' because you know you would be risking pain for both of you. However, you might be guilty of unwitting comparison, either because you don't notice you're doing it, or because it's entirely in the imagination of your current. There's the catch – you don't have to say a word to introduce comparisons. If you and your new love are doing something that she knows you once did with your ex then the comparison is just under the surface anyway. So try to do new things, create new habits and hobbies that are based uniquely around your new relationship.

Don't relive old battles

She doesn't want to know how evil your ex was. You might think it's a confirmation of how much better things are now but she will be at best bored and at worst horrified by how you still haven't gotten over your ex. If you're still grumbling and resentful about the ex then you haven't got her out of your head and you need to work harder on moving on not on airing your grievances. Save the grumbles for your mates. As long as you stand your round they'll stand your stories.

Don't kid yourself

Staying friends with the ex sounds like a splendid thing and doubly so if there are children involved but as with so many things be careful that you're not duping yourself. Being hostile to an ex speaks volumes about unresolved issues but going over the top about being buddies can mean exactly the same. It's a rare ex-couple that doesn't still harbour all sorts of issues about the old relationship and you may both end up kidding yourself that all is well rather than accepting that there are problems that aren't going to go away. Be absolutely honest about why you're still in touch with her. Do you still need/want/miss her? Are you one hundred per cent sure you're not hankering after a make up? Because if you are then it's a certainty that your new love will instinctively pick up on this. Actually she may decide that's the case whatever the truth.

"I still miss my ex.... but my aim is improving" **Traditional**

Don't create a triangle

No, your current doesn't want to go out with your ex in tow. She may say that's fine but she's proving how strong she is. You may feel extremely manly being out and about with not one but two conquests but sooner or later this will blow up in your face. And as for sex with the ex? Don't even think about it. Seeing your ex lover as a fall back or stand by for sex means you're ignoring the damage you're doing to yourself by not moving on.

Here's an idea for you

Still in touch with the ex? Why? Don't be vague about it – write down a list of reasons and sort them by importance. If 'children' top the list then yes you're going to have to work out a relationship to minimise the pain all round. If 'having a laugh' is the best you can come up with then it's time to decide whether you are potentially prepared to jeopardise your current relationship for that.

Sorry!
x

60. Making up doesn't have to be so hard to do

The Fonz isn't the only one who finds it hard to say sorry. Sometimes we all do. We're just not always that good at it.

You're a manly man but you're also human so you will make mistakes and have stupid rows about silly little things. At which point you have a problem because one thing we men are seriously bad about is saying sorry.

Just do it

Say to yourself out loud 'I'm sorry, I didn't mean it but I've acted like an idiot'. Was that so hard? Now go say it to her. Remember to say you've acted like an idiot not that you are an idiot because if she's still angry there's a high chance she'll snap back 'yes' and it's less upsetting to be told you've acted like an idiot than to be called one.

Say it without speaking

Sometimes the written word is way more powerful than speech and heated moments are a good example. If you've just upset her (and probably yourself in the process) then it may help cool things down by writing down your apology. Keep it simple, keep it honest, don't put in any 'buts', and tell her you love her. Now email it to her, text her, or write it on a note and place it where she alone will find it.

Make a reminder board

If you don't have one already then create a collection of pictures of the good times; of the two of you doing all the things that matter to you and have mattered over the past. Then make it a rule that when you're having an argument you have to both take a look at the reminder board and ask yourself whether the argument is really worth it. Of course if the best picture you can come up with is the two of you in the rain at Cleethorpes then this is a potentially risky strategy.

Commemorate past rows

I once knew a French couple who bought each other pot plants in honour of famous rows they had had. The idea was that the plant was not just a way of saying sorry, but also a reminder that they had rowed over things before and come through it. They had a small forest of these things but it turned out that they knew each one. Challenging them I pointed to one plant and asked what it was. Turned out it was called 'Châtelet' – the name of a Paris metro station. It seems he had agreed to meet her outside the entrance. Châtelet has more entrances than any other metro station (on the planet I think). They both laughed with embarrassment that they'd even had a row over that and the system seemed to work for them.

"Words are a wonderful form of communication, but they will never replace kisses and punches" **Ashleigh Brilliant** *(cartoonist)*

But don't...

Rely on cheesy gifts. Women know full well that flowers, while usually appreciated, can be a lazy way of avoiding the real business of saying sorry and meaning it.

Wait for it all to go away. By all means wait for things to cool down, but acknowledge that you've had a spat and say sorry for arguing even if you aren't sorry for disagreeing. Pretend it will all go away and you risk festering sores.

Expect her to make the first move. You should be manly enough to take it on yourself to take action. No matter how wrong she was. At least get the ball rolling and say you're sorry you got angry.

Here's an idea for you

Take a leaf from basketball and try the 'Time Out' trick. Often rows get worse because one or the other partner pulls away and withdraws out of frustration and anger. Instead of doing that agree to a time out so either person can call time at any moment and you both back off for an agreed period – say ten minutes. After that you have to come back together and start again, rather than just let it simmer.

Because all work and no play makes Jack an axe-wielding maniac. And we wouldn't want that now, would we?

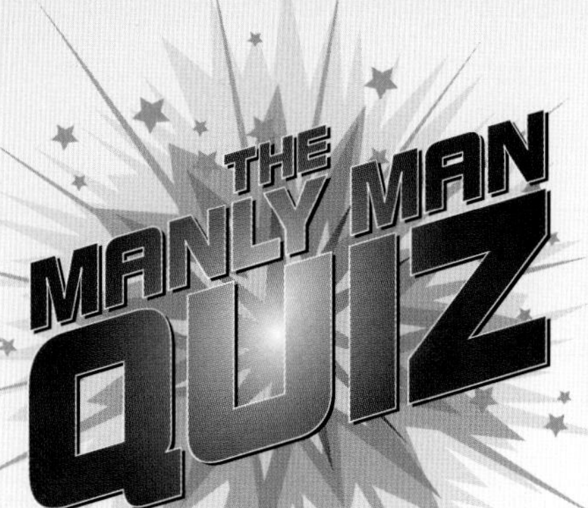

First past the

Read on for tips on being a real man's man.

You're in a smart restaurant and she expects you to choose the wine, do you:

1. Without looking at the menu ask if they have your favourite St Emilion?

2. Pick the one right in the middle of the price range?

3. Look for one with a familiar noun in the name; nun, bull, that sort of thing?

You're in a casino, do you

1. Take your usual seat at the baccarat table?

2. Head for the roulette wheel and bet on a colour?

3. Elbow the pensioners aside and play the slots?

Your 'speed dial' numbers include:

1. Your tailor, a designer florist, and a brace of maître d's.

2. Your loved one, your best mate, that nice little bistro.

3. Pizza delivery, offie, bookie.

st... or non starter?

Mainly 1s: Always a pleasure to see you Mr Bond. Read on though – even you might learn something.

Mainly 2s: You know how to enjoy yourself, but there's a whole lot more out there if you take a little time to read some of the next few ideas.

Mainly 3s: If belching and scratching yourself don't count can you honestly claim to have a hobby? You really need to take a long hard look at some of the ideas that follow.

61. Lap dancing clubs

Rules of engagement

Sooner or later, you're going to end up in a lap dancing club. Trust us, you will. So what's the etiquette?

The average strip club doesn't bring out the best in the average man. When booze, money and naked women are in the same place, most guys go a bit mental. The best thing that can happen to you is that you'll wake up the next morning with a headache and an empty wallet and say to yourself: 'what was I thinking?' The worst is too awful to contemplate.

Always keen to help you out, we have conducted extensive first-hand research into how you ought to behave by asking the experts: the girls who work there.

The first thing to do is to pick a venue to suit your aspirations and budget. The big, corporate clubs often attract the most beautiful girls (these days, most come from Central and Eastern Europe or South America), but are geared towards guys with expense accounts. If you are lap dancing on a budget, there are smaller clubs, and some pubs. They are a bit more rough-and-ready, but often more friendly and tolerant. The web pages at www.undressedtokill.com have location and reviews for the UK.

At the high-end clubs, the girls are constantly dancing on stage. They will come and ask you if you want a table dance or a private dance – the prices vary. A table dance means they will stand in front

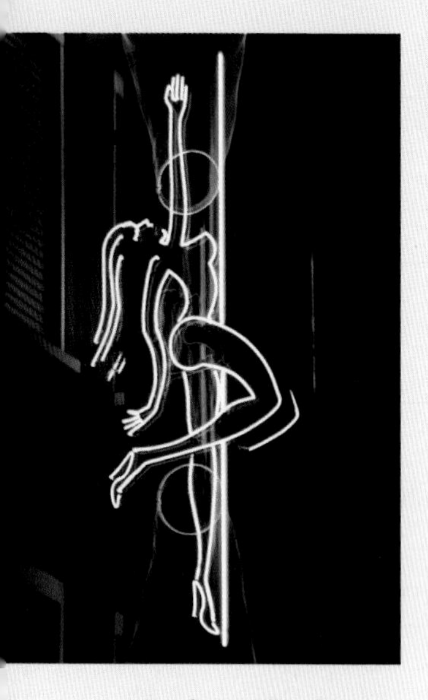

Here's an idea for you

Many lap dancing clubs employ about twice as many girls as they need to at peak time. In the late evening when the crowds show up, this can get manic as girl after girl hits on you. If you want a more relaxing time with your mates, a drink and a chat and maybe a dance, pop in during the early evening.

of you and dance for one song. If offered, a 'private dance' will take you to a closed off area, which might mean more nudity or a more intimate experience (within the terms of the law and their licence), and a standard price is £20. If you don't want either of these, just say, 'no thank you', firmly but politely. At some of the bar venues, the girls will collect change in a glass from the punters before they dance on stage. The going rate is £1. Don't try and get out of paying, it's cheap and insulting. Every club you will visit always works as cash only. Stripper clothes don't have a pocket for a credit card terminal.

The other essential pieces of advice are: be friendly and don't break the rules. Be friendly to the bouncers, who have zero tolerance for trouble and don't want to debate with you. Be friendly to the other punters, it's not a competition. Most of all: be friendly to the girls. When a beautiful woman wiggles her way towards you, batting her eyelashes and asking your name, this shouldn't be a problem.

Clubs have their own rules for the distance between you and the girl in your lap dance, the cost and the duration. Ask the bouncer or one of the girls. If you break the rules, you may get a nasty slap. The girls hate gropers, and will warn each other about you if you transgress. Many of them work 12-hour shifts in very high heels among very drunk men. When you pinch their bums and palm their breasts, they often miss the humorous element. This is especially true in a private dance, where the exposed bits of the dancers are so close you can touch them. Don't. If you don't trust your wandering hands, sit on them. And don't lick any part of the girls: they don't like it.

The second pet hate: customers who smell bad. If you want anything more than minimum service at maximum distance have a shower before you go out. Wear clean clothes.

Take care of those two and you're well above average. As a result, the girls might want to talk to you. Many of them are smart and interesting, but they get asked where they are from, when they came to the UK, whether they like their work and whether they have a boyfriend at least 20 times a day. Ask them something original, about their lives, or what they like to do when they are not working, or have a joke with them and you'll get better service. Tell them the truth about yourself if you want a long conversation. They know you've got a girlfriend; they aren't asking to replace her.

We shouldn't need to say this, but we will: don't start conversations by telling the girls they have gorgeous tits, and look them in the eye when they are talking to you. You get plenty of time to look elsewhere later.

"The major civilizing force in the world is not religion, it is sex."
Hugh Hefner

62. Car trouble

Lifting the bonnet

You don't have to be a mechanic, but let's face it, there's nothing very manly about standing around by a dead car with no idea of what to do.

When there's car trouble the first thing you do is pop the bonnet and look under it with a worried look, right? But do you have a clue what you're looking for? Fact is that breakdown is not the time to pop the bonnet at all – you should have done that long ago. A little bit of routine maintenance goes a long way towards avoiding car trouble – and means that if you do break down at least you don't have to look completely clueless.

Popping the bonnet

Don't wait for something to go wrong. Go pop that bonnet now. That's not as easy as it sounds – in fact just popping the bonnet is your first test of motoring manliness and it's not one you want to have to go through with an audience unless you've mastered it beforehand. The bonnet release could be under the steering column, below the dashboard on the driver's or passenger's side, or even in the glove compartment (although that's usually just Rolls Royces). Some Fords even have the bonnet release hidden under the Ford logo on the car's grille – which makes you think they're deliberately trying to ridicule those of us not man enough to know where to look. Men traditionally hate manuals but if you can't find the damn thing then that's what you have to look for next.

Here's an idea for you

Breakdowns do happen, and even manly men can't always know why so at least be suitably manly about waiting for help. Keep your RAC/AA membership up to date and have a survival kit in the boot. That means a warning triangle, a bottle of water, a blanket, a reflective vest and a road atlas so you know exactly where you are when the nice men ask. That way you won't look helpless while you wait for help.

Bonnet up, now what?

Checking your fluid levels is probably the simplest and most effective thing you can do to avoid car trouble, starting with the oil.

First find the dipstick – the thin rod that slots into the engine. Take the oil level when the engine is cold if possible and do that by pulling the dipstick out, wiping it, putting it back in and pulling it out again. You should see the level of the oil from the residue on the stick. There are two lines clearly marked on the stick and if the oil level is between them you're fine. If it looks closer to the lower of the two put some oil in. The oil goes in through the filler cap on top of the engine. Just be sure you don't confuse it with the water filler cap – if in doubt smell it. The car handbook tells you the right type of oil to use.

Water is in a small tank, usually marked 'water' (doh). There is a minimum and a maximum level and the coolant level should be between the two. Don't take the water filler cap off if the engine is hot or else you'll release steam, leap backwards, bang your head on the bonnet and swear a lot.

There's also a plastic bottle or tank for water which is tucked away to one side. That's for your windscreen washers, it doesn't heat up, so you can pop the top of that any time it takes your fancy. If you've got a rear wiper you'll also have a rear washer bottle.

"I want to die in my sleep like my grandfather... Not screaming and yelling like the passengers in his car."

Will Shriner, *comedian*

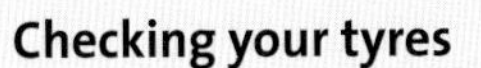

Checking your tyres

1.6mm is the legal limit of tread and that's measured into the grooves on the tyre, not into any cracks or holes you might find. In fact the wear must be even across the tyre to be legal. If they're looking balder and more desperate than Bruce Willis it's time to get new ones. Uneven wear may be a sign of more serious problems and you'll want to have that checked.

Know your tyre pressures (manual time again) and check them at the petrol station using the air nozzles.

63. Cheat's cuisine

How to host without skill or effort

Special occasion looming? Naturally, the smart move would be to serve up a cordon bleu foodgasm but (a) you haven't got the ability and (b) you can't be arsed. Time to cheat.

So you eat ready meals – who doesn't? Except that this time you've got someone coming round for dinner, or it's a romantic occasion, or there's a growing feeling that you're just a loafer in the home. Fraudulent cooking is one of the finest arts for the aspiring cad to master. Skill with food conveys an air of worldliness, an understanding of the finer things in life, a practical ability in the kitchen and it can get you out of all kinds of scrapes by suggesting simultaneously that you are pulling your weight in the household and of course you love her.

The bottom line is that you are going to go out and get that supermarket ready meal because it's cheap and easy and even you know how to heat up lasagne. It's where you go from here that decides whether you are going to be hero or zero come suppertime.

Presentation is everything. Slap your pasta down on the table in its tinfoil package and you might as well pack your bags. Instead make a big fuss of needing to be left alone in the kitchen (this is why chefs develop their melodramatic flair) so no one can see what you're up to and remember to dispose of the wrappings very carefully indeed. The rest of the devilry is in the detail.

Lay the table with side plates for bread and butter. Have the butter itself in a ramekin (those little white bowls you always thought were ashtrays) and remember to lay out separate (larger) glasses for water as well as those for wine. Remember the candle – not only does it look romantic but it hides a multitude of sins when it comes to your food. Big white plates always work best and all food that's brought to the table should be in a serving dish (the plastic microwave tub doesn't count).

Garnishes are by far the easiest way of making dull grub look like haute cuisine. Fresh herbs are the best and the Manly Man team's favourite recommendation is Delia Smith's tip of throwing a handful of fresh basil leaves over any pasta dish – tastes great, looks pro.

If you're really pushing the boat out and trying to make up for major misdemeanours then get hold of some edible flowers for a garnish. Cheese shavings (reach for the vegetable peeler) or ground nuts also work wonders. A swirl of cream (or yoghurt if weight conscious) will transform even tinned soups, stews, and curries, especially if you then dust it with a bit of ground paprika. Judiciously placed olives will do the same for hummus, tsatsiki, and pretty much any other dip. If you're going to have good old veg, then remember that baby versions of the corn, carrots, cabbages et al. not only look exotic and cute but also cook faster (result!).

A few easy touches can transform the simplest of things. Shop-bought meals are usually quickly recognised so go for the fancy premium versions available from the more up-market supermarkets and then slice mozzarella on top, melt it and garnish with fresh herbs so it looks different. A baguette or piece of pitta is bread but slice it diagonally, toast it and pour a little olive oil on it and it becomes cold-pressed, drizzled crostini. You didn't know you had it in you, did you?

Here's an idea for you

Check online for gourmet delivery companies that deliver the ingredients and instructions. Leaping Salmon blazed this particular trail by delivering top-quality ingredients to culinarily challenged Londoners. The meals come in kits, already washed, sliced and measured, just waiting for you to throw together, heat according to instructions and then emerge triumphantly to general applause (as long as you remember to hide the instructions afterwards). The idea has caught on and similar outfits are offering the meal kit approaches at mainline stations and on the Internet. Don't forget that all the above tips are still applicable, even if you've craftily ordered out.

64. Fake being well read

Given that we're still judged by what we read, how do you fake being well read if you've flipped through nothing but porn and Harry Potter since school?

Are you the kind of guy who gets annoyed about the fact that, however bad the book, and however good the TV drama, you will always get more cred for having read a book than for watching the TV?

Victoria Beckham ('Posh Spice') once confessed to 'never having read a book' in her life and was immediately ridiculed by all and sundry. She quickly took it back. While it's fair to say that ridiculing Posh is fair game at any time, it's interesting that even bubblegum pop eye-candy can't be seen to be poorly read – it's an admission too far for anyone, it seems. So if your cultural tastes lean more to Spice Girl than Solzhenitsyn then this is what to do.

First off consider what your goal is in trying to pull this off. Are you attempting an all-round performance with a view to creating an aura of sophistication and culture, or are you trying to impress (or simply keep up with) someone who is themselves better read than you? Think carefully because the answer will define your strategy.

If you've never really read anything more taxing than cereal packets yet need to pass yourself off as the bionic bookworm then you're going to have to put in a little bit of legwork. You might even have to read something. Not much, though – that would be missing the

point. For a start don't bother with any of the big fat ones (not that you were going to anyway). There are short cuts to cultivating your literary savoir-faire – reading a couple of short poems, for example, preferably in a foreign language, will go a long way.

If you realise you are expected to know a novelist then don't go for the favourites but instead find something short and obscure. Most of the big boys have written the odd short story or novella on the way to fame and the more weird and wonderful the better. Use this to head off any direct questions about the other books you've read. For example, if anyone starts talking about Hemingway's *For Whom The Bell Tolls* you need only nod and mumble something about the seeds for the novels being sowed early in the (satisfyingly) short stories.

A brilliant tip for just-add-water intellectualism is to skim a copy of Schopenhauer's *Essays and Aphorisms*, which provides bite-size nuggets barely longer than the jokes in a Christmas cracker. Because they are philosophical musings on just about anything, they are also ripe to be brought out on almost any occasion. Use discretion when doing this, though; the person who insists on coming out with the same phrase over and over doesn't come across as well read, just well annoying.

Good phrases for the bluffer include lots of vague adjectives ('authoritative', 'entrancing', 'hypnotic') and a couple of equally vague themes ('alienation', 'timelessness', 'loss of innocence'). String these together and you're on a winner. Try it. You can sum up anything from Chekov to *Charlie and the Chocolate Factory* as a 'hypnotic study of alienation and loss'.

Here's an idea for you

Get a copy of **How to Become Ridiculously Well-read in One Evening: A Collection of Literary Encapsulations,** *edited by E. Parrott. It's a collection of humorous poems summarising the classics. The odd thing is that, while it is meant as humour, much like spoof history book* **1066 And All That,** *it nonetheless gives you some great thumbnail sketches of the literary greats and an insight into what a well-read person's reading list should feature.*

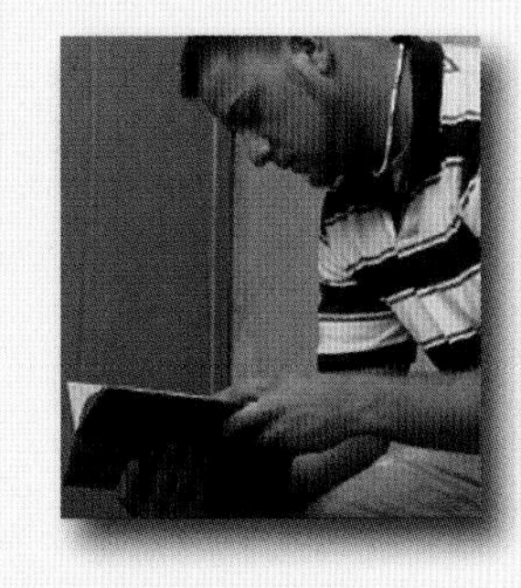

By the way, if you're pretending knowledge of books you've never read and it looks like you're going to be rumbled, don't forget that even those who really have read the work are unlikely to remember much detail. This is doubly so if they also read hundreds of other books and have been doing so for a long time. So a risky (but very satisfying) strategy is to infer that you read the entire works of an author years ago in your youth when devouring all the world's literature. This is harder to pull off if you're closer to sixteen than sixty but only literature professors can quote chapter and verse from books they've read. There is even a way to reverse this and head off the rumbling. When someone is detailing a precise scene or character, smile fondly and suggest that this freshness is because of their having only just discovered the writer. Then glaze over gently and nod as if casting your mind back to those days when you too were gauche enough to get excited about Gogol or Proust.

You can sum up anything from Chekov to *Charlie and the Chocolate Factory* as a 'hypnotic study of alienation and loss'.

65. Bluffing it as a wine buff

A few easily affected mannerisms and well-chosen phrases will help you get away with it when you're posing as a wine buff.

Anyone planning to fake it in the world of wine needs to remember just one thing – actions speak much, much louder than words. There are two pieces of simple logic behind this strategy. The first is that there are a few easily performed rituals that will instil such confidence in your oenological prowess that neither professionals nor amateurs would ever question the pearls of vinous wisdom that might drop from your lips. The other is that really accomplished wine buffs tend to shroud themselves in a mysterious air of silence – it is only the amateurs who drone on about malolactic fermentation and yeasty autolysis.

Here's an idea for you

Take a tip from wannabe rock stars the world over and practice your sniffing and slurping routine in front of a mirror at home. The first stages of spitting practice can be done with water over a hand basin. Remember that even bluffing requires practice.

Seven confidence-instilling rituals

While the half hour required to practice the following might seem onerous, remember that it can take a lifetime to equip yourself with the knowledge required to be a real wine bore.

Step 1: When picking up a bottle, never look at the label before pouring. This will send out a subliminal message that you are the sort of person who can identify a glass of Chateau Rip-Off at fifty paces. Those who can barely tell red from white should simply sneak a sideways glance a second or two later.

Step 2: When pouring a glass of wine, never serve yourself with more than the equivalent of a double spirits measure.

Step 3: Leaving the glass on the table, place your forefinger and your index finger either side of the base of the stem and gently rotate the glass as though moving it round a ouija board. Your manner should be deliberately casual and slightly distracted and you should talk about some trivial, unrelated subject in the way that surgeons do while performing open-heart surgery on TV hospital dramas. This will give the impression that tasting wine is something that you do all the time – and could happily do in your sleep.

Step 4: Continuing your conversation – and affecting the same slightly distracted manner – hold the glass at arm's length at a forty-five degree angle, ideally holding it in the direction of a source of natural light and frown slightly but don't pass comment. Tipping the contents of the glass over your shoes will obviously give the game away.

Step 5: Next, lift the glass to your face in one swift movement and immerse your nose deep into the body of the glass. Breathe deeply as you would with an inhaler.

Step 6: With another swift movement, sip from the glass and swill the wine round your mouth while gently sucking air between your lips. If you suck too forcefully there's a chance that you will inhale the wine and cough violently, creating a Jackson Pollock style pattern on your shirt, so suck with care.

Step 7: If there is a dedicated spittoon, accomplished spitters can provide a really convincing finale by discharging a fine stream of wine from their lips. (When you are really good, your aim and range should be sufficient to take out a fly on the other side of the room.)

Learning to sit on the fence

A few pre-rehearsed comments will speak far more loudly than a litany of fact and half-baked opinions. Ideally these should be as non-committal as possible (it's always embarrassing to wax lyrical about a wine, only to discover that it was badly corked or mistakenly poured from a bottle that was opened a fortnight beforehand). Remember that wine appreciation is a bit like abstract art – in the same way that one man's paint spill is another's abstract expressionism, one man's vinegar is another's vinous nectar. Also avoid commenting on anything too specific such as its origin, grape variety or vintage – wild guesses will inevitably get you into trouble.

The following all-purpose phrases can be said about any wine. They will satisfy amateurs and shouldn't raise the suspicions of professionals:

'What a VERY interesting wine.'

'Very cool climate.' [This is worth a punt since almost all good-quality wines are made in cool areas.]

'Amazingly deep colour.' [All wine is an amazingly deep colour.]

'It would be interesting to see how it responded to another year or two in bottle.'

'Goodness, isn't it fascinating to compare this with the 1999' (or whichever was the preceding vintage).

66. Local heroes

What should a good wine taste like?

Some of the best wines have an extra dimension: as well as being delicious they also express the winemaking tradition of the area where they were made. And the best needn't cost the earth.

What should a good wine taste like? 'Fabulous' is the obvious answer. If only it were so simple!

Wine falls into two categories: the stuff that reflects the winemaking tradition of the region where it was produced and the sort that tastes as though it could have been made anywhere in the world where the sun shines enough to ripen grapes. There's not much wrong with the latter; the huge advances in winemaking technology in the last decade have made it possible to produce good-value wines virtually anywhere. What sets these two kinds of wine apart is something that wine buffs call 'typicity' – meaning that they conform to a certain style that is typical of the wine's birthplace. How important is this quality? If wine is enjoyable to drink, surely to worry about typicity is nothing more than splitting hairs? Possibly. But a world without wines that reflect their origins would be very boring. Which would you rather do? Drive hundreds of miles through the unchanging landscape of the American plains or wind your way through the ever-changing scenery of France, Italy or Spain?

When it comes to wine, variety is undoubtedly the spice of life. While the consistency of 'global' wines might offer a convenient option for everyday drinking, the highs and lows are provided by wines that taste of the place they come from. There are parallels between winemaking and cookery. The people of every region of the world have their own tastes in food that are influenced by the available ingredients, the climate and the gastronomic tradition that has evolved over the years. Precisely the same is true of wine.

A sense of place versus a suggestion of terroir

Describing a wine as having a 'sense of place' could easily be confused with suggesting that it expresses terroir. Though terroir does contribute to the sense of place, the typicity of a wine has more to do with winemaking tradition – the style of wine created by techniques such as oak ageing and blending. The grim reapers of the wine world might make gloomy predictions that typical wines are being replaced with ones that have no regional characteristics, but the fact is that these two kinds of wine can coexist happily side by side.

"No-one escapes from his individuality."

Arthur Schopenhauer

Taste test – REDS

To distinguish between these two kinds of wine try comparing the following:

- Inexpensive Chilean Merlot + good-quality Rioja

Taste test – WHITES

- Inexpensive Chilean Sauvignon Blanc + good-quality Sancerre

Compare and contrast

In each case, ask yourself which of the two wines in the glasses before you could have been made anywhere in the world and which has an idiosyncratic feel that is all its own.

Where to find typical wines

Although it is easy to see typicity as a quality that is peculiar to European wine regions such as France, Italy and Spain, some New World areas are developing their own styles and winemaking traditions. For instance Sauvignon Blanc from Marlborough in New Zealand tastes very different from Sauvignon from Western Australia, and Barossa Shiraz has a style different from Shiraz made in South Africa. Here are areas where you are likely to find more typical wines that are true to local tradition than homogenous 'global wine':

Old world

Bordeaux
Burgundy
The Mosel Valley
The Loire
Rioja
The South of France
Tuscany

The new world

The Barossa Valley
The Clare Valley
The Hunter Valley
The Margaret River
The Napa Valley
Sonoma

Here's an idea for you

Typical wines tend to be part of a gastronomic tradition. Try drinking wines that are typical of an area with corresponding regional specialities, e.g. bold southern French red with cassoulet, and Muscadet with seafood.

67. Put your palate through its paces

Understanding a wine's flavour is a much more complex art than you might imagine. But rest assured: with plenty of time, practise makes perfect.

Although smelling a wine seems a straightforward action (no more difficult than smelling a flower or a pint of milk really), tasting it is more tricky, because different areas of the palate appear to respond in different ways to different types of flavour.

"I am tempted to believe that smell and taste are in fact but a single composite sense, whose laboratory is the mouth and its chimney the nose."
Brillat Savarin

For this reason the basic principle of tasting is to swill the wine around your mouth like mouthwash to get as much of the wine in contact with as many of your taste buds as possible. Often it can help to aerate the wine by slurping a little air into your mouth through pursed lips. This can require practise. (If you get it wrong there's a danger that you'll splutter a mouthful of wine down your front.)

Assessing flavour

The basic aim of tasting is to try to judge: the wine's acidity, sweetness, how well the sweetness and acidity are balanced, bitterness, how long any of these qualities stay in the mouth (known by wine buffs as their 'length').

The tools

You will need: suitable glasses, still mineral water, paper labels (if blind tasting), water biscuits (if you are spitting) a large receptacle such as a Champagne bucket, a notebook and pen.

The procedure

Everybody develops their own technique, so experiment until you find a tasting style that you feel happy with. But you might begin using the following procedure:

1. Hold up to a window (professional tasting rooms always have a good source of natural light for this purpose) and note the colour. Is it dense, pale or somewhere in-between? You might also want to judge the wine's viscosity, i.e. whether it leaves a transparent coating on the sides of the glass.
2. Next, swirl the wine around in your glass (this helps to release its aroma) and then lower your nose into the glass, taking a deep breath that will gather the full effect of the wine's aroma. Don't even think about moving to the next stage until you have fully explored the scent – or lack of it – provided by the wine.
3. Now sip a small amount of wine, running it all over your palate, sucking a little air in after it.
4. Either swallow or spit – a procedure that can take years to perfect (the ideal is a fine stream of precisely aimed liquid.
5. Between wines it can sometimes be useful to clean the palate with water and/or a biscuit. You don't need to do this every time you try a new wine – just when you feel that you need to.

Taking notes

There are plenty of reasons for taking notes, including the fact that they provide a record of wines that you have liked should you wish to experience them again. More important is the fact that note-taking forces you to focus on what you are tasting and to try to articulate your thoughts.

To spit or to swallow?

If you are of drinking age, you won't need any advice on this. Some people feel that they haven't really tasted a wine until they have swallowed – although there are no taste buds in the throat, so technically it isn't necessary. Others find that even a hint of alcohol can dampen their objectivity. One option is to spit when you are making an in-depth analysis and later in the evening to swallow. With time you will soon find your ideal method.

Here's an idea for you

To find out how your senses of taste and smell are inextricably linked it isn't necessary to delve into the anatomy of the mouth, tongue and olfactory system. Simply try the following test: taste a glass of wine that normally bursts with flavour and aroma while at the same time holding your nose. What more evidence do you need?

68. Keeping your palate on its toes

Even when you're focusing on a limited number of grape varieties and styles, it's useful to venture occasionally into uncharted territory.

In order to understand wine you need initially to keep the number of wines you focus on to a manageable selection. But in doing this you will only scratch the surface of the huge range of styles and grapes on offer.

Even on the first leg of the path to vinous nirvana, it is important to expose your palate to other styles of wine without letting them cloud your understanding. There are a huge number of wines that no one except a few hardened wine buffs is aware of. Plenty of wines are made purely for local consumption, such as Austrian Gruner Veltliner, Swiss Chasselas, Italian Aglianico, Uruguayan Tannat and Canadian Ice Wine. Though initially you should keep these wines at arm's length, they will eventually be essential for pushing your taste buds to the extremes – just as the best fitness training programme will exercise muscles that you don't normally use. The chances are that you won't like them. But even if you don't they will offer flavours and aromas that your palate and nose wouldn't otherwise be subjected to. They will stretch your senses to the extremes of their experience.

"One should try everything once, except incest and folk-dancing."

Sir Arnold Bax

The secret to tasting offbeat wines is never to get too involved. You don't need to know a great deal about wine in order to enjoy it. It doesn't really matter whether Gruner Veltliner, Tannat, Aglianico or Eiswein is a grape or a style of wine. Nor does it really matter whether they come from Austria, Uruguay, Italy or Canada. What is far more important is that you, your palate and your nose are receptive to them. Of course, when – or if – you find an offbeat wine that you like, that might be the time to investigate the winemaking tradition from which it springs.

Where to seek the weird and wonderful

Although wine is made everywhere from Austria to Zimbabwe, many of the more obscure winemaking regions are devoted to classic French varieties such as Cabernet and Chardonnay. For some really extreme experiences, try wines made from local grape varieties.

- **Austria** – Gruner Veltliner might twist the tongue – but its taste should also keep you on your toes.
- **England** – English wines may not be to everyone's taste, but varieties such as Seyval Banc, Schonburger, Huxelrebe, Bacchus, Kerner and Ortega can't fail to stimulate the palate.
- **Germany** – Plenty of strangers here. Try Scheurebe Silvaner, Lemberger and Dornfelder.
- **Greece** – Ignore the new generation of modern wines and try the native Greek varieties such as Agiorgitiko.

- **Mexico** – Try the fabulous, obscure Petite Sirah grape, which will put predictable Cabernet in the shade.
- **Switzerland** – Go off piste with local specialities such as Chasselas, Arvine and Amigne.

How food can help

When tasting unusual wines such as these, start by doing so in quite a formal way, noting the flavour, aroma and colour so that you are able to make as objective a judgement as possible. However, having done so, it is essential that you have food at hand; few wines are created to be sampled in the formal environment of a tasting. The best option is a dish from the wine's country of origin – for example Chasselas with fondue, Mexican Petite Sirah with chilli and Agiorgitiko with a lamb kebab. It is remarkable how wines taste completely different when experienced in the context of the gastronomic tradition in which they were produced – it also explains why wines might taste delicious in their country of origin but strangely alien once you return home.

Here's an idea for you

Good sources of unusual wines are restaurants that specialise in offbeat cuisine such as German, Lebanese or Swiss. Good Greek, Cypriot and Turkish restaurants also tend to have a wide selection of wines from the Mediterr?anean. Most of these specialist restaurants are likely to have wines that it would be difficult to buy anywhere else. These restaurants will also give you the opportunity to taste the wines in a gastronomic context in which they might not taste quite so weird.

69. All fired up

Summer is here – it's time to barbeque

There's the promise of a sun-filled day and you get the feeling that you want to entertain – summer's here and it's the season to barbecue.

When the weather is bright and you are in the mood to socialise, then the time is right to eat alfresco. But let's be realistic about cooking outside.

Very few people take the time to learn the most basic skills. However, they're so simple that it seems ridiculous to suffer burnt sausages or undercooked chicken, blackened fish and shrivelled burgers.

Timing is everything. So, while you don't need to approach it like a military operation, it is an idea to have a plan for the hour or two that precedes the arrival of your guests. Have meat already marinating, have lights set up ready for when the sun goes down, have seats in sociable groups around the patio and have salads prepared. Let's consider the elements that make up the perfect barbecue.

Type of barbecue

Do you want to cook by gas or charcoal? It's probably just me, but cooking by gas always seems to be the cheat's way out. If you look at it in terms of restaurants, then a gas barbecue is a perfectly respectable but uninspiring bistro while a charcoal grill is more of a quality, five-star affair. I know people who are perfectly happy with gas and say how easy it is to get the grill going and cook food

"Give a man a fish and he will eat for a day. Teach a man to fish and he will eat for a lifetime. Teach a man to create an artificial shortage of fish and he will eat steak."

Jay Leno, *comedian*

without burning it – but don't wimp out. Some things in life present a challenge and perfecting the art of cooking with a charcoal grill is one of them. The object of the exercise is to enjoy the food, after all, and the smoked-in taste of 'genuine' barbecue food only comes with a real fire. The Rolls Royce of the barbecue world is a Charcoal Weber and it's worth every penny (even if it does spend several months of the year parked in the garage).

Guests

You need to have a rough idea of numbers in order to buy the right amount of food. Two to three portions of meat per person, or two of meat and one of fish, is a good guide.

Food

Are you having standard barbecue fare or are you going to put together something more interesting? Think marinated fish kebabs, garlic prawns and stuffed tomatoes. If you buy a decent barbecue you'll get some recipes in the manual but do take the time to search around for more unusual ones. Once you have become governor of your grill you can cook sweet and savoury, small portions and whole joints – so don't just stick to sausages and burgers and hot dogs every time you fire up.

Do try to be reasonably accurate in judging the amounts when buying your meat or fish. Anything that's been left outside waiting to be cooked, and which doesn't get used, will have to be binned. Salads, breads and side dishes can go back into the fridge for the next meal so you can go to town on these. New potatoes are perfect as an accompaniment and have the advantage of being delicious both hot with butter and great with mayonnaise and chives when they have cooled down. And if you know that there will be vegetarians, why not buy a small 'throwaway' barbecue on which to prepare vegetable kebabs or veggie burgers?

Drink

Do remember that you need to provide soft drinks for the drivers – and also bear in mind that whoever is in charge of the barbecue should remain sober for safety reasons!

Lighting

Whether you have fully functioning exterior lights or simply rely on garden flares stuffed into terracotta pots filled with sand – which can double up as ashtrays so you don't have a garden full of butts in the morning – doesn't matter, but you do need something. If the barbie is swinging you want to be able to linger outside long into the night. A 'pub style' garden heater provides warmth and a soft glow, and is now relatively inexpensive.

Be ready to put in preparation time before your barbecue starts and it will be a sure-fire success.

Here's an idea for you

Cleaning a barbecue ranks alongside going to the recycling bank as one of those chores you put off for days but know you've got to face some time. Make sure that leftover charcoal is removed on a regular basis and cut down on the worst of the cooking detritus by lining grates with foil. Remember to soak them in soapy water after the unit has cooled.

70. Guess who's coming to dinner?

Entertaining the boss

You need to plan a menu and put together a formal dinner party for the boss...

When the occasion calls for fine food, the best wine and a beautifully dressed table, it's important that nothing gets rushed.

If you have been employed by the same company for any length of time, the chances are that you will have spent a certain amount of time socialising with your boss. Whether it's office drinks, client cocktail parties or company family days, some events are business-related and others purely social. What can happen at the family occasions, is that your partner can land you in it...

Here's the scenario. You introduce your partner to your boss's partner and you quickly realise that they have a lot more in common than you and your boss. So much so that your partner says to the other person, 'Why don't you both come over to our house next weekend?' Once the invitation is out there, you can't take it back. After you've confirmed the details and moved on with a polite excuse, you then take your partner away to a quiet corner and smack them sharply round the back of the head. Then you start to panic.

(And if you don't, then you're not normal.)

Right, the first thing is: don't let the idea scare you. It had to happen at some point and at least this way you'll get it over with. Who knows, you might even enjoy it so much that you repeat it in the future… hmm. Seriously, just think how much good it might do your career if your boss sees the sparkling, entertaining, relaxed, amusing, witty individual that is concealed behind your tough, serious, stressed-out work persona.

"Nothing ever comes to one, that is worth having, except as a result of hard work."

Booker T. Washington

The first thing to plan is who else to invite along and what sort of meal to prepare. Try to avoid making it an entirely work affair. If a few of your closest friends can be trusted not to embarrass you then include them, plus one or two work colleagues with whom you enjoy socialising. If everyone that you are planning to ask has children, then why not make it a family barbecue? There are plenty of distractions with kids around and everyone can get involved with burning the burgers and tossing the salad. This makes for a relaxing environment, even considering that the boss is there. Who knows, maybe they have hidden barbecuing

talents and will be in their element? If you can't rely on the weather, then still ask families over but arrange to host a buffet instead. If your boss doesn't have children, then don't make it a child-friendly affair. Arrange a dinner party or evening buffet.

Here's an idea for you

If the prospect of cooking a dinner for your boss and having them in your house for several hours fills you with fear and trepidation, there is an easy alternative. Arrange to have cocktails instead. Issue an invite that gives a very specific time range: 'Come for drinks between seven and nine.' Then if things are going well at 9 p.m., you can allow it to drift on. However, if it has been a bit of a minefield full of social gaffes, you can give the wink to a couple of friends and get them to instigate the winding up of the event.

Perfect planning

There is no question that you are probably going to be nervous at the prospect of the boss coming to dinner, and a sunken soufflé, a corked bottle of wine, a set of linen that isn't ironed or a messy bunch of flowers should all be avoided.

The point of the occasion is either to impress or get to know the person and to do that you need to be relaxed. For that to be the case, I would strongly recommend that you do not attempt to cook anything very tricky (no soufflé) or anything that could go wrong at the last minute. Stick to recipes that you know look good and are almost guaranteed to come out right every time. Another important point to bear in mind is that you do not want to be stuck in the kitchen all night. The point of the occasion is to spend time with the boss, so it would be good to include one or two courses on your menu that can be prepared in advance.

This is why it can make sense to have a buffet; you'll only need to disappear when you want to clear plates or restock platters. The other advantage is that people can mingle and move around and you can probably accommodate a few more guests.

Who knows, you might actually enjoy yourself!

71. Make mine a double

How much booze to buy for a party

It can be complicated, so here's how to make sure that you have the right amount of alcohol for your event.

We've all been there. It's late at night and the fridge is empty of beer, the cocktail cabinet is a desert and so it is deemed sensible to start on the leftover bottles of red wine. If I had a pound for every person who blames their hangover on a combination of grape and grain, I would be very rich. Estimating the amounts of drink is never going to be easy and your budget is a major factor in the equation.

You can't predict how long people will be around, but I would suggest a good proportion of those invited will last until the end and there's nothing worse than the drinks running out. So be as generous as your wallet permits with your allowance per person. To estimate how much you might need to spend on alcohol, you can expect this to be approximately half as much per person as you spend per person on food.

Let's think about drinks at a venue. Some of this applies equally to drinks at home, too. Heddy, a top bar manager, has organised the booze and the bar at countless events. His most salient piece of advice is 'know your guests'. He knows that if you have a group combining one or two generations of adults and children at a sit-

"Drinking makes such fools of people, and people are such fools to begin with that it's compounding a felony."

Robert Benchley, *author*

down dinner, they will generally drink far less than guests at a buffet party of friends celebrating a twenty-fifth birthday.

One of the first decisions that he asks people to make is whether they are going to run an open bar, pay for the wine and beer and allow people to buy their own spirits or whether they want to put a tab behind the bar to cover all drinks. Be clear which option you favour so that there are no misunderstandings on the night.

If you are going to put an amount of money behind the bar then ask the manager to keep you informed about how much money has been spent. I would suggest that you want to know when half of the money has gone and again when about 80% has been spent, so that you can monitor the situation and won't get a shock. Don't tell people how much money is in the kitty, but it can be an idea to mention to one or two close friends that it will revert to a paying bar when the money runs out; this will get round.

Have a discussion with the bar manager about what you want the bar staff to say to guests when the money has actually gone. The best approach is to tell people as soon as they approach the bar rather than wait until they have placed their drinks order.

So here are some points to consider:

- Is it a formal occasion? People drink less at a ceremonial affair than during an informal and lively event.
- What time of year is it? In the summer you need to up the amount of soft drinks and beer.
- What time of day is it taking place? You'll need less booze during the day than you will in the evening.

- How old are the people who are coming? Older guests drink less; a younger group will consume more.
- Are you serving food? People also tend to drink less when they are eating.

In general, at a sit-down dinner you should allow two large glasses of wine per person. This is about two-thirds of a bottle of wine and while it doesn't appear to be that much, think of it in these terms: sixty people at the meal equates to a hundred bottles.

If you are buying a lot of wine the advantage is, of course, that you can negotiate on the price per bottle. Remember that you also want to include soft drinks such as juice or cola if there are going to be children at the event. Just a note: if you are going to incorporate toasts, allow two glasses of champagne per person. You can expect to get five glasses per bottle. And please don't be troubled about ordering bottles of mineral water. Ask the staff to put jugs of iced water on the table and instruct them to make sure that they are monitored and refilled as required. This is enough for most people's needs.

Are you planning an evening buffet? Then allow three to four drinks per person for the event. If the party is going to run for a long time, say more than five hours, budget for four to six drinks per guest.

So now you know what you need, get to the bar and order your first drink.

Here's an idea for you

If you are concerned about the quantity of alcohol that is going to be consumed, arrange with waiting staff not to leave bottles on the tables. That way you limit automatic refills. It's a fact that people are much more wasteful with wine when it is left on the table than when it's being served on request.

72. Winning ways with cocktails

Cocktails are a party in a glass but as with parties that can mean a sophisticated soirée just reeking of class, or a teenage cider party that just reeks.

If you're the mature side of eighteen then it's high time you had this cocktail thing sorted out. When you walk into a cocktail bar, or when someone insists that they're celebrating and your usual half of lager just won't do then you don't want to dither. You should be able to pronounce firmly and with confidence the name of the drink you are going to have without so much as looking at a menu and you should know exactly what goes into it. The rules of cocktail drinking are simple:

Rule number one – no plastic monkeys.

You're a man remember, so you don't need to dress up your drink with what looks like a selection of Christmas cracker toys. Sensible cocktails don't come with the toy box on top, and if you're in a drinking hole so naff that it slaps them in there anyway then quietly remove all the debris before raising the glass to your lips.

Rule number two – no stupid names.

Any drink that has to sell itself with the words 'knicker', 'nipple', 'sex', or 'orgasm' is for overexcited teenage boys and the desperately sexually repressed. Avoid.

Rule number three – don't drink anything where you don't know one or more of the key ingredients.
Be honest with yourself, you don't even know where Curaçao is, let alone whether yellow or green taste different to each other (they don't).

Rule number four – blue is not an appropriate colour for an alcoholic drink.
Roughly speaking the more garish the colour the more garish the vomit in a few hours time.

"One martini is alright, two is too many, three is not enough."

James Thurber

Rule number five – ideally a cocktail is based either around a single alcoholic drink, or one principle drink with another adding greater depth to the first.
Think martini. What it should not be is a random selection of equally strong drinks thrown into a glass like a bunch of rowdy soldiers packed into a small room. They will fight, and you will lose. Think Long Island Iced Tea.

The answer is to have a repertoire of just a few simple drinks, each for a different purpose. Tastes vary of course but suggestions would include:

Martini; the old standby. If you are drinking martini and the barman asks how dry you want it, remember that means how little vermouth is added to the gin (or vodka, if it's a vodka martini). This ranges from a ratio of 2:1 to 15:1, or as some insist just showing the vermouth bottle to the gin without actually pouring any in.

Manhattan; sounds smooth and cultivated though since it mixes sweet vermouth in with whiskey (whiskey = Irish, whisky = Scotch) it's not as dry a drink as a martini.

Here's an idea for you

Mojito; the caipirinha factor you can make at home – grind some fresh mint into a class with a teaspoon of sugar, add lime juice, then fill it up with white rum and soda. Nobody agrees on an official ratio for rum and soda so you're free to come up with some rubbish about this being the way you were taught to do it in Maputo/the Ritz/the Rat and Ferret.

Caipirinha; delicious, has that Latin suave thing going for it, and you're never going to have any cachaça around the house so you might as well drink it when you're out.

If at home then a very different rule applies. Unless you're mixing cocktails for yourself (unlikely, but if so then you sir are definitely a better class of hopeless drunk) the chances are that you're mixing for someone else. So the rule is that you want to impress them but not have too many fancy ingredients to get wrong or have to substitute. So think;

Martini; again, you can't really go wrong and all you have to do to seem hyper suave is remember the olive.

Sea breeze; vodka and cranberry – simple, fresh, barely a cocktail at all but it comes with a name so you can sound cool offering one.

73. Getting hog whimperingly drunk without the hangover

The morning after. The words alone have us reaching for coffee and shades. What on earth can we do to dodge that hell? Well, just find the time it takes to read this idea.

Booze: it's not big and it's not clever. It shrivels your liver, puts pounds on your paunch and hoovers the content of your wallet. Worst of all, it leads to the inevitable revelation, usually around two in the morning, that you – yes, you – are in fact the greatest dancer in the world and you don't care who knows it. Then, before you know it, the next day dawns and you've got a pounding head, bleary eyes, and that yummy baboon's armpit sort of feeling in the mouth. Frankly, if that's all you wake up with, you can consider yourself lucky. But wouldn't it be nice if it didn't have to be that way?

The obvious way of dodging hangovers would be not to get drunk, but if you wanted that kind of advice you could have asked your mum for it. There are alternatives.

Here's an idea for you

The jury's still out, but pills alternately known as RU-21 and KGB can be bought at a pharmacy to combat hangovers. Forget stories that the KGB developed them to help agents win drinking competitions – you're still going to get wasted, but the idea is that they speed up the breakdown of the acetaldehyde. The catch is you have to remember to take the pills when you're plastered, including before 'the last drink' (there's a last one!?), which in practice makes them less than reliable.

Before you get drunk

The old college-boy stories about lining your stomach with milk are partly right. It's not that you can literally 'line' your stomach; it's the simple fact that your body will process the alcohol more steadily if it's absorbed along with food, so eat before your jiggle-juice bonanza.

Choose your poison

'Gin makes you sin', 'whisky makes you frisky', 'beer before wine, you'll feel fine' – lyrical verse, doubtless, but entirely fact free. What matters is clarity, purity and quality. The active ingredient in booze is ethanol, a natty little substance, part drug, part food, which your body happily gets to work on to transform so as to metabolise the sugars. So far, so good, except that en route there is a by-product called acetaldehyde: this is vile stuff and is largely responsible for the next-day nasties.

As ethanol goes stale it produces more acetaldehyde, so drinking last week's opened bottle of wine is a bad idea (tip – try finishing it off in one go first time around). The same applies to wines or mixes which are in the process of being distilled or fortified into something stronger. This means cheaper hooch made from low-quality ingredients is likely to pack a sucker punch. Avoid dodgy rum, sherry, et al. if you want to avoid the hangover from hell. And don't even think about 'shooters', in which the colour and sugar drown out any point in using good ingredients.

The other quotient is the congener count. Congeners occur naturally in fermented and distilled drinks and have been identified as another something that increases the hangover factor. Helpfully, the congener count comes with a rule of thumb that even the deeply bladdered can remember – the darker the drink, the higher the hangover risk. Thus port is one of the highest on the congener scale, vodka one of the lowest. It's not, strictly speaking, a congener factor, but drink anything green or blue and you're asking for it.

Remember this isn't the only factor – a poor-quality vodka can easily make up for its low congener count with an extra helping of acetaldehyde. That's the reason why you sometimes hear the boast that such and such booze can be drunk without risk. A product called Bismark schnapps seemed to be a likely contender but, in the end, the *Manly Man* team found that disproving such claims was just a matter of downing enough of the damn stuff.

During the drinking

Avoid carbonated mixers: fizzy drinks get you smashed faster, and that affects your drinking decisions (hmmm, a single malt, or one of everything in the optics?). Above all drink water – as much of it as you can before going to bed. Don't take headache pills in advance as this will put an extra strain on your liver and your liver don't love you no more as it is.

Next day

Ginger is great for settling the guts – try juicing some with apple. Water is good but an isotonic sports drink will get to your cells even better. Vitamins and minerals are also called for. NO, having a hair of the dog isn't a good idea and points the way down a slippery slope.

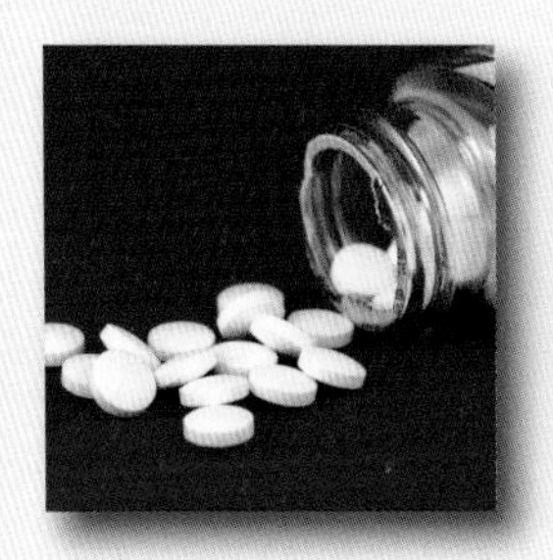   

74. Beating the bookie

There's a gambling proverb: 'In every bet, there's a fool and a thief'. The thief is getting away with it. Problem is: how do you recognise when you're the fool?

At this point, you're probably expecting a (literally) foolproof scheme to win cash when you gamble, like the sort of things blokes tell you down the pub which seem to make perfect sense, such as continually doubling the money you put on black in roulette, or which cards to twist on in blackjack, or the name of a dead cert in the 3.20 at Sandown. If you've ever taken their advice, and we really hope you haven't tried the roulette one, we can confidently tell you now: you're the fool.

In gambling terms, the key to getting away with beating the odds is to bet big when you have an 'edge' – that is, the odds are slightly in your favour – and bet nothing when you don't. It sounds simple, but hardly anyone bets like this. We bet when we think we will win, or when – even worse – we feel lucky.

Luck has nothing to do with this. If you genuinely believe your special lottery numbers mean you are more likely to win the jackpot, get over it. They are just numbers. Gambling is a game of chance.

Here's an idea for you

Check out the Internet betting exchanges. They are popular with smart punters because they offer the chance to find fools. On an exchange like Betfair or Betdaq, you're not making a bet with a bookmaker, you are making it with another individual, and individuals are a much softer touch than a professional bookie. The trick is to spot your fool first. If you want to bet that Manchester United will lose, for example, you might get much better odds from someone who is a United fan, whose judgement is subjective. Betting exchange odds are, in about 80% of cases, better than those you could get from the bookies.

So compare the odds of winning with the return on offer, and when those odds are in your favour, you're getting away with it. For example, there might be a 50% chance that a horse will win a race. However, if its odds are even money, the bet isn't an opportunity for profit, so don't bet. If there was a 51% chance it would win at the same odds, then you are getting away with it. Spotting the extra 1% and backing it is your edge.

This starts with your choice of game. Lotteries are often a poor bet, with a huge margin for the lottery company, and comparatively few chances to win. If you play the lottery and own power tools, you are about as likely to win the jackpot as to be killed in a bizarre DIY accident.

The clever lottery player will get an edge by buying tickets only when there's a big rollover. If, thanks to a massive jackpot, the value of the prize money being given at one draw exceeds the value of the tickets bought for that draw, you have an edge – even though your chances of winning on a single ticket are still the same ... millions-to-one. You might buy lots of tickets for these rare draws, never play the rest of the time, and that's theoretically an edge over the game – though it might take several thousand years to pay off.

The scarcity of a clear edge that no one has appreciated is why a professional horseracing gambler who spends seven days a week on research might make six bets a year rather than six bets a race like you do. Trouble is, as soon as someone else spots that edge and backs it, the bookies cut the odds. The reward is smaller, and so if you don't have a bet on, the edge has gone.

The principle of finding someone less smart to take your bet is why poker, played online or in a casino, is also popular with serious gamblers. You'll know whether you have the talent to play poker and win by following the old poker player's rule: look around the table for the mug. If you can't see one, it's you.

Unlike casino games like roulette (set up to guarantee that the house always wins if you play for long enough), poker is played against other people. Study strategy and apply it with discipline and you have a long-term edge over 'lucky' (translation, 'loss-making') players which they can never comprehend.

Alternatively take the advice of one professional gambler we consulted: 'How do you guarantee you'll make money out of gambling? Become a bookie.'

"Depend on the rabbit's foot if you will, but remember it didn't work for the rabbit."

R.E. Shay

75. Gamesmanship

True cheating is not the way to win at sports because the detection-risk is very high. Instead try gamesmanship.

Stephen Potter, a master chancer, once described gamesmanship as being the art of beating your opponents without actually cheating. This comes down to a number of sneaky but not illegal tricks of wrangling the situation so that your opponent starts out with the disadvantage of being bothered, irritated, angry, and generally (literally and metaphorically) playing with the sun in their eyes. It's easier to do than you might think.

Try this with a friend. Tell them that all they have to do is to talk 'normally' for a minute. Take turns. Chances are you'll end up giggling at the idiocy of it and just how stilted you sound yourself when you try it. It's because we suddenly lose the fluidity of a natural action when we have to focus on it. Filmmakers will tell you that it is nigh on impossible to get someone to walk up to the camera without freezing or striding with all the naturalness of an Action Man. If you've ever seen a cheap local cinema ad in which the owner of a garage chews his way through a one-line endorsement, you'll recognise the syndrome. Quite simply if we focus on it too much we can lose the ability to walk or talk smoothly, so what do you think it does to the sportsman?

There are many ways of unleashing the savage weapon that is self-awareness, ranging from the way you dress to the briefest of comments. Turning up badly dressed is a wonderful wile because it works on a number of levels. Firstly it encourages people to underestimate you, which is always an advantage, but more

importantly it makes them suddenly aware of what they look like themselves. Someone who shows up in an old school sports kit or something clearly borrowed and ancient is saying 'I never really play this sport', which by comparison immediately makes their properly kitted-out opponent look like they take it far too seriously and may even be an 'all the gear, no idea' wannabe. It only takes one successful rally/shot/move from the opponent in the rags to make the other look a fool and, more importantly, feel one. Combine that with the ignoble art of 'dinking' (see opposite) and you have a lethal combination for winding up far superior opposition.

"Daring ideas are like chessmen moved forward. They may be beaten, but they may start a winning game."

Johann Wolfgang von Goethe

The other technique for unleashing self-awareness is the way you talk to your opponent. Compliments can be double-edged, even lethal if used properly. Emile Zatopek, the legendary distance runner, famously came to prominence by turning to the then champion mid race and asking him if they were running at a fast enough pace. Flustered the champion replied 'no', sped up, lost his timing, and with it the race. In a similar vein the compliment of death can be applied in almost any one-to-one sport. Try this when next playing golf/squash/polo. Go up to your opponent and say in terms of obvious admiration 'that was a superb shot – could you show me just where you placed your hands to achieve that?' In showing you, they will have to think about something they've probably never thought about before. It will be a small miracle if they manage to reproduce that shot in a hurry.

The beauty of gamesmanship is that, unlike cheating, it can be done in the open, and can even work if the opponent is aware that that's exactly what you're playing at.

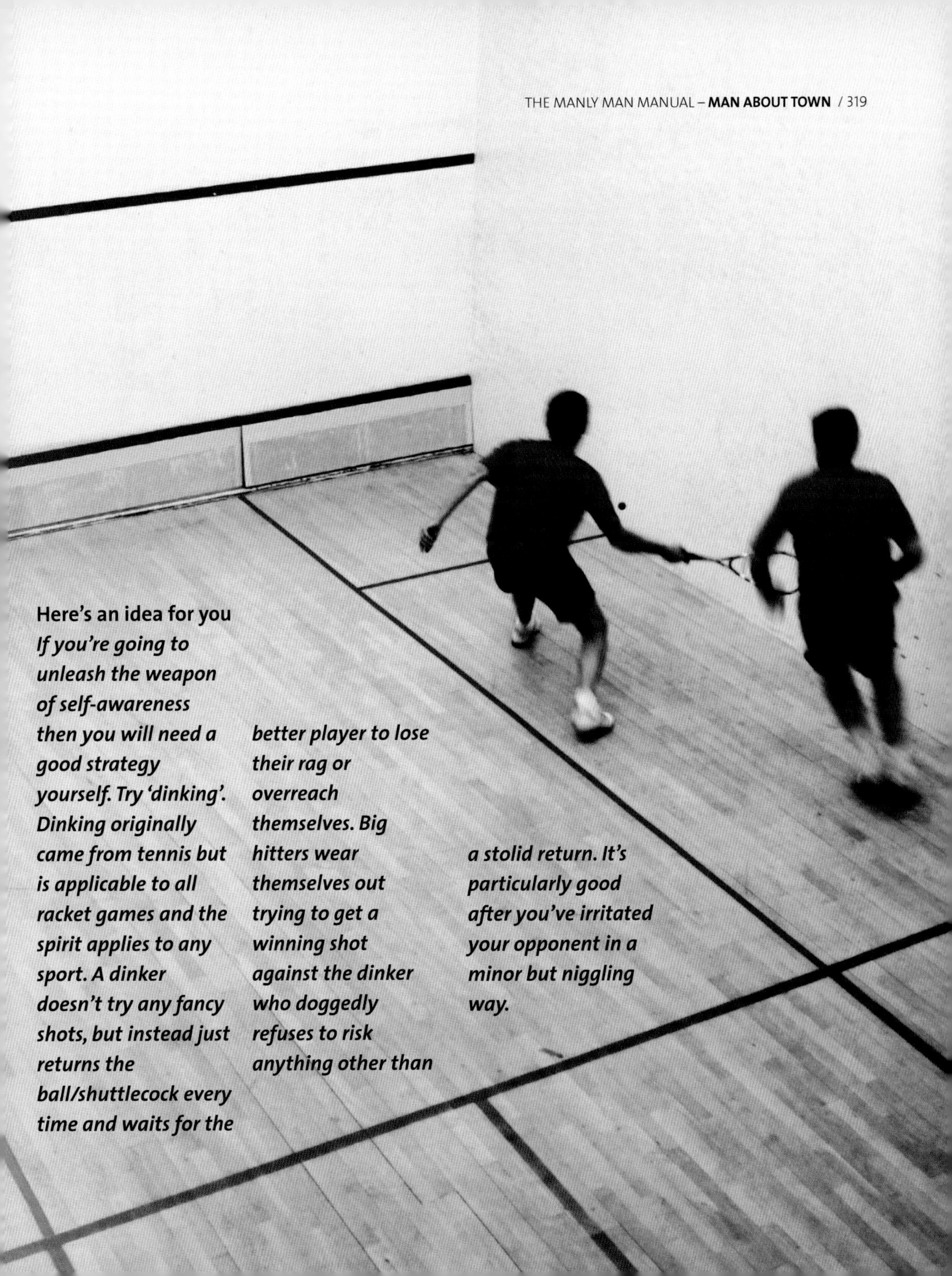

Here's an idea for you

If you're going to unleash the weapon of self-awareness then you will need a good strategy yourself. Try 'dinking'. Dinking originally came from tennis but is applicable to all racket games and the spirit applies to any sport. A dinker doesn't try any fancy shots, but instead just returns the ball/shuttlecock every time and waits for the better player to lose their rag or overreach themselves. Big hitters wear themselves out trying to get a winning shot against the dinker who doggedly refuses to risk anything other than a stolid return. It's particularly good after you've irritated your opponent in a minor but niggling way.

76. Playing poker with panache

After decades of neglect, poker has re-established itself as an essential skill in a gentleman's repertoire – right up there with the ability to unhook a bra with one hand, or carry four pints back from the bar without a tray. And it is every bit as likely to get you into trouble if you do it wrong. You may not get slapped, but your reputation can take a hammering, irrespective of whether you win or lose.

Smug, arrogant winners rarely get invited back to play again, and have trouble finding people to play at their own tables. And bad, petulant losers exclude themselves from tables everywhere when they throw their toys out of the pram. Losing money is never fun, but it's part of the game. Far worse is not being invited to win it back again.

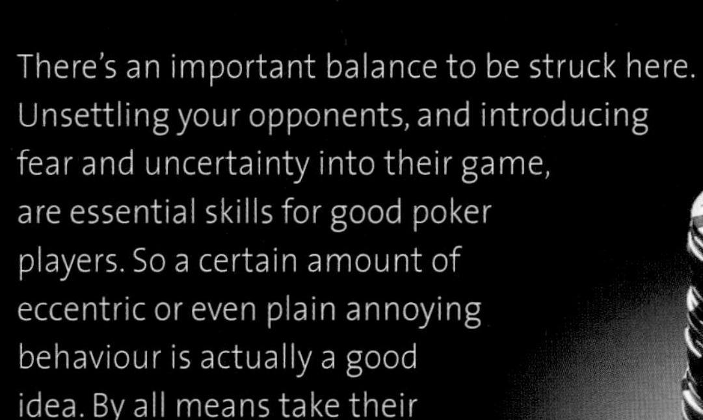

There's an important balance to be struck here. Unsettling your opponents, and introducing fear and uncertainty into their game, are essential skills for good poker players. So a certain amount of eccentric or even plain annoying behaviour is actually a good idea. By all means take their money – that's literally part of

"Whether he likes it or not, a man's character is stripped bare at the poker table; if the other players read him better than he does, he has only himself to blame. Unless he is both able and prepared to see himself as others do, flaws and all, he will be a loser in cards as in life."

Anthony Holden, *Big Deal*

the deal. But do it without style or grace, and you'll soon find yourself a poker pariah.

The key to losing with style is to understand that however good you are, there will be times when outrageous luck will defeat you. You know the drill: you know have a one in four chance of getting that last card to complete your winning hand, only to be beaten by a novice who flukes a 22-1 shot on the river.

We all know the guy who whinged for days afterwards about his bad beats, irritating his opponents and gaining a reputation as just another big girl's blouse. Don't be that guy. If you know that you worked out the odds correctly and played the hand properly, you also there wasn't anything else you could do. Console yourself with the fact that you played a better hand than your opponent, pour yourself another drink (although see opposite) and concentrate on scalping him next time around.

If you find that you're getting angry about losing, take a few deep breaths and sit out a few hands while you recover your composure. By all means mutter quietly to yourself while you do this, but under no circumstances rant at your opponents about what lucky bastards they are. Remember that folding is actually a sign of strength, not weakness, and that compulsive callers and bluffers always get caught out by better players in the end. The smartest players make a point of folding when they know they don't have the cards, and you'll steer clear of the bad beats by following their example.

Finally, don't be too smug if you get it all right and walk off with everyone else's cash. Gracious winners gain a lot of respect from their opponents, even if it sounds grudging at the time. You'll soon learn that even if you played immaculately, calculated all the odds perfectly, raised every pot at exactly the right moment and folded hands where you knew you couldn't win, you'll probably still be accused of being a jammy git. By all means needle your opponents back if you know them well enough – but if you don't, smile modestly and remind them that they'll probably get it all back next time around. That way, there may actually *be* a next time.

Here's an idea for you

Don't drink too much when you're playing poker. Drunken players are orders of magnitude more irritating than sober ones, and they're far more likely to lose. Stick to soft drinks or beer unless you're happy to lose your reputation and your trousers; and be extremely wary of opponents pouring you large scotches. They're really not doing it to make you more interesting.

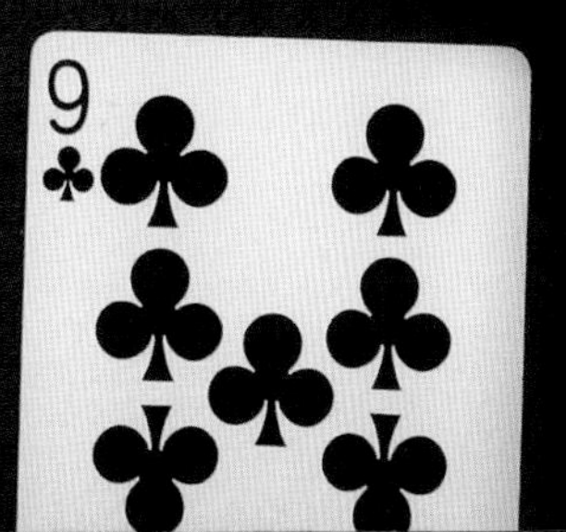

77. Throwing a poker party

Poker parties provide unique opportunities for spectacular chaos and discord, few of which will enhance your reputation as a man who knows how to throw a decent soirée. There's nothing quite like the combination of booze, testosterone and competitive games to liven things up really quite dramatically, especially when there's money involved – as you'll soon discover when prising apart old friends fighting drunkenly over a pile of chips laced with broken glass.

These things really do happen. Poker is a highly competitive and fundamentally gritty game – that is rather the point of it, after all – but it should also be a game of considerable skill and sophistication. So your poker party needs to reflect that, allowing just enough of the all-important bar-room factor into the mix to make it really interesting too.

How do you achieve this blend of style and sleaze? First, a word on taste. Don't be tempted to 'theme' your poker party – and especially avoid serving cocktails with tacky poker-esque names. Your reputation as a man of style and class is at stake here, after all. So keep things simple and elegant. Feed everyone en masse before play starts with something quick and easy, and provide snacks during play to keep them going late into the night. Keep the drinks flowing in moderation, but be careful not to overdo it – drunken novices are likely to be scalped by more experienced players and will end going home in their underpants, which can seriously damage your relationship with your cab company, not to mention your friendly local bobbies.

Here's an idea for you

It's a safe bet that at least one player will need reminding of the order of winning poker hands – usually the one drinking G&Ts from a pint glass. It's a good idea to print up a few cheat sheets listing these for the benefit of the novices or drunkards – a simple trick that can stop people betting their trousers on losing hands and avoid brawls over whether or not that straight flush really does beat four of a kind.

And so to the game itself. Before you start, make sure you have two full packs of cards ready and counted – one in play, one shuffled ready for the next hand. Avoid those 'novelty' cards you bought in Amsterdam – suitable for those late-night solo games, perhaps, but less than salubrious in anything but the least polite company. Remember that the choice of poker games for your party has a big impact on the smooth flow of the evening. Texas Hold'em may be only game in town for serious players these days and it's a great game for parties too, but a little variety goes a long way towards keeping people interested and engaged.

'Dealer's choice', in which people take turns to select the game for each hand, is often the best way to go here, but it's wise to discourage people from choosing too many of the wackier versions. Be especially wary of games with absurdly complex rounds of betting and bizarre wild cards, which are likely to confuse your guests and interrupt the flow of the table. Make a list of suggested games (Hold 'Em, a couple of stud variants, standard draw, and a classic or two such as Anaconda and Indian poker should suffice) – but be prepared to accept new suggestions if the assembled players are all in agreement.

Make sure that you explain the house rules to people in advance, especially as far as betting is concerned, and have the confidence to enforce them. Poker chips may look good on the telly, but they're a bit

over the top for casual games and enforce a buy-in arrangement that may not always be popular. It's often better to get people to bring a bagful of coins – 10p, 20p, 50p and £1 especially. Set betting limits that are affordable and realistic for the guests you have in mind, and remember that even low-stakes games with 10p antes and £1 maximum raises can result in big pots.

Above all, be prepared for a long night. You may be the one left in your underpants at midnight, but a good host keeps the game going until the last player drops...

"Last night I stayed up late playing poker with tarot cards. I got a full house and four people died".

Steven Wright

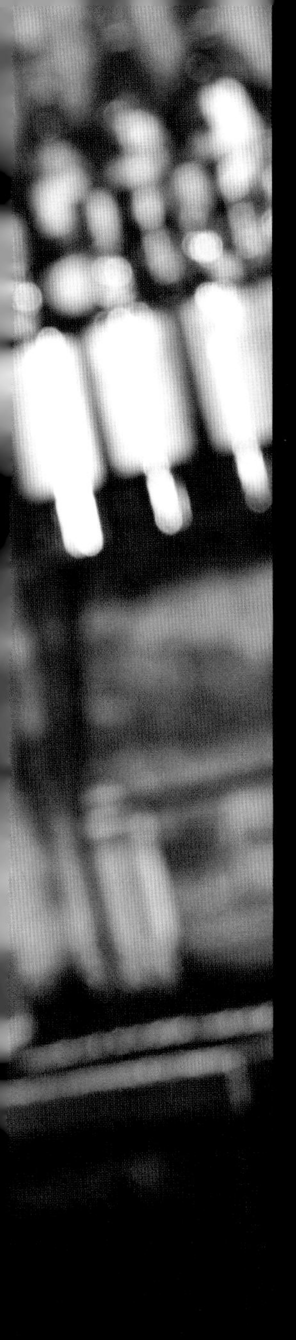

78. Pubs
A user's guide

What could be more simple than a pub? A place of ease in which to while away the hours with a refreshing glass of something or other while enjoying the cheery company of others. Rubbish. Pubgoing is an ancient proving ground of manliness and still the acid test of whether you fit in and get on with your fellow man.

The Social Issues Research Centre studied 800 pubs (it's a tough job but...) and came up with a few quite handy observations.

Getting served

Position: Two spots stand out for making eye-contact; opposite the till (because the staff return to that after each order), and next to someone being served. The SIRC concludes that the latter is the best since experienced bar staff may see the 'till position manoeuvre' as the strategy of choice of queue jumpers (which of course, being a manly man, you are not).

Pantomime: The 'pantomime' is what the SIRC calls the mute dance we all do to indicate we are waiting. There are variations on the dance moves, but within strict limits. Wave like a drowning swimmer, bang, tap, or call out and you've broken them. If anyone else grumbles loudly about dying of thirst it means they are a regular/the owner and under no circumstances should you follow suit. Instead, hold the empty glass in front of you, tilted slightly and

assume a look of quiet hopefulness. On eye contact raise your eyebrows and lift your chin slightly. Any more and they'll have you down as a tourist and treat you with the contempt you deserve.

Buying Rounds

Everyone knows someone who manages magically to be first out of the taxi and last up to the bar and everyone despises them. Rightly. If you're skint then say so up front and allow your fellow manly men to make a plan. That might be a loan, a kitty with you putting in whatever you can afford, someone paying your way or at worst call a suggestion that you come back when you have the cash. Any and all of these are better than the slow dawning that you're trying to avoid payment.

"I have two ambitions in life: one is to drink every pub dry, the other is to sleep with every woman on earth."

Oliver Reed

Rounds are the unspoken rule of manly drinking. Nobody ever told you that when you started, and nobody ever needed to. Even the academics at the SIRC concluded that "why is round-buying so important to native

pubgoers? Because it prevents bloodshed... buying your opponent a drink is a sort of symbolic handshake, which proves that you are still mates."

Avoiding fights

You might think that the true manly man doesn't avoid fights because he's well hard. That thinking only works, however, if you are a) a cage-fighting champion, b) only ever found in pubs with the rest of your regiment, c) already drunk. The rest of us are aware that the price of dentist's bills alone rule out fighting as a sensible hobby. Far manlier to avoid the whole sorry fiasco by following these simple rules:

- **Look confident**. Stand tall, head up, and don't look like a potential victim.
- **Keep your cool**. They're drunk ok. So whatever they said about your religion/team/mother just let it go.
- **Avoid eye contact**. There's a tendency to stare back if you think someone's looking at you. If it's Kylie that's fine. If it's a bloke then just look away.
- **Walk around large groups**, never create a path through them.

Here's an idea for you

There is a temptation not to be the first round buyer on the belief that the first buyer will always end up paying for more rounds than the last. The SIRC, however, has the last word;

RESEARCH FINDINGS: "We observed that, on average, 'initiating' round-buyers (those who regularly buy the first round) spend no more money than 'waiting' round-buyers (those who do not offer a round until later in the session). Yet 'initiating' round-buyers are perceived as friendly and generous, and enjoy great popularity among other regulars, whereas 'waiting' round-buyers are less well-liked, and often regarded as miserly." So now you know.

79. Dancing

Staying alive

If you are a member of CND (Confirmed Non-Dancers) the golden age was the early 1970s, when real men leaned on the bar with a pint of Worthington E, occasionally condescending to hook their thumbs into their jeans pockets for five minutes of elbow-wiggling to 'Born to be Wild'. This is not recommended for the modern male.

For many men, the idea of going out dancing offers much in the way of humiliation. We can't make you a great dancer overnight. That's the bad news. Now the good news: look around you. The UK is, generally speaking, a country where males don't dance well. We're all in this together.

If you secretly want to join in, the following should not be your role models: early period John Travolta; would-be cool dads; anyone at a wedding.

For CNDs, John Travolta and Saturday Night Fever have a lot to answer for. It made disco cool. It made a generation of women wish that their boyfriends were great dancers. And somewhere in the world, right now, a girlfriend is dragging her glum partner onto the dance floor as the first bars of 'Staying Alive' spark up, saying, 'Oh come on! It'll be fun!'

Faced with this, there are two approaches for CNDs. There's an embarrassed shuffle or the ironic disco pose - the one where you do that thing with your arms like a lawnmower and then point at the

ceiling. Both display your discomfort and self-consciousness. So let's not start here.

Unless he hung out at Wigan Casino (look it up) your would-be cool dad is rarely a role model either. Not least because he might have grown up in the 1970s. Dads are well-known for pretending to be enthusiastic ('this one's got a good beat!') about music they secretly hate. It's best to actually like the music you dance to. If you adopt an uncooperative club policy with your pro-dancing friends, you'll end up in places where you hate the music. Take part in the discussion about where you go, and you might go somewhere where you feel happier cutting a rug.

"Dance first. Think later. It's the natural order."

Samuel Beckett

People at weddings show the effect that excessive drink has on your dancing. A couple of drinks can be liberating, can take the edge off. More than 12 can be dangerous to the people on the dance floor around you. As with driving, sex and operating heavy machinery, excessive alcohol consumption before dancing gives you misplaced confidence in your ability to perform.

So if you really want to get a handle on this dancing thing, you could always learn from an expert. Lots of places have Latin American dance lessons for example. Dances like samba and salsa may look impossible, but they have very simple steps, because they are designed for ordinary people to enjoy. Latin dances are proof of the saying that dancing is the 'perpendicular expression of horizontal desire'. Who wouldn't want some of that? After a few weeks, you'll get the hang of it, loosen up, start to move those hips, and enjoy what you're doing. And that's the secret of dancing everywhere in the world in any style: relaxation and enjoyment. When you stop thinking about every little movement, it starts to come together.

If you don't fancy formal lessons, clubs that have South American nights usually open an hour early to teach newbies the steps. You won't be an expert in an hour, but the experts who turn up later aren't there to watch you dance, they're too busy dancing. Learning to dance is also a great date; or, if you're feeling adventurous, possibly a great way to meet a date.

Ultimately it comes down to whether you want to hang around on the edge sneering at other people or have a go yourself. About 35 years ago it might have been cool to be a CND, but that is one fashion that's never coming back. Not everyone can be a great dancer, but everyone can show up, and that's the main thing.

Here's an idea for you

If you're going out to a club, you don't have to dress up elaborately in uncomfortable clothes. You're going out to enjoy yourself. Dress casual, be yourself, wear clothes that don't involve sucking in your belly and which you can work up a sweat in. If other people want to dress like corseted peacocks, let them.

80. Being Bond

The quintessential Manly Man

The name's Bond, James Bond. Oh come on admit it: you've looked into the mirror and said that, probably while flipping a real or imaginary Zippo into the bargain. We all know it's a bit sad but every man on the planet has dreamt of being Bond – and for good reason.

Bond is really a collection of adolescent dreams – driving fast, seducing women, knowing everything, fighting well, saving the planet, and each generation has added to and updated his list of accomplishments. So much so that's it a bit of shock to go back to the original books and find a slightly hidebound 'blunt instrument' with some seriously bizarre beliefs such as the idea that homosexuals can't whistle (*The Man with the Golden Gun*). Fleming's Bond also had an eyebrow raising taste for women with boyish bums, even prompting Noel Coward to ask him "really, old chap, what *could* you have been thinking of?"

It's also been pointed out that the original Bond's sexcapades were a lot more modest than his celluloid incarnation. Kingsley Amis (a Fleming friend and fan) noting that in the course of an adventure Bond rarely gets off with more than one girl – "just about what an English businessman of average attraction and income might hope for on an average business trip".

So if you really want to be Bond you can forget the unlimited sex and cars with machine guns. Indeed you can forget the gadgets

"I'm looking for Commander James Bond, not an overgrown stunt man."

Ian Fleming *[on meeting Sean Connery]*

altogether as the real Bond preferred to rely on his bare hands and tried and trusted old fashioned approaches. Real Bondage means learning skills – commander Bond does his homework to perfect lock picking and card sharping – not twirling flashing toys. Which is rather handy really since it means that we can all be a bit of a Bond without waltzing around in a tuxedo or having to fork out for an Aston.

General Theme

The critic Christopher Hitchens describes the Bond aura as "a distinctive blend of fine leather, good tailoring, and club-land confidence" and that timeless appeal is what you should aim for.

Clothing

The tuxedo is only rolled out for casinos, for the rest of the time Bond is clearly a believer in a few well tailored items. He is usually to be found in a dark blue suit and shares his creator's tastes in short

sleeved shirts thereby combining classical elegance with a readiness to travel. It helps if you have bulging muscles to show off if you really want to carry off this look as both Connery and Craig demonstrate but Fleming and Moore managed well enough. Your watch should have the minimum of buttons and a simple classic Rolex is ideal. Luggage should be limited to a single pigskin attaché case.

Shaken, not stirred

What that means is that the vodka and vermouth of the martini are brought together either in a cocktail shaker or by stirring with a spoon. Shaking it mixes air into the drink and is said to give a colder martini and was the preferred choice of Ian Fleming. On the other hand Somerset Maugham argued the case that "A martini should always be stirred, not shaken, so that the molecules lie sensuously on top of one another". I doubt you or I would honestly be able to tell the difference and since Daniel Craig's Bond rather memorably makes the point that he doesn't give a damn I think we can all draw a line under this particular discussion.

Here's an idea for you

With all the shaken/stirred debate it's often forgotten that the golden rule of Bond is that the vodka should always be made from grain, never potato. You might also want to sprinkle some grains of black pepper into your vodka (if it's any good they will sink) as Bond has been assured by Russian contacts that this helps remove impurities.

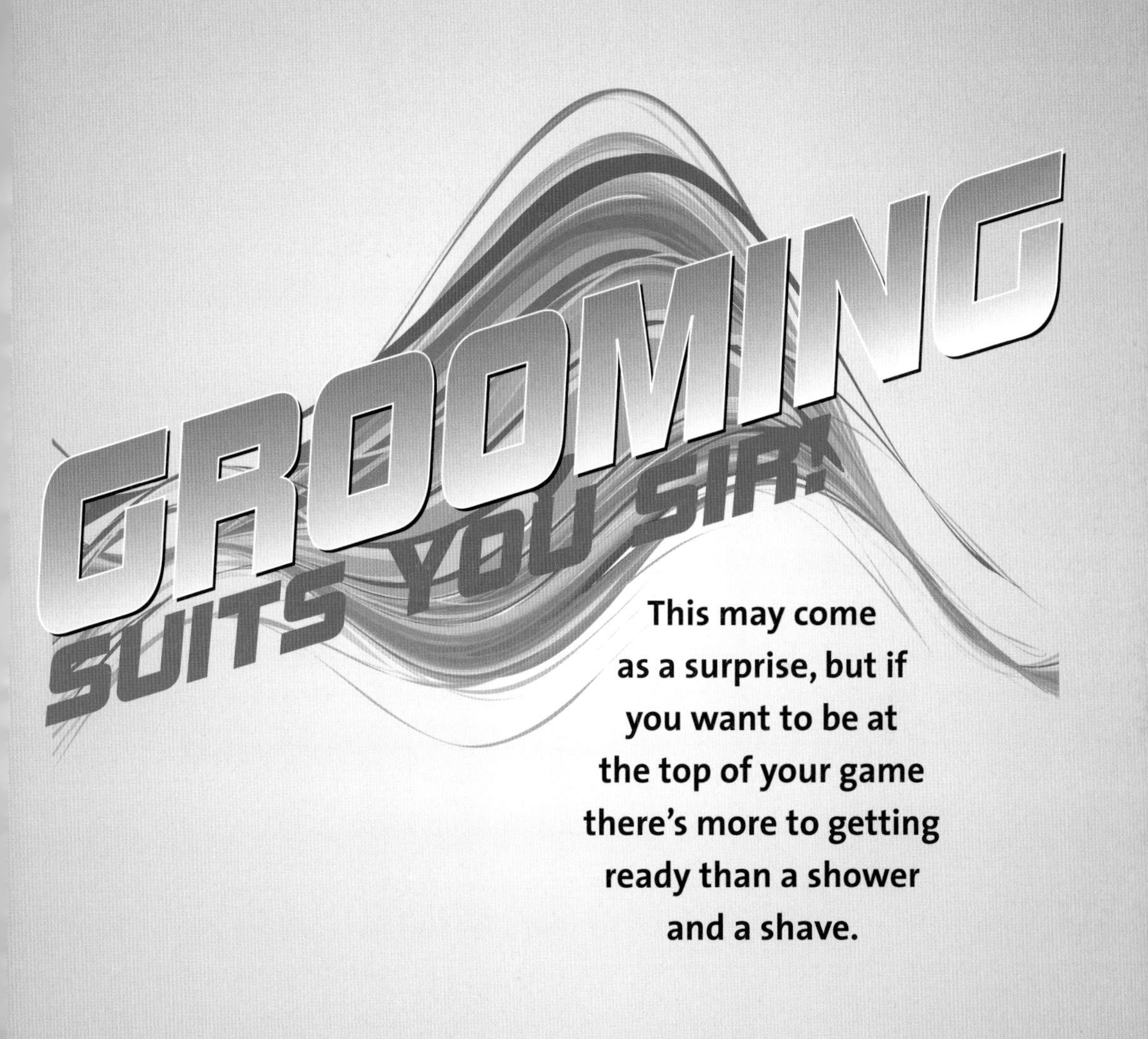

This may come as a surprise, but if you want to be at the top of your game there's more to getting ready than a shower and a shave.

THE MANLY MAN QUIZ

Manly man o

Take the quiz then read on for insider grooming secrets...

It's looking a bit thin on top: what do you do?

1. Ask the hairdresser to come up with an appropriate style.

2. Shave it to a number one.

3. Flares came back, why not comb overs?

Do you have a moisturising routine?

1. Certainly, twice a day along with the facial scrub.

2. I occasionally pinch a dollop of hers.

3. Are you calling me a poof?

Your smartest jacket does up with:

1. A single button.

2. Three buttons.

3. Velcro.

caveman?

Mainly 1s: You're not afraid to be called metrosexual and quite like to see yourself as a bit of a dandy. Just remember that there's a fine line between dandy and fashion victim.

Mainly 2s: You make an effort alright, but it is an effort, not something that comes naturally. Read on for a couple of cheats to sharpen your edge.

Mainly 3s: Be honest, if Homer Simpson did designer, would you be the target market?

81. Avoiding fashion faux pas

It's fine for us to give you advice on what to wear. But before you start thinking about that, you've got to appreciate what you shouldn't be wearing.

The problem with having choice is that it can give us guys the opportunity to make the wrong choices. The list of male fashion faux pas in long, but most of the worst offences are simple enough to avoid.

Problem one: you're wearing too many colours, or the wrong combination of colours. More than three colours at once is always wrong. The colours you combine should be complementary, which means they produce grey if you mix them, or should be closely matched to each other. Complementary pairs include red and green, or purple and yellow.

But, and this is a big but, you have to wear a colour that's right for you in the first place. Strong primary colours make pale skin look 'washed out'. If you have dark colouring, you're much better suited to strong reds and purples. If you want to know what's right for you, you can pay for a consultant to tell you, or you can ask your girlfriend, who will be dying to throw away half your T-shirts for exactly this reason...

Here's an idea for you
Sort your clothes in your wardrobe properly – separate the winter clothes from the summer clothes, solids from patterned shirts, neutrals from the bright colours. It makes assembling an outfit quicker, and shows up where you're missing an essential item. Most important of all, a good wardrobe keeps your clothes clean and crease-free. If you don't have a wardrobe that's big enough for this task, buy one before you buy anything else.

Problem two is similar: don't wear too many patterns. Mixing stripes and spots and checks makes you hard to look at. By all means wear a striped tie with a striped shirt – but not with a pinstriped suit as well. If you're worried about this, buy solid coloured suits in neutral colours. You can look interesting by investing in good quality brightly-coloured shirts and ties. Some brands, for example Oswald Boateng, combine deep colours to stunning effect.

Problem three: wear the clothes like they are meant to be worn. That means washing them when they are dirty, repairing rips, removing stains, and ironing them. If this is beyond you, make sure you have a good dry cleaner that does small repairs, and pay someone to do your ironing. Your trousers have belt loops, so always wear a belt that's the same colour as your shoes. Don't do up all the buttons on your suit jacket: if it has two, only do up the top one. If it has three, do up the middle one, and in an extreme circumstance, maybe the top one, but never the bottom one. Never put your hands in your jacket pockets, and don't pack your pockets with useless junk that makes you look like a bag of nuts.

Buy the right size. Big, baggy clothes are a way of hiding. If you're overweight, big clothes make you look even fatter. Learn to use cut and fit to make the bits that should look big to look big, and the bits that should look small look small.

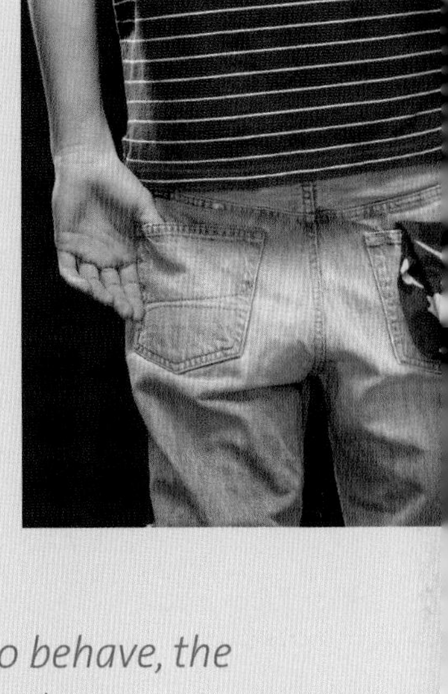

Some of the most grievous crimes against fashion are committed by fashion's biggest fans; they buy everything that's fashionable every season, and bung it all on at once. By all means refresh your wardrobe, but mix and match fashion with your favourite clothes. Sporting too many labels is also a common problem – many designers seem to like making you into a walking billboard by writing their name all over your clothes. A large, classic logo can be kitsch or iconic. Too much simply shows a lack of self-confidence or self-awareness, and it makes you hard to look at.

Finally: you live in a country where it's cold one day and hot the next. Dress for the weather, and that means fabrics as well as cut. Thick wool trousers and socks will make you sweat in summer, as will most synthetics. Wear a linen jacket in winter and you will look like someone in the arrivals lounge at the airport. And never, ever wear your sunglasses indoors, or after dark. People will laugh at you behind your back.

The weirder you're going to behave, the more normal you should look

P. J. O'Rourke

82. Dressing yourself slim

Time to lose weight. While you know a good diet and exercise are the real answers, you'd actually like to look lighter right here, right now. Here's how to make the Fat Boy look Slim.

Time to fess up: it was you that ate all the pies. As if you were ever kidding anyone in those baggy tracksuit trousers and oversized sweatshirts. Just as Mr Comb-Over is the only person in the world who thinks his hairstyle is hiding rather than accentuating his baldness, Mr Huge Baggy-Clothing is not camouflaging the wobbly bits, as he hopes, but rather labelling himself straight off as Lardy Arse Love Handle Man. So stop it right now. Women have known for years how to make themselves look slimmer just by what they slip on, now it's our turn. We both know that there's nothing wrong with your body; there's just a little more to love than there used to be. Even so, there's no need to show the world that.

For a start you want to lose the baggy and don't even think about the tight. Baggy clothing may make you feel more comfortably camouflaged but the very nature of loose clothing means it will only

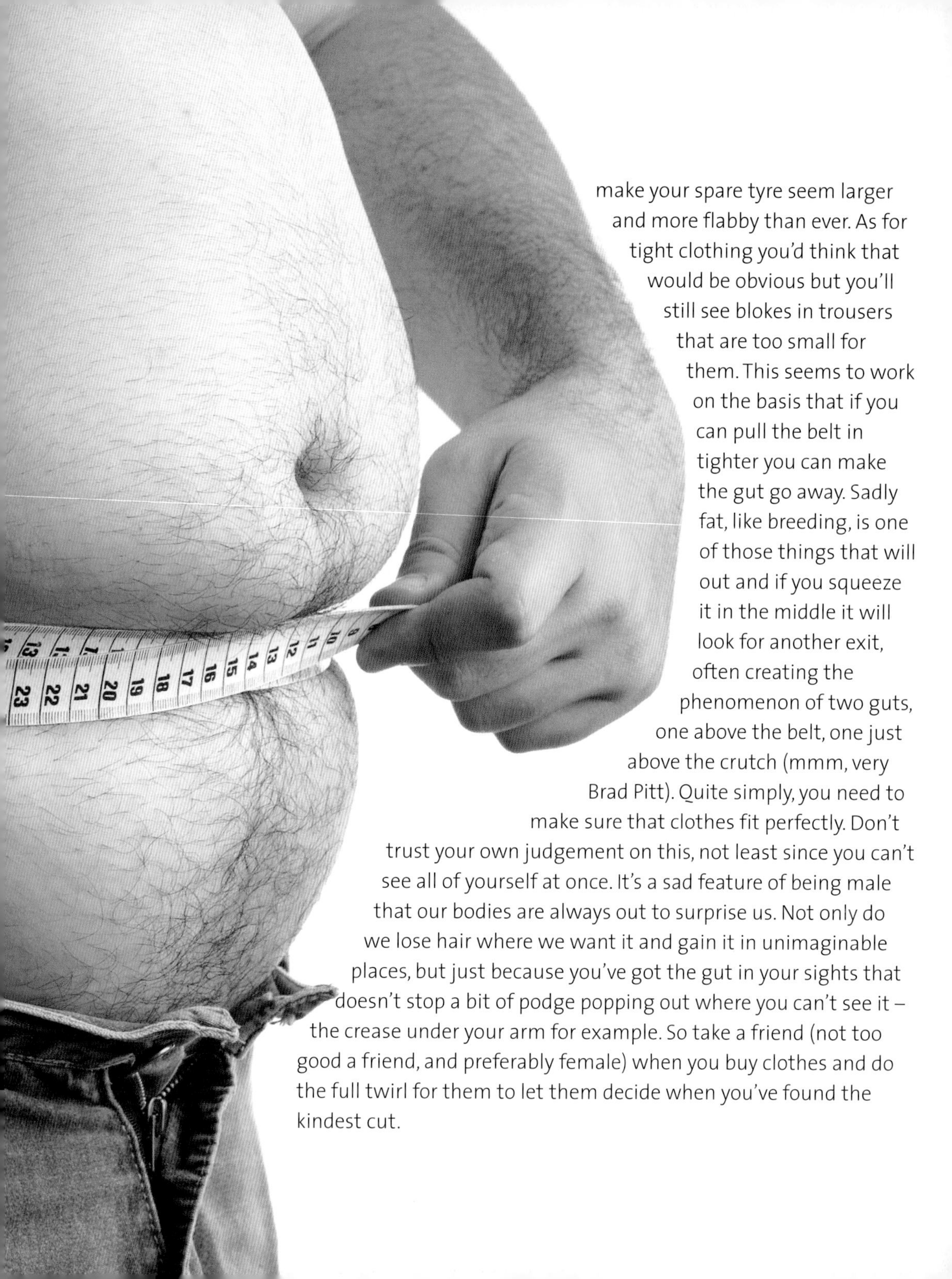

make your spare tyre seem larger and more flabby than ever. As for tight clothing you'd think that would be obvious but you'll still see blokes in trousers that are too small for them. This seems to work on the basis that if you can pull the belt in tighter you can make the gut go away. Sadly fat, like breeding, is one of those things that will out and if you squeeze it in the middle it will look for another exit, often creating the phenomenon of two guts, one above the belt, one just above the crutch (mmm, very Brad Pitt). Quite simply, you need to make sure that clothes fit perfectly. Don't trust your own judgement on this, not least since you can't see all of yourself at once. It's a sad feature of being male that our bodies are always out to surprise us. Not only do we lose hair where we want it and gain it in unimaginable places, but just because you've got the gut in your sights that doesn't stop a bit of podge popping out where you can't see it – the crease under your arm for example. So take a friend (not too good a friend, and preferably female) when you buy clothes and do the full twirl for them to let them decide when you've found the kindest cut.

The debate about double breasted and single breasted jackets rages on as ever but the general feeling is that they should be long enough to hang below your bum (yes it does look big in that) and that a well-cut double breasted jacket is far better for making your torso look longer and slimmer. It's all part of the oldest optical trick in the book, which is that horizontal lines make you look wider (so bin the hooped rugby shirt) and vertical lines make you seem longer and loftier (cue the pin stripes).

Similarly, if you're a little vertically challenged, try to avoid cardigans and jackets with more than three buttons because they are intended for the long of torso and will often make you look dumpier. Matching the tops and the trousers in terms of colour and design will help them blend into each other and help visually lengthen the whole outfit. Fashion writers insist that dark colours are more slimming so make a start with black and charcoal.

Oddly enough, platform heels probably won't help because they suggest you're self-conscious about your height. You might want to think about 'lifts' instead which slot into your shoes and subtly add a bit of height.

Here's an idea for you

Since it's your waistline that's the problem, why draw attention to it? Big shiny belt buckles are a no-no. If you're wearing jackets try wearing braces because the belt itself is one of the things that catches the eye. Take that mobile phone out of your trouser pockets and put the wallet in a jacket pocket – these add unsightly lumps to your profile. Make sure your trouser legs are long enough to cover up your socks and continue the long elegant line of your body (ahem). Gorblimey trousers that don't reach the end of your legs don't make your legs look longer, they just make your lower half look dumpier and wider.

83. A man for all seasons

Making your wardrobe meet any challenge

You've got limited time, money and wardrobe space, but you need a wardrobe that can adapt to any challenge. Some guys pull it off, so why shouldn't you?

If we had been writing this 100 years ago, we'd have had to go into great detail about when you put on black tie and white tie and whether you could be seen in town in a pair of suede shoes.

Life is a lot more fun now. You can wear most things in most places, but the breakdown of strict rules has given rise over recent years to crossover abominations such as the T-shirt printed like a dinner jacket and jeans with a sown-in crease down the front. Having an adaptable wardrobe doesn't mean wearing a different coloured pair of trainers to royal Ascot. It means looking right at all times without having to bring a suitcase out with you in the morning.

Think about the balance of your life, and reflect that balance in your wardrobe, but be prepared to break out once in a while. If you spend most of your waking hours in meetings, then we're sorry for you –

Here's an idea for you

The test of your wardrobe is when you pack for a few days away. You need clothes for the beach or the meeting room or the nightclub or the restaurant or the bar, and only a fop carries a big bag. So, if it's a business strip for example, take one classic suit in black or blue, but match it with very different shirt-and-tie combinations so you don't look like a man with only one suit. Visualise where you will be, whether it will be hot or cold, think through the full outfit, and lay out combinations until you can cover everything with as few pieces as possible. Don't forget, an outfit always includes shoes.

but more importantly, you're going to have to invest in suits and jackets, and if you're going out from the office, learn to adapt that look. If you have a fetish for denim, invest in at least one pair of jeans that will look right in a flashy restaurant.

Being adaptable means striking a balance: be confident that you fit in without having to copy the guy sitting next to you, but don't be arrogant and assume that people always have to adapt to you, whatever you are wearing. It all comes down to a few really essential items.

A really good half-casual three-button jacket or even a blazer is top of that list. Think of the sort of jacket that looks good with jeans, but doesn't look out of place with a pair of trousers either. The material matters: in winter thick wool, corduroy or moleskin, and in summer a lighter cotton. Blue and black are easiest to match, or a neutral shade in summer. Quality loafers, jeans, a white or coloured shirt and that black or blue jacket gets you past the door in most environments. Don't try and wear your suit jacket like this – the cut and style is usually too formal, so you will just look like a man who's wearing his suit jacket.

The same goes for the standard office shirt. If you want a shirt that means you can throw off the tie at the end of the day to go out to play, wear a more casual cut with a soft collar to work, or even a button-down oxford in a bright colour. You could also wear a vigorously striped shirt with a plain knit tie, and simply change into your jeans at the end of the day. Bright stripe shirts and jeans go well together – as long as the shirt is cut close and sharp. Ties and jeans don't go together in any circumstance, and nor do formal shoes and jeans if you don't want that off-duty-copper look.

"Who the hell wants fourteen pairs of shoes when they go on holiday? I haven't had fourteen pairs in my life."

Brian Clough

Some items of clothing should have 'wear anywhere' printed on the label. The chief among these is your beloved leather jacket. What do you mean, you don't have one? Stick to a classic style, and scour every vintage shop and designer store until you find one that feels right and smells good. In this jacket you can go to the football, impress a date or look like a man of the people at the theatre. It will never need ironing and will look better the longer you wear it. If you don't know what to wear, wear it.

In no particular order, the following are also smart and casual, depending on how you wear them: a black or grey V-neck (with shirt, with T-shirt, never next to the skin. Remember Michael Douglas in Basic Instinct? We still wake up screaming); a good denim jacket; quality leather belts; black loafers and really good classic trainers. Once you start thinking like this, there may be a few items in your wardrobe you never wear. Give them to charity. Hoarding is for people who don't know what they like.

An adaptable wardrobe also needs to stick to as few colour palettes as possible and not too many patterns. White basics (shirts, T-shirts) will go with anything, as do your jeans and your dark jacket, but that doesn't mean that everything goes. This is good discipline for you, because you don't look good in every colour, and spots probably don't suit you.

84. Greatest hits

Why a few classics can go a long way

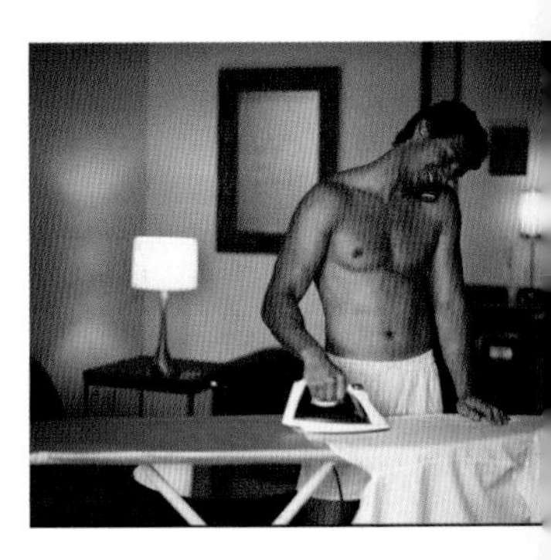

It's no accident that followers of fashion are called 'victims'. The truly stylish man rises above fashion – he knows what he likes and where he likes to buy it from. The secret is a well-planned wardrobe of classics.

Here's the actor Richard E. Grant describing his summer wardrobe a few years ago: 'six black T-shirts, six pairs of Pumas and one pair of Levi's'. This is the fashion statement of a man who knows where he's going, but who carries a small bag when he goes there.

Lots of guys have been wearing the same clothes for the last 15 years, replacing them like-for-like when they begin to fall to pieces. This in itself is not stylish: it's often just boring. But at least half your clothes should deliberately not be fashionable.

The key to this is making sure you're well stocked with the authentic classic basics of the male wardrobe.

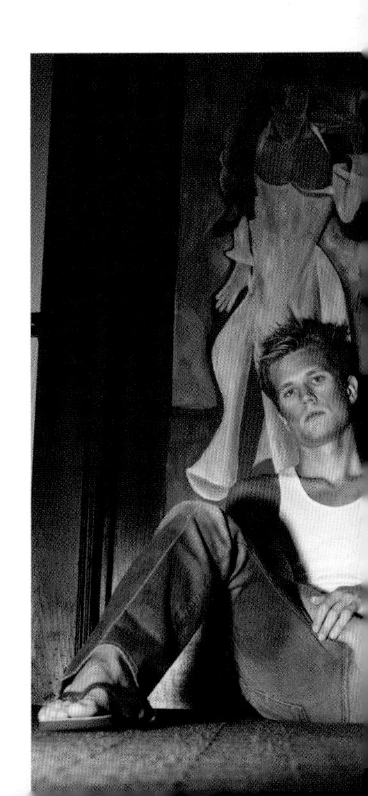

More important than ever: the right jeans. Today, your jeans can take you anywhere from the beach to a three-star restaurant, but they have to be the right pair for you. Avoid this year's fashion, whether it is skinny, baggy, ripped, bleached, or whatever 15-year-olds are wearing. Anything with bits of material sown on or a large prominent logo is out (nothing is more out of fashion than the last thing that was in fashion), but apart from that, there are few rules. Find a subtle brand that works for you, whether it's Lee, Diesel,

"If people turn to look at you on the street, you are not well dressed"

George 'Beau' Brummell

Carhartt, or the old standby – a pair of Levi's. Don't skimp on cheap denim, because a good pair should really start looking good after a year or so, which is about the time that your cheap jeans are falling to bits.

You're going to need a couple of good white cotton shirts – get a cut that flatters your body and don't wash them with anything that isn't just as white. The same goes for your T-shirts. It doesn't matter whether you like M&S, The Gap or Armani, you'll need plain black and white Tees. Ditch the black ones when they fade, and a little bit of lycra with the cotton really, really improves the fit.

Our climate changes from freezing to tropical, often on the same day, so you need to carry this through to every essential item. Some things can't be skimped on – for example, a quality classic leather jacket – so thank your god for outlet stores and January sales.

The rest of your shirts, ties (simple, strong, easy to match – use solid colours and simple stripes), socks, underwear (quality please – the person who's going to see it is someone you want to impress) express your confidence in who you are, and so stick to brands you like and trust rather than hopping from shop to shop until you buy the nearest thing in desperation. If you like the Mod aesthetic, stock up with classic Fred Perry, John Smedley and Ben Sherman. If you're a classic Brit, Paul Smith and Richard James. A cool American look means your first stop for shopping might be Calvin Klein. Wear brands that reflect your values in an understated way – for example, Welsh brand Howies (www.howies.co.uk) makes limited edition organic denims and practical jackets that are equally good in a club or on a mountain bike. Put some time into looking these out: visit good department stores and just occasionally pick up a clothes magazine. That time gets paid back later, when you can shop for a season in one afternoon using your usual route through town, and you always know what size to look for.

When looking for iconic pieces – such as a Harrington jacket or retro Adidas or Fila sportswear for example – always buy the real brand, and not some lazy high street look-alike. Don't trade your integrity for convenience or price: you wouldn't pay to watch a crap football team just because it was playing in the same shirt as the side you support. But equally, don't be a brand slave. It's better to buy second-hand authentic items than cheap copies: you might find something that is exactly what you're looking for, and totally unique.

There's no harm in buying a real winner item in more than one colour. Many guys make the mistake of thinking that classic means black. Black is easy to match, but strong colours and even prints mean you can be classic but never dull.

Remember, this is your life, not a series of fancy dress parties. After the age of 30, trying to look like anyone except yourself is demeaning. You were given one, and only one, personality, so use it.

Here's an idea for you

It's not rude to politely but firmly lay down the law to relatives who insist on buying you clothes. Tell them the brand you like, your size, and be clear what you like and dislike. Even better, preselect what you want, and put it aside for them to pick up for you. People often like to buy you 'something different' – in other words, something that they like and you don't, which is a waste of everyone's time and money.

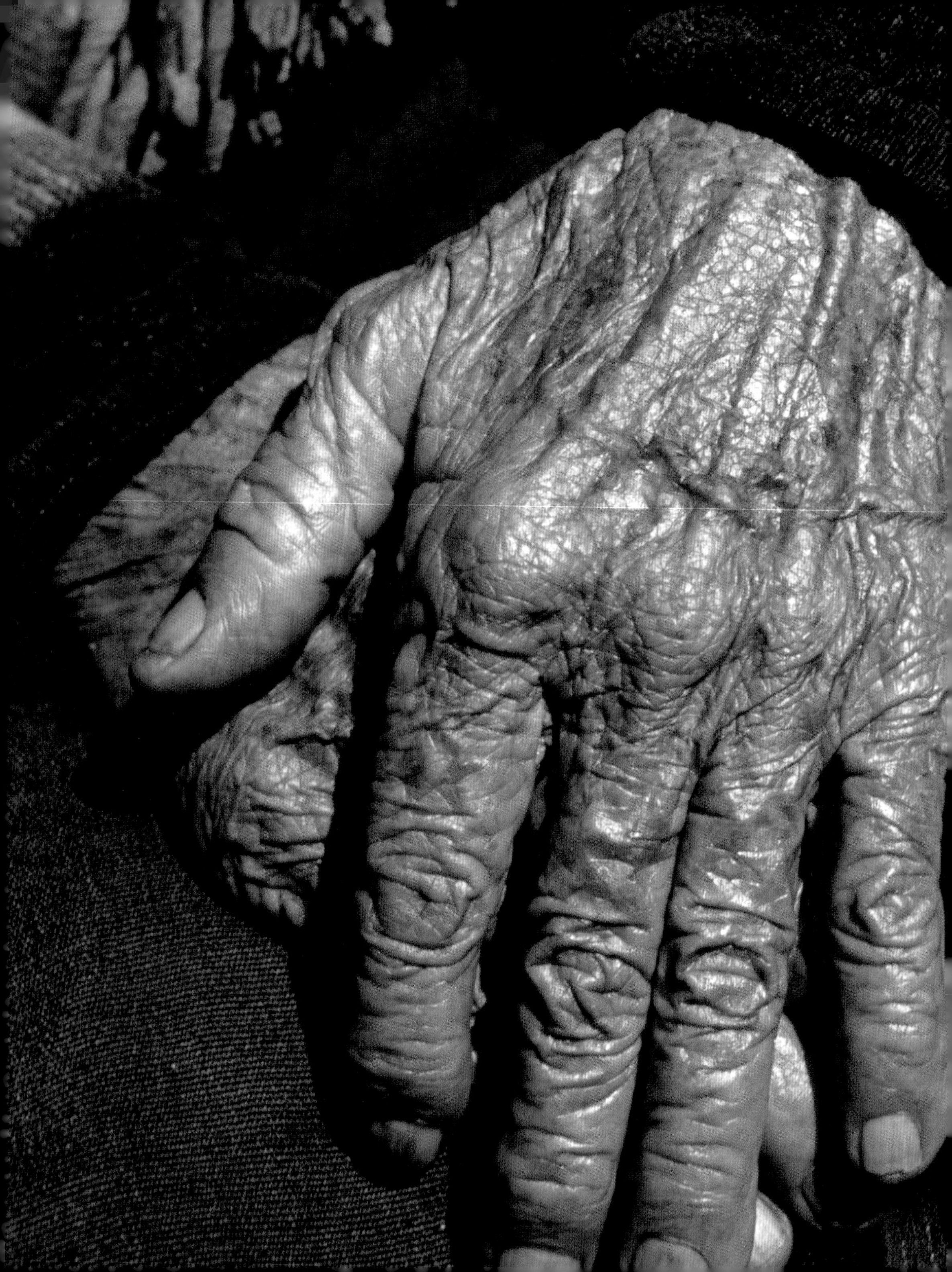

85. Skin care

Because real men moisturise, but more often than not they have to rely on adverts to tell them what to choose.

Ok so we understand that men use face care products, that bridge is behind us. The problem is that unlike women who are brought up understanding what an exfoliator is we can't really turn to our mates in the locker room and ask for advice on moisturiser. Not if we want to go back to that gym. So here's face care in a nutshell.

Skin Type

First know your skin. There's nothing sissy about caring for your skin any more than there is about caring for your liver. It's your biggest organ, your first line of defense against infections and unlike all the rest of your organs it's the one most prominently on display (if it's not the most prominent you need to see a doctor). Not all skins are the same though, and before you splash out and splash it on all over you need to be sure you're buying the product that fits your face. There are six main types of skin; normal, dry oily, combination, sensitive, and problem.

Normal – you lucky, lucky man. Little oil, no flaking, and no spots.
Dry – cold and dry weather causes dry patches and a little flaking, maybe around the nostrils or eyebrows.
Oily – oily skin is tough and elastic, which is good because you're less likely to wrinkle, but it's prone to spots, which is not so good because we all kind of hoped they were a thing of the past.
Combination – this is a pain – you get oily areas around your nose but often dry skin around the edges of your face. If that's the case then you have to treat each area accordingly.

Here's an idea for you

Baffled by all the products? Don't pick one out yourself then. Just tell her you're ready to take the plunge and moisturise. Bet you she'll be happy you're taking care of yourself and she will be much more patient than you at navigating the grooming section and asking the right questions of the sales staff.

Sensitive – you're fine. Right up until you swim in a chlorinated pool, borrow someone else's soap, or go out in strong sun. Then you're not fine.
Problem – If you have this then you know about it already. If you're not an adolescent but have teenager acne, or sore spots then see a dermatologist.

Products: Every day;
Cleanser – a cleanser takes off the dirt and helps ungunge pores. Cleansers tend to be pretty neutral but the oily skin can benefit from more acidic brands while dry skins do best with a cream. The trick here is the cleanser you choose shouldn't leave your face feeling tight or worse (if it feels like you've had a face lift you need to change product fast). Mix with warm water, smear it on your face, rinse gently off. Dry.

Toner – this cleans our pores and in particular helps restore your skin's balance after shaving. If you use a cleanser that is pH-balanced you can probably skip this step.

"A mans face is his autobiography. A woman's face is her work of fiction."

Oscar Wilde

Moisturiser – this is supposed to help the skin retain its water, which should make you look less wrinkly. Don't confuse this with anti-ageing creams which are of highly questionable effectiveness. Moisturiser won't turn back the clock, it will just help reduce the damage and help with those bags under your eyes. Very good for dry skin. Not a good idea for those with oily skin, although there are oil-free versions for that purpose. Massage it in with your finger tips in the morning.

Beware products with alcohol and menthol as they are probably cheap and will dry out your skin's oils. If you have oily skin ask about an astringent and avoid oily products.

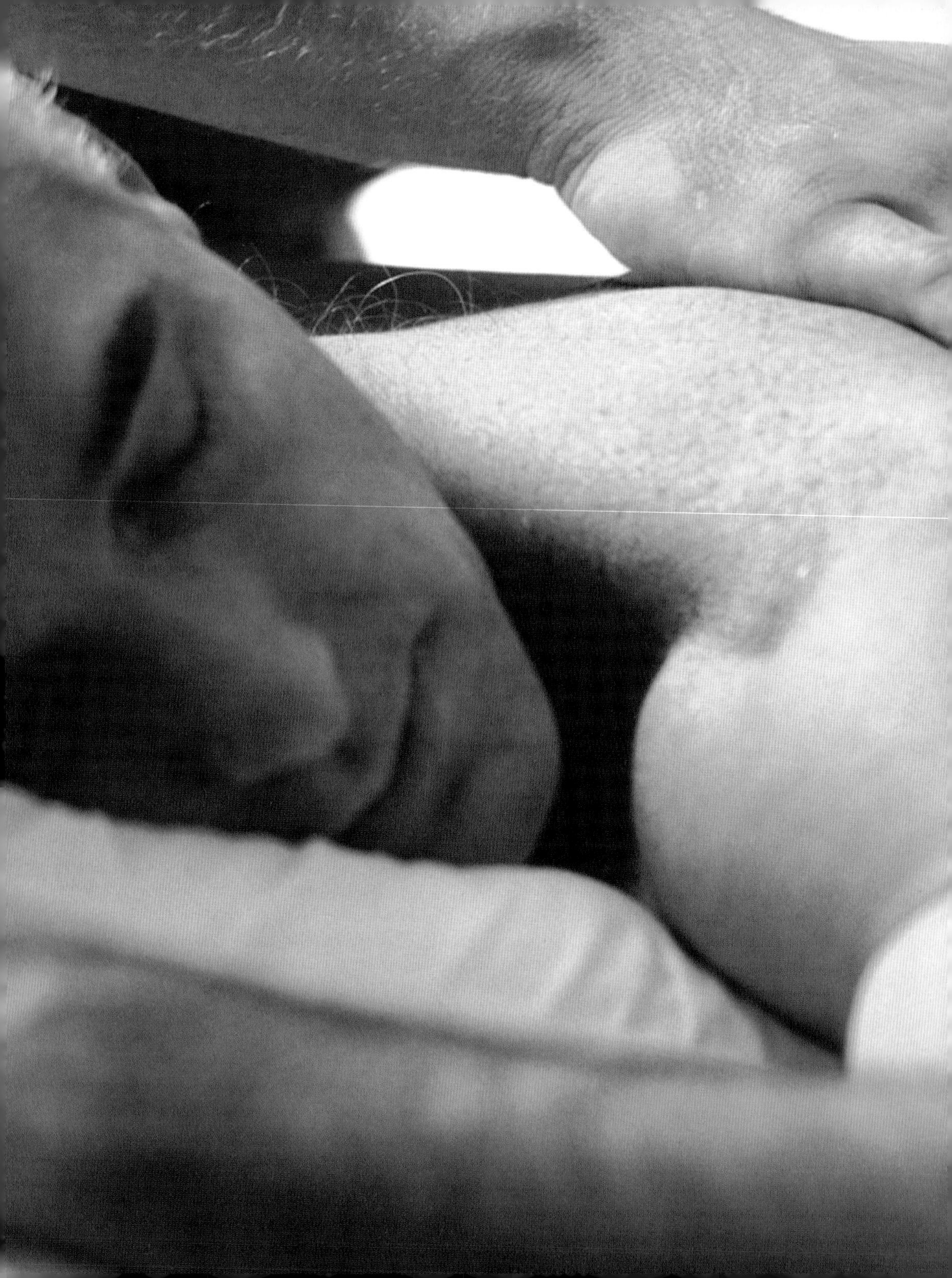

86. Spoil yourself

Spas aren't just for women. Take the plunge for a day and come back a new man. Or at least smelling like one.

Men hesitate to go to spas, seemingly in the belief that they offer the same kind of distractions as San Francisco massage parlours. Most men only try out a spa because they've been dragged along to accompany her highness but once there they usually enjoy it, because once you lower your guard, it's actually really nice to lie back and be fussed over. Here are a few things you can safely treat yourself to without getting all worried about your masculinity.

Manicure/Pedicure – this is one for her really as you'd be surprised how much women tut over the state of our nails. Men don't usually care too much so spas go to some effort to rebrand manicures and pedicures to make them sound more manly; 'Man Hand Maintenance' is just one example, suggesting that the staff are about to set to work with spanners.

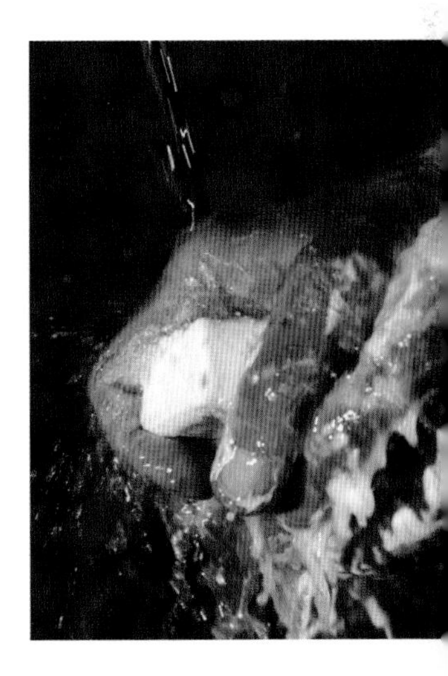

Facials – a great starting point as you don't have to take your clothes off, and since you probably don't normally spend a lot of time fussing over your face you may well be surprised by the results. Best of all she'll love it and be much happier to get close up to check out those results afterwards. Just don't shave before you go in for a facial.

Deep tissue massage – top manly treatment because it's associated with sportsmen but useful for anyone with the odd nagging twinge. The idea is that your muscle tissues don't always align themselves properly after hard use and the massage will help with that.

"Sometimes there is a bit of hurdle in getting men into a spa, but once they go, they're usually hooked."

Susie Ellis, *spa expert*

Be warned, it involves deep and firm finger strokes which means it can be uncomfortable, particularly in really knotty areas, but the sensation of wellbeing afterwards should be worth it. You don't have to have run a marathon to benefit from deep tissue massage – it's also great simply as a stress buster.

Saunas and steam rooms – another great way of dealing with muscular pain and stiffness as the heat and humidity warm and relax your muscles making them easier (and less dangerous) to stretch. As such they work best as a prelim to a massage. You may also be offered mud treatments where you get to sit around with warm gloop on your skin. Get over how daft you look and revel in the feeling. Be aware that it is considered bad form to do anything in a sauna, including rubbing or scrubbing yourself so see it as being a bit like a game of statues.

Thalassotherapy – catch all term for pretty much anything involving seawater and seaweed, or marine mud. Don't worry it's all been cleaned before it gets to you so you're not going to end up covered in crabs and barnacles. Many claims are made for the benefits of thalassotherapy but really the various treatments come down to a cleaning and exfoliating process with a bit of pampering thrown in for good measure. Find out exactly how rigorous the processes are as some places seem to think cleanliness is best achieved by hosing you down like riot police with protesters at the G8.

Thai massage – nothing to do with the kind of Thai massage you heard about in Bangkok, this is a system of gentle stretching and pressure starting from the feet upwards and taking in the energy lines and acupressure points on the way.

Here's an idea for you

Still unsure about the idea of a spa? Then see it as an extension of the gentleman's club – a temple of manliness to which you retreat to be treated in the style you truly deserve. Pick a spa attached to a sports club (golf clubs are a good example) and you'll find yourself surrounded by a reassuringly familiar locker-room atmosphere.

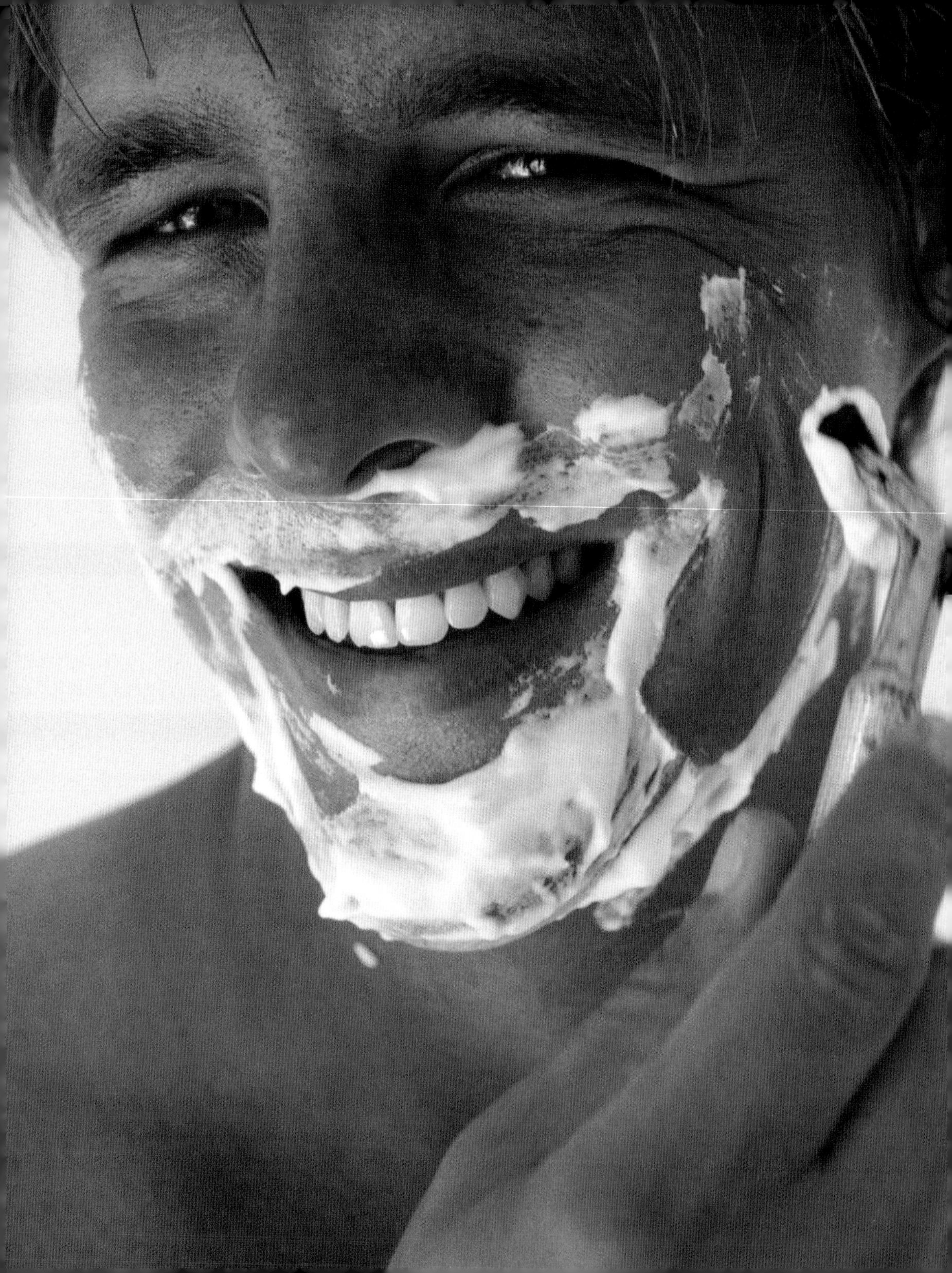

87. Close shaving

You're a grown man so you've mastered shaving. Hmm, that rash and the blood spots on your shirt say otherwise. Admit it, you need help.

It seems we spend an average of about five months of our lives scraping metal blades over our chins in order to look pretty. Sadly there's no figure available for how many months we then spend swearing and trying to cope with the damage but there are a few tips to try and ease the pain.

First of all don't shave first thing. Neither your skin, nor your brain are ready for it yet. Give them both a bit of time to wake up so that your hand is more steady and the fluid that collects in your face during sleep can drain away exposing more of the stubble.

Don't ever shave in a hurry. Short of forgetting your trousers there are few better ways of looking like a complete muppet when you get to work than having razor nicks all over your face.

Exfoliate – if you still think that's something they did in Vietnam with Agent Orange then it's time to join the twenty first century. These days it's ok for men to exfoliate which means using a facial cleanser to scrub off dead skin cells leaving your face fresh and your stubble all the more exposed.

Get yourself one of those magnifying shaving mirrors and make sure the light is bright. If you're relying on the basic bathroom single bulb then at least make sure it's a strong enough wattage that you can really see what you're doing.

"If you teach a poor young man to shave himself, and keep his razor in order, you may contribute more to the happiness of his life than in giving him a thousand guineas." **Benjamin Franklin**

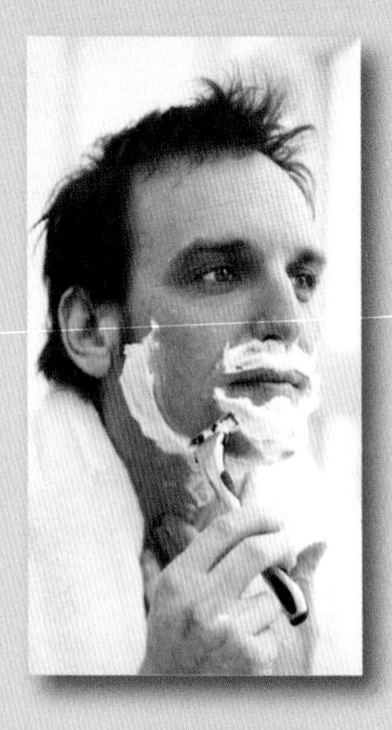

Wet your face first with warm water before slapping on any shaving cream. The theory is that it helps swell the stubble making it an easier target.

Don't just spray some foam on like whipped cream on jelly, this is your face and what you do next can make or break your whole day. Instead massage a cream with soothing aloe vera thoroughly into your jaw. There are razor blades which come with aloe vera strips built in. If you believe that does the trick then you probably also buy those disposables with eight or nine blades because the man on the telly told you they were eight times better.

Don't be tempted to use an old blade. Don't mistake an old blade for a new one. Yes, we've all reused and got away with it but at least have two separate places to keep the old and new ones completely clear of each other.

If you have delicate skin then make each stroke in line with the direction of growth. Yes that does mean that the 'upper cut' stroke is wrong. Shaving against the grain increases the chance of rashes and irritation.

Rinse the blade after every stroke in hot water.

Finally slap on an oil-free moisturiser to protect the skin. Take it easy on products that have alcohol and menthol in them, they may be all tingly, but they're strong stuff and you don't want the tingle to turn to forest fire on your face.

The chances of cutting yourself are in direct proportion to the importance of your meeting that day. If you're spending the day in front of the telly you will have a perfect shave. If you're putting your business plan to Donald Trump in an hour you will emerge from the bathroom looking like you washed with a barbed wire face flannel. If you do look like you were shaved by Mack the Knife and serious meetings beckon then it's time to reach for a styptic (aluminium sulfate) pencil. It's not nice, and it's going to hurt but it will stop those cuts long before the alternative of dabbing frantically at them with loo paper.

Here's an idea for you
Styptic pencils do the do when it comes to stopping bleeding but they are undoubtedly a harsh way to treat your skin and for the soft and sensitive types that can cancel out the benefits. So for a more gentle approach try using lip balm on your war wounds.

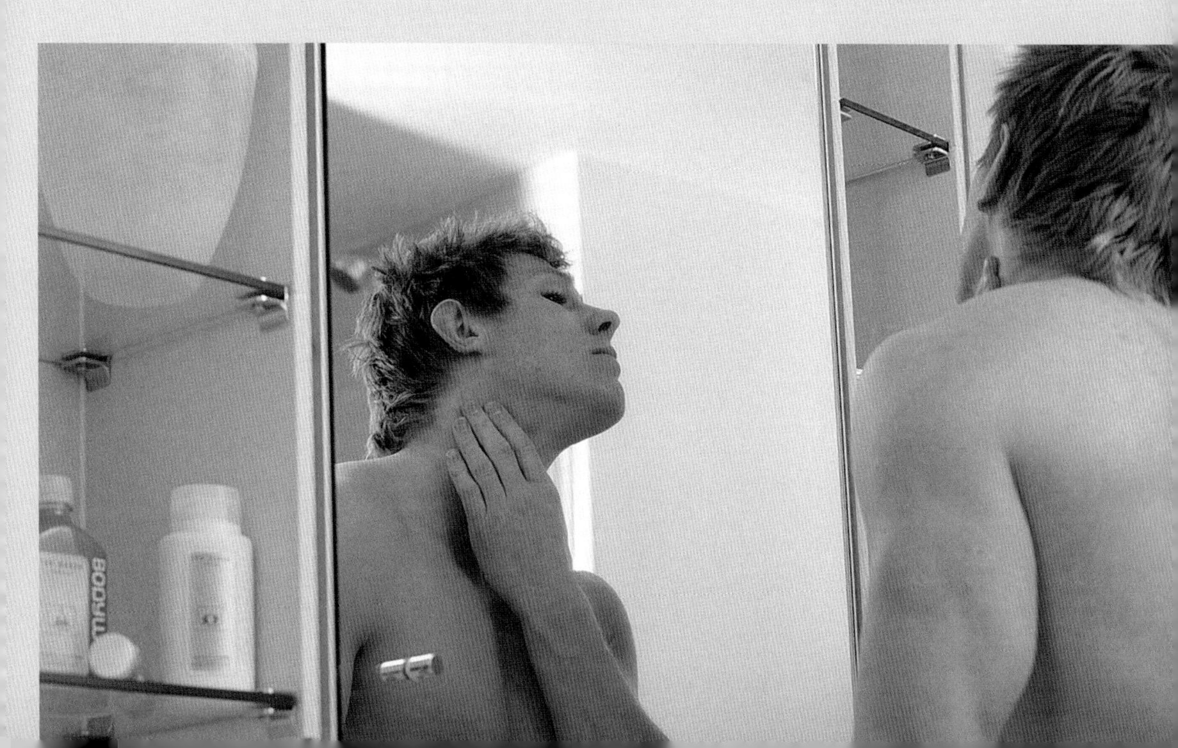

88. Go bald gracefully

Getting away with going bald is an important life skill for men. You'll need a frame of mind in which reality shines through and acceptance is your goal. Tough it out.

If you become a baldy badly, schoolchildren will throw stones at you and relatives will look at photographs of you whenever they want a good laugh. You don't want that.

The only men who don't worry about their hair falling out are the ones who have already lost it – which amounts to around three in ten men approaching the end of their thirties. The other seven are loudly making jokes about how their friends are getting a bit thin on top while anxiously checking the mirror and secretly eyeing the shampoo shelf in the supermarket for the bottle that promises extra volume.

It is important to accept that everyone has already noticed. It doesn't matter how carefully you have been combing to hide your bald spot, or how often you have avoided windy days, remember that the only person denied a really good look at the top and back of your head is you. Everyone else caught on to the fact you are losing your thatch long before you did.

Your motto should be: hide nothing. For example, when you start to feel the crown of your head pressing against your fingers, it's natural to comb your hair a little more carefully. Soon, you're avoiding going

Here's an idea for you

Don't wear a hat everywhere because you don't want people to know you're going bald. It's like attaching a flashing sign to your head saying 'embarrassed bald man'. What did you think when you saw that guy today wearing a hat for no obvious reason? You thought, 'He's going bald'. We rest our case.

out in the rain. Your barber notices what you're doing, and leaves that area a little longer. You start to experiment with hair products that keep this piece of hair in place. You set your alarm twenty minutes earlier so you can reattach your hair using hairspray. Then one day, a few years later, you realise that you have turned into Bobby Charlton.

During this time you fooled precisely nobody, and all those hours in front of the mirror are hours you will never have back.

Many men believe that women don't like bald men. This is not true. Women don't like flabby, sweaty, ignorant, self-obsessed men who love their cars more than they love their girlfriends. Compared with this, the exact amount of hair you have on your head is a mere detail. This means that if you're worried that no hair means no girlfriend, the first step towards getting away with encroaching baldness should be a visit to the gym and the launderette, where you can fix the more urgent problems that you can do something about.

Step one: get a decent haircut. Less is more. The closer your remaining hair is to your head, the less different it looks to the bits where there isn't hair: think Bruce Willis. Having your hair clipped short actually makes you look like you have more hair, not less – or just stops people looking, because there's no furtive bald spot to seek out. It also has time management benefits because you'll no longer have to carefully arrange your hair every morning. Haircuts are cheap and take five minutes. Plus you don't have to waste time and money on conditioner, because you don't need to use it.

Step two: groom well. Use the extra time liberated by your new hairstyle to think about the other nine tenths of your body. If you have thick tufts springing from your ears, nose and back, your loved ones will not treat this as compensation for the lack of hair on your head, so clip and wax. Also, you may have noticed that girlfriends have entire wardrobes of clothes with which they attempt to accentuate the bits of themselves that they like, and draw attention away from the bits they don't. They're on to something here; after all, they fooled you with it.

Always remember that, men – male pattern baldness is the price we pay for getting the better deal on almost everything else in life, so stop whining and hiding your head. Don't even think about hair transplants and weaves and liquids that cost £30 a month. Even if they might do something to begin with, they'll stop working as soon as you stop buying them. If baldness is good enough for Sean Connery, frankly it's good enough for you.

89. Back, crack and sack

You know what we mean

For those of a squeamish disposition now is the time to look away.

Like it or loathe it, women are not the only ones now expected to be silky smooth. Where once upon a time a man with the physique and body hairline of a silverback gorilla was a thing to be admired he is now just as likely to find himself on the receiving end of subtle hints about removing body hair. Subtle hints like 'ugh'. So here are the choices.

Shaving – fine for your face, but forget it for anything below the neck. Yes, some cyclists do use razors for shaving their legs (why they do that is a whole other question) but you've had years of shaving your face and you still cut it so what do you think you're going to do if you try that approach on any other bit of your bod?

Depilatory cream – promises painless and easy hair removal. Problem is that they can often be a skin irritant and they just don't seem to last as long as the adverts suggest. Besides, you're going to need help to reach bits like your back and if you think this could lead to a playful frolic with the girlfriend you haven't thought how un-erotic it's going to be for her.

Waxing strips – waxing strips are just a bigger version of what happens when you have to take a plaster off your leg. And you know how much that hurts. The upside is that the effects are good. The downside is that it takes more skill than you would have thought.

Electrolysis – pretty much permanent. Hair roots are zapped with an electrical current and they shouldn't grow back. Downsides are that it's expensive and usually requires several sessions before you've nuked all of those pesky follicles.

Laser – much like the above with the same up and down sides.

Professional hot waxing – probably your best bet. Lasts the longest for the money but you're probably still looking at a monthly visit for an averagely hairy back.

Sugar – really much the same as the above, although it does have it's own loyal following, most notably for the dreaded crack and sack area.

As for the c & s if you're not actually working in the porn industry then the big question is whether you really have to. Because it means a world of pain even if the silky smooth feeling afterwards is highly liberating (or so they tell me). If, however, you are determined to bite the bullet (better bring your own, you'll need it) then sugaring is done by applying a mix of sugar, lemon and water to the skin, either by hand sugaring (a thick past is smeared on and pulled off) or by strip sugaring in which a spatula is used to apply a thin layer of paste, a cloth strip is then laid on that that and pulled off taking sugar and hair with it. Which all sounds fairly pleasant until you remember that a) these are your crown jewels we're talking about here, and b) that's another man doing the application. It takes all types.

Here's an idea for you

Don't have a shower before you go, don't sunbathe before you go. Both will make your back more vulnerable and you have enough pain in store already. Don't have a shower or expose your newly bald back to the sun for a day afterwards either and when you do shower go easy on shower gels – try to stick to a natural soap with fewer harsh chemicals. Because there's no point in going baby bum smooth if you're only going to get spots.

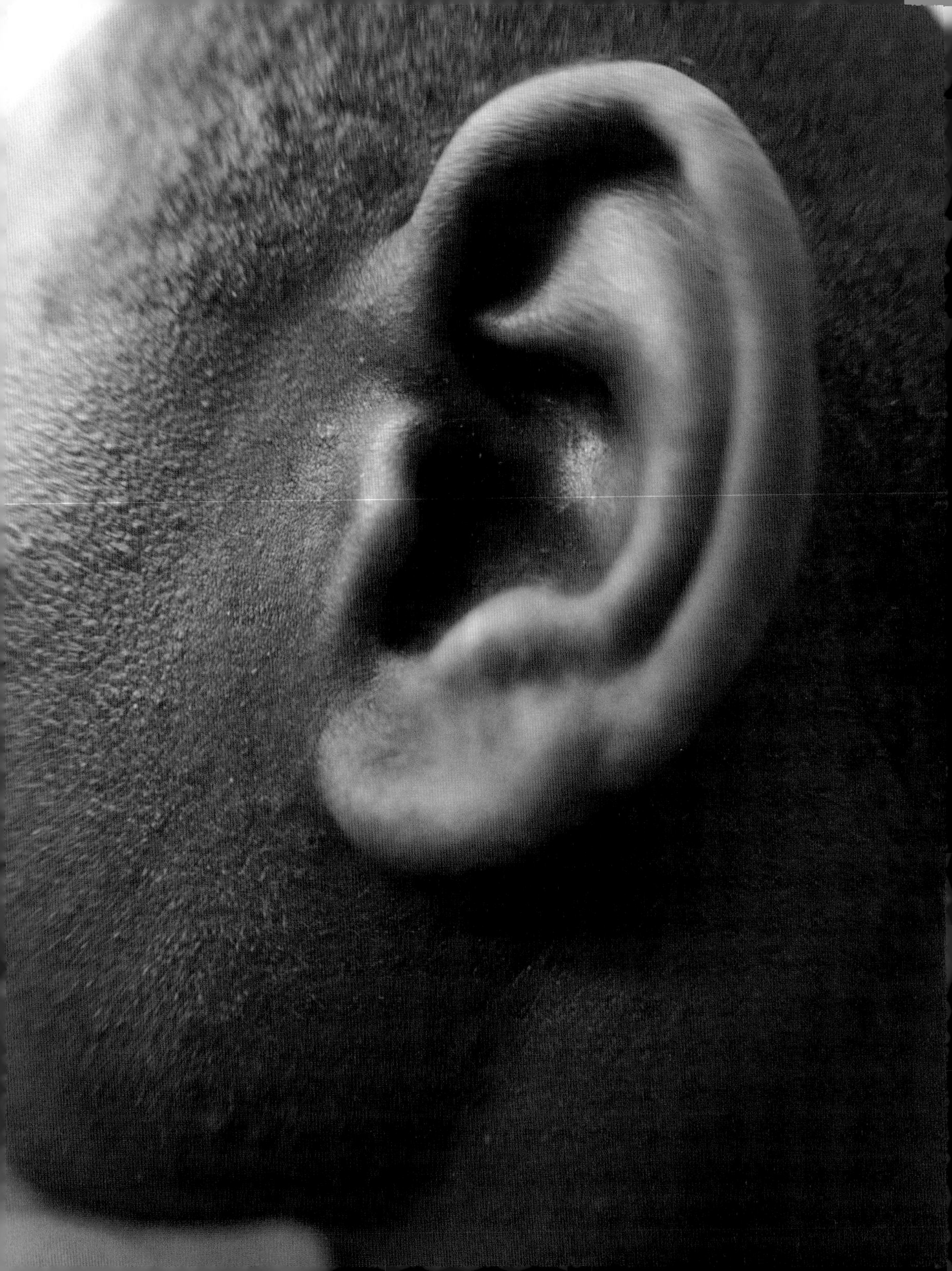

90. Eyebrows, nose, ears

Trimming places you never knew existed

It's one of life's great ironies that just as the thatch on top of your head starts to thin, the hair sprouts afresh in places you never dreamt of. Like your ears.

I vividly remember the first time. She was an attractive hairdresser and we'd been maintaining that level of bouncy banter that's just the professional side of flirting when she made a slight throat-clearing noise and asked if I'd like her to trim the ears. Ears? Why, had I turned into Spock? But no, looking closely into the mirror she was quite right and my ears were now each sporting a fine little hairpiece of their own. I think I aged about twenty years on the spot. The men in white coats aren't 100% sure about why hair growth increases on our ears, eyebrows, and nose but there's a theory that it's related to DHT which is also the cause of baldness. DHT stands for dihydrotestosterone so yes it does prove that you're only growing ear hair because you're a real man, not that this is likely to cheer you up. In any case there's no point ignoring it – you've just got to get on with it if you don't want to end up looking like you have hedgehogs frolicking above each eye and a couple of Spaniards tucked away in your nose and ears.

Here's an idea for you

A pair of scissors is good for wayward eyebrows but better yet is someone else who knows what they're doing with a pair of scissors. Next time you're at the barbers don't be shy, ask them to trim the brows while they're up there.

Nostril forests

First up don't pluck nose hair. Not only is it ridiculously painful but you risk tearing the delicate skin on the inside of your nostrils. Instead get a nose hair trimmer. There are two main types; either a rotating blade spins in one direction, or an oscillating blade goes left to right. In practice the difference is negligible. Pay a little extra and get a cordless variety.

Ear plantations

There are two amusing areas for ear hair. Tufts on the inside that sprout outwards, and a little thatch that puts in an appearance on the outside of your ears. The stuff on the inside can usually be mown with the same device you use for your nostrils. The hairs on the outside are best dealt with by an electric razor. Never be tempted to use a normal razor to tackle your ears. You'll end up with nicked lobes and anyone who realises what you've done will double up with laughter. Not manly.

Eyebrows

Eyebrows can be plucked if you have wayward hairs appearing out of left field, but if that's the case then the advice is to use a good pair of slanted tip tweezers as pointed ones are more likely to rip the skin. The best time to pluck is after a shower when your skin is soft and the hairs are likely to offer the least resistance.

Chances are, however, that the problem isn't a single wayward strand, it's a number of hairs that have started growing longer and thicker leaving you with brows like draft excluders. That's fine if you enjoy scaring small children but not so good for your urbane man about town look. A pair of scissors is the obvious way to trim errant hairs; just comb the brow upwards and then use the scissors to trim the over long hairs.

If you're tackling your own brows remember to stay well clear of the lower line of the eyebrow. Why? Because if you pluck or trim that you'll be guilty of shaping the brow and only women and drag artists are permitted to do that.

"No-one is born with perfect eyebrows"

Linda Evangelista

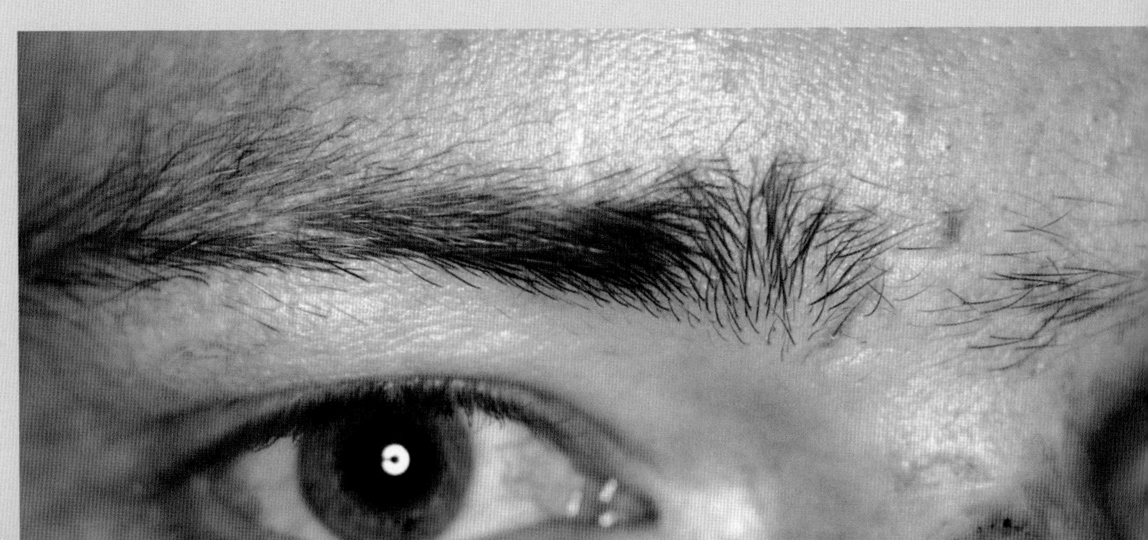

91. The great smell of...

Once upon a time a famous boxer could advertise cologne and we'd go out and buy it. These days we're a little more aware, well aware enough not to want to smell like a boxer anyway.

On second thoughts maybe we haven't come that far. If you go by sales alone then it's clear that a very large number of us think that all we need to do to smell great is spray ourselves with a certain mass market deodorant. This product is advertised by guys who spray themselves with the stuff in anticipation of being apparently devoured alive by marauding hordes of the fittest looking women on earth closing in on them in a frenzy of olfactory passion. Which is what I believe advertisers refer to as post-modern. They're not really saying that you spray it on and you pull, oh no, of course not. Yet at the same time the underlying message is very clear that if you unleash an entire aerosol of this stuff on your torso then you are clearly about to undergo death by sex. Dream on.

Choosing a scent

Good male scent is not a mass market thing. Different scents smell different on different people due to skin types. Unless the scent in question is actually an industrial strength chemical strong enough to wipe out natural skin tones. Which is where our mass market sprays come in.

"I love the smell of napalm in the morning"

Lieutenant Colonel Kilgore; *an expert on the subject of mass market perfume*

To know what smells good on you go to a good department store and try a number of scents but don't just spray them straight onto your own skin or else you'll quickly be overwhelmed by the mix and become incapable of smelling any one clearly. Besides you'll also smell like a tart's window box and people will stare at you on the way home.

Instead spray the ones that interest you onto small pieces of cardboard which you cunningly have in your pockets. The experts suggest that you also have something else to smell to 'clear your palette' in between testing each one so you don't get confused by lingering elements of the previous scent. A small bag of ground coffee will do the trick.

If finances allow then consider having two or more scents for different times of day. All men love those heavy scents described as having 'overtones of leather and tobacco' but they can be a bit rich for work and daytime. Something based around notes of citrus is usually a better bet for that because it smells clean and fresh. Save the strong stuff for the evening.

Examples of citrus based scents include favourites such as Kouros (Yves St Laurent), Armani (by Armani), and Dolce and Gabbana (you've worked this one out already haven't you).

Applying a scent

Whatever you do don't splash it on all over. Remember the advertisers would like you to empty that bottle in two applications so you buy more but you will stink since it's very hard to control the precise amount of a splash. Sprays are a better bet since they give a measured amount. If you don't have a spray then tip a small amount into your palm and rub that on.

Remember you're not a woman so don't spray it onto the inner wrist or neck. These are warm and exposed and so give off the scent fast which is fine for a woman but a truly manly man is interested in a long slow burn effect for a more subtle scent. Try applying it to your chest or the backs of your shoulders instead. Unless you insist on wandering around with your shirt off that should mean that it's covered and lasts longer.

Here's an idea for you

Bought/been given a scent in a splash bottle? Make it last longer, and avoid the risk of overdoing it by decanting a little into a simple spray bottle (from any chemist). Now you also have a small bottle you can take with you to work for daytime use. Just don't ever let anyone see you using it.

92. Suits you sir

Whether going to your wedding or going to court, there are times when nothing else will do: you will need a good suit.

Young lads no longer start dressing like their fathers as soon as they leave school, a collar and tie is not now a prerequisite if you are going to a football match, and it's now casual Friday on most days of the week – but sooner or later you need to add a good suit to your wardrobe. At this important juncture, most of us go out and buy a bad suit instead.

A good suit makes you look, and feel, a bit like James Bond. Depending on your error, a bad suit marks you out as a pimp, an exhibitionist or a sausage with buttons on.

Don't skimp. You're looking at a few hundred pounds at least for a quality garment. The most important reason is the fabric. You want material that won't sag, bobble and go shiny in a couple of months, and that will drape properly. Everything looks good in the shop, but scrunch the sleeve of the jacket in your hand. The material should spring gently back, without holding the creases. All-wool is traditionally what you're looking for, but some modern suits mix wool with synthetics to make something that's luxurious but lightweight, so this isn't a rule. Cotton can be hardwearing for a basic suit but doesn't drape as well; linen looks lovely on the hanger, but you'll freeze in winter, and it crumples in summer – which makes cheap linen a definite no-no.

Buy a solid colour as your basic everyday suit: dark blue, charcoal grey or black. Splash out – you will look better in one £600 suit than in any

of three £200 suits, but if you're spending everything on one garment you'll need a suit you can wear everywhere. It's tempting to be the nonconformist, and select an amusing tartan. Excellent at film premieres, but a little odd at your uncle's funeral. Remember, George 'Beau' Brummell, the greatest British dandy, wore only grey suits. With a good basic suit you can use a bright shirt to create an impression, but you can also wear it to the office.

Now you need to think about cut. For many years, the three-button jacket has held sway. This suits many body types, as long as the jacket is the right length, falling just below the seat of your trousers. A longer, two-button jacket is now common, which nips in nicely if you are tall and have a waist to show off. Double-breasted suits are available for off-duty yachtsmen and middle-aged deputy sales managers, but probably not for you. The trick is not to be constrained by this week's fashion – a good suit could last for years. Try everything with an open mind. Trousers most commonly have a flat front, though a single pleat is just acceptable if you want some room to manoeuvre down there. Two pleats will often make it look like you're wearing a nappy when you sit down, and waistcoats are generally best left for snooker players.

And so you come to the try-before-you-buy stage. You can't do this in a hurry. It's wise to take someone with you, who can point out problems you might not see. Does a single vent make your bum stick out like a duck? Does the collar poke out from the back of your neck? Is the jacket bunching under your armpits? (In case you're wondering, these are all bad).

To look slim you need the suit to follow close to your body, but it needs to fall naturally in a smooth line without bunching. You should be able to do up the jacket, which should hang naturally when not buttoned. It's tempting to buy suits by mail order, because you hate shops and they look good on the models. These men are not shaped like you.

Why not go one step further and have a tailor 'make' for you? 'Made to measure' suits offer a good fit but a limited range of styles. Your suit is cut from a basic template to match your measurements. For the best and most expensive fit, a 'bespoke' suit is cut entirely to match your body, every aspect according to your wishes. You will need an opinion on lapel size, type and number of pockets, where the waistband of your trousers sits, button positioning, colour of lining, and hundreds of other details. If in doubt, your tailor will suggest what's best for your body.

For made-to-measure, you will need to spend at least twice as much as you would off-the-peg, and for bespoke, costs are usually at least four figures – though away from Savile Row and the big names, prices are cheaper. Ask for a price before you commit, because you can't back out later; but you will get a unique suit that makes you look like yourself, only much better. It will still look new and stylish many years later – which might come in handy if you are wearing it to court. A custodial sentence can seriously date your wardrobe.

"A dandy can never be a vulgar man."

Charles Baudelaire

Here's an idea for you

If you get excited about this, and want to understand the history and finer points of tailoring, you can do no better than to consult a small book called 'The Englishman's Suit', by the late Sir Hardy Amies. You will never again make errors such as having a double-breasted revers on a single-breasted jacket, which for suit-literate people is like claiming to support Chelsea United.

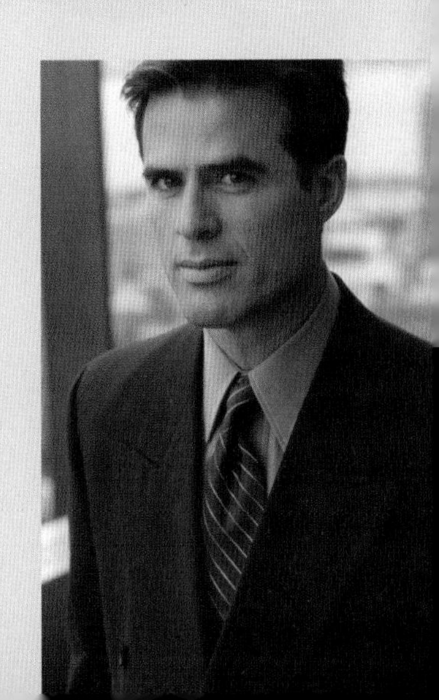

93. Best foot forward

Get the shoes wrong and the best-planned wardrobe in the world falls apart. Get them right, and people really notice.

You don't need hundreds of pairs of shoes if you want to make in impression. A few well-chosen pairs will do the trick. Really good shoes last for ever, are comfortable and practical, and they don't just match your clothes, they say something about your personality.

The exact shape of the toe, the size of the heel and the cut of the uppers changes from season to season. You can follow the trend, or you can choose to ignore it and buy the time-honoured classic styles. But with shoes, this season's fashion is always a variation on a standard style – a good shoe should last for years, so try not too buy into too many feet fads or you'll have a season of fashion and several seasons of being painfully out of fashion.

You need at least two pairs of leather shoes: a black pair, and a brown pair. The black pair is for work, to wear with your suits, and for formal occasions. The standard model, with a

"I still have my feet on the ground, I just wear better shoes" **Oprah Winfrey**

shiny toecap, is known as an Oxford. It's the most versatile shoe, because you can wear it with anything from a pair of chinos to a dinner jacket. Be prepared to pay top whack for this type of shoe, because you want good quality, thick leather, but a supple shoe that's not going to give you blisters.

If the shoe has those little patterned zigzags and punched dots in the leather, it's known as a 'brogue' – either an Oxford brogue (like a slightly fancy Oxford), a 'half brogue' (the toecap wraps around the toe, and there's a matching heel piece) or a 'full brogue' (the fancy leather goes all the way down the side). The brogue is the best style for a slightly less formal brown pair, which look good with light coloured trousers, with jeans, or occasionally with a blue suit (naturally, with a brown belt and toning accessories). Again, quality pays: this type of shoe looks best when it has acquired a little wear and the leather has a patina from being polished.

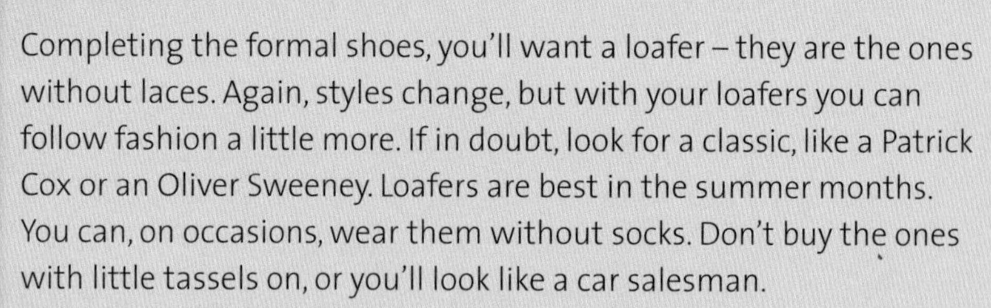

Completing the formal shoes, you'll want a loafer – they are the ones without laces. Again, styles change, but with your loafers you can follow fashion a little more. If in doubt, look for a classic, like a Patrick Cox or an Oliver Sweeney. Loafers are best in the summer months. You can, on occasions, wear them without socks. Don't buy the ones with little tassels on, or you'll look like a car salesman.

Boots are a subject all of their own. Recently the cowboy boot has made a comeback, but most Brits look odd in them, because it's not part of our culture. If you're an urban kind of guy, why not look for that timeless classic, the Chelsea boot? This low boot has elasticated sides and a formal look, and works with jeans, but is at its best with a sharply-cut suit that's narrow through the ankle. They're been cool for 40 years, they're not going out of fashion tomorrow. Otherwise, Australian bootmaker Blundstone makes chunky practical boots created for the outback that are a great anti-fashion statement even if you don't know any sheep.

Everybody wears trainers, but don't wear the pair you wear to the gym in the street, and don't be seduced by flash and gigantic heels that look like they have some type of piston arrangement floating inside them. Instead of buying from anonymous chainstore sports shops, seek out a discerning supplier of classic and innovative trainer brands – the major names now make limited editions and retro styles which are far more individual, and rarely cost more. If you try on a retro style you like, why not check online – eBay is a good source – to see what variations you can get that aren't in the shop?

Finally, you need something for hot weather. No socks, just a classic sandal or flip flop. Birkenstocks aren't for hippies any more, and they feel like your feet are being caressed. Surf brands from Australia, Brazil or California have worldwide credibility, and are made to withstand the rigours of the beach.

Good shoes can be pricey, so it's tempting to shop in the sale and buy something a bit too big or a bit too small because it's discounted. You can have the bargainest shoes in the world but, if you're shuffling because your feet pinch or you're tripping because your shoes are falling off, it's better to be barefoot.

Here's an idea for you

You paid good money for your shoes but why do you insist on coating them with strange paint-like goop? Buy proper shoe polish, two brushes, one to put the polish on and one to scrub it off, and a cloth to shine them, and clean them at least once a week. It takes three minutes. If you want shoes to keep their shape, use shoe trees inside them. If you have suede shoes, use a spray-on suede protector and a wire brush, and don't wear them in the rain.

94. Knotty things – ties

Whilst it's true that Ronald Reagan was fond of 'bootstring' ties with silver clasps those of us living in the real world stick to normal ties. Usually given to us by someone else.

Ties are probably not top of your shopping list. If you had to wear them at school then you probably spent more effort trying to turn them into a badge of rebellion than you did studying for exams. If you first encountered them in the workplace you see them as a functional necessity. So why would you want to buy one now?

The answer is that ties are a case where quality, not quantity, is the name of the game. Ties are eye-catching. Their whole point is to draw attention to themselves (although by the same token they then act as visual conductor down to your waistline which can be unfortunate). One thing for sure is that a cheap tie drags down any suit to its own level.

Choosing a top tie: material
Keep it simple; stick to silk. There are different qualities of silk but it's easy to distinguish good silk just by its smoothness. A tie should always be lined and 100% wool is probably the best material for that.

"Because more men are going to work without a tie, it becomes even more powerful ... Ties are more than ever a signifier of power and success. They inspire confidence. The less common and popular it becomes to wear a tie, the more I shall."

Dylan Jones, *Editor of GQ*

The cut

Good ties are cut 'on the bias' which means across the roll of fabric. It's more expensive because it's more wasteful of material but it makes for a straighter tie. To check just knot a tie and let it fall over the back of your hand. If it falls straight then it was probably cut on the bias, if it tries to twist then it wasn't.

As an added reassurance that you're buying the real deal look for the 'bar tac'; a single horizontal stitch at the broad end of the tie that stops the material of the tie from pulling apart. In any good handmade tie the bar tac should be neat and without any bunching around it.

Tie dos and don'ts

Clip-on ties are only acceptable for those people likely to be grabbed by the tie and threatened. If you're a bouncer then a clip-on could be a lifesaver. For any other occupation if a clip-on is part of the uniform then the only sensible thing to do is get a new job.

Ties should just come down to the waistline. Only twelve year old school kids think it's cool to have a tie that's ten centimeters long. If you're a very tall guy then you'll need a longer than average tie. So get one.

Ties should always be darker than the shirt they're on. A white tie on a black shirt is fine if you're in show business, or you usually go accompanied by Italian men packing guns. For the rest of us it's a no no.

As a general rule a tie should be no wider than the lapel of your jacket. Wide lapels, wide tie, skinny lapels, skinny tie.

The size of the knot should be defined by the type of collar. A wide collar gap asks for a wide knot (probably a Windsor), a narrow gap means a Four In Hand is probably your best bet.

If your tie has a pattern then the main colour should go well with your suit (but not be so similar as to blend into it) and the secondary colour should ideally carry on the theme from your shirt.

Here's an idea for you
There's a sneaky way to tell if it was cut 'on the bias'; because a good tie will always revert to falling straight no shop should have a problem with you trying a tie by tying it. If they know the ties aren't cut on the bias, however, they will fret about you putting twists in their ties.

95. If you want to get ahead, get a hat

Baseball caps are all very well but sooner or later you're going to wonder about getting a hat, and where fifty years ago that would have made you nothing more than normal it's now a choice that's just as likely to mark you out as eccentric or as mad as a, er, hatter. So it pays to know what you're doing.

By 'hats' we're not talking about caps, hoodies, or anything with Kangol on the front here. We're talking about real hats, with brims. The sort of thing that in days of yore people would doff. Doffing has pretty much gone the way of the dodo but hats are still with us.

Hats serve many purposes; they can be protection against the sun, they can keep your head warm, frame your face, and emphasise your broad shoulders. Realistically though, the reason why any modern man wears a hat is to make a bit of a point about standing out. Which oddly enough, is pretty much exactly the opposite of the baseball cap etc. which are all about fitting in. It's your call.

Choosing a hat

Although there are as many reasons to wear a hat as there are hats to wear the commonest hat 'looks' break down to 'urbane' and 'adventurous'.

Urbane

Fedora – The definition of the smooth look is the fedora. From Humphrey Bogart to Hasidic jews it is the hat of choice for the city slicker. Which makes it a testament to the flexibility of the hat that it also tops the list for adventure hats – think Indiana Jones. Fedoras don't have to be felt; it's a style not a material so you can also have a panama style straw fedora but felt is the commonest choice. In case you're confused a trilby is just a British name for a fedora and a pork pie hat is a variation on the fedora with a narrower brim.

Panama – Pub experts will happily tell you that a true panama is one that can be rolled up. In fact panamas come in all sorts of styles, including broad brimmed. If you find yourself in a trivia contest on the subject you can always pull out the information that Panama hats are in fact made in Ecuador (especially the town of Montecristi) from the leaves of the panama-hat palm. The panama is right up there with the lightweight linen jacket as a sign of summer, and is often used as stylistic shorthand for 'gentleman abroad'.

Adventurous

Leaving aside caps (which tend to be better suited for real adventure) the adventurous look is often a classic

"Grab your coat, and get your hat, leave your worry on the doorstep, just direct your feet, to the sunny side of the street."

Dorothy Fields, *lyricist*

Here's an idea for you

Having trouble with hat sizes? Forget all that 7 and one eighth stuff as the actual diameter of hats sizes varies enormously from one maker to another. Just go try the thing on in person, feel for something that doesn't fit too tightly and doesn't fall over your ears. If you find (as always seems to be the case) that you fall in between two sizes go for the big one – too many hats have been bought in the hope that they'll stretch a bit whereas in fact felt and leather hats tend to shrink slightly.

hat style but made in a more rugged material. A lot of Indiana Jones fans swear that the Indy look is best achieved by modifying an Australian Akubra 'Drover' rabbit fur fedora.

The Stetson is actually a brand rather than a style (named after John B Stetson) but has become synonymous with the cowboy and cavalry hat and has a significant following to this day. Leather is sometimes used instead of felt for a more hardcore look although if you really want toughness and practicality then hemp hats by the likes of Tilley may prove a better bet. Let's face it though, in most cases a hat is about image, not practicality.

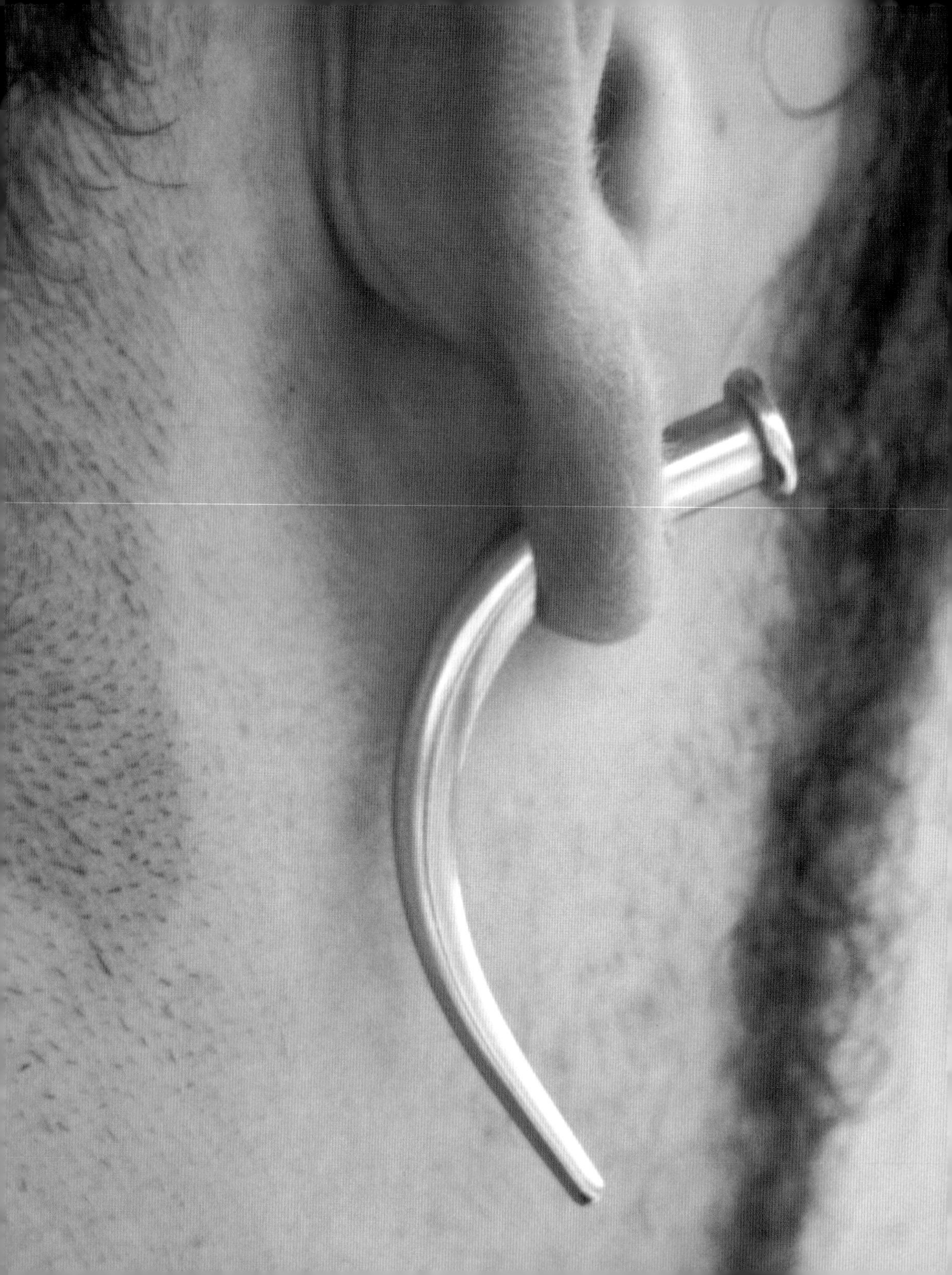

96. It's just a little prick – piercings

There's nothing new about men having piercings. There's evidence that Egyptians and Romans indulged in nipple and navel piercing, and if you want a gentleman role model the Prince Albert penis piercing does indeed take its name from Queen Victoria's hubby.

Think carefully before going for a piercing. While something as mundane as an ear can be done in any high street more delicate areas require specialist skill and even then there are associated risks. The dental industry absolutely hates tongue and cheek piercings and you will too if you end up having to pay for new crowns because you chose to have a piece of metal in your mouth tapping away at your enamel. There are plenty of examples of navel piercings causing fainting, infection, and even blood poisoning and I'm sure we don't have to paint the picture of how scary it can be if anything south of the belt line swells up and goes bad. Don't get a piercing on a whim, and never get one when drunk. Instead take your time, think long and hard about whether you will regret the piercing for personal or professional reasons, and sleep on the thought for a couple of weeks before looking into it any further. Bear in mind

“I think men who have a pierced ear are better prepared for marriage. They've experienced pain and bought jewelry.”

Rita Rudner, *comedian*

that not all piercings are equal and that some (nipples for example) heal up very fast, while others (most penis piercings) may well be with you forever even if you stop wearing the stud or ring. Other things to think about include:

- Ears are commonly pierced with a spring loaded gun – that's ok for ears but not for anything else and makes rather a small hole. If someone proposes a gun for anything other than ears then go elsewhere.

- All piercers must have an autoclave (steriliser) and that should be complete with maintenance certificates which should be proudly on display.

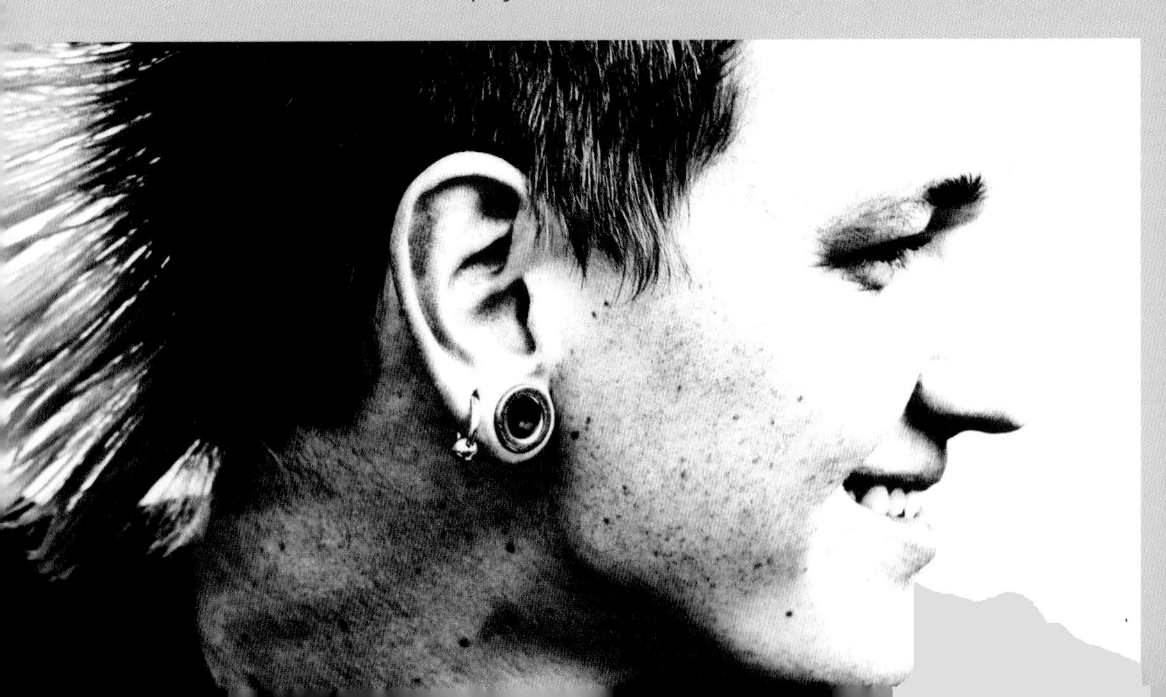

- Given the choice between surgical steel and titanium go for titanium every time. Surgical steel may have varying quantities of nickel in it and that has been linked to allergies.

Piercings and places to play with;

- **Ampallang** – through the glans from one side to the other.
- **Apadravva** – as above but vertically, top to bottom.
- **Dydo** – through the ridge of the glans (I'm wincing just writing this) be warned it can tear (now you're wincing too aren't you)
- **Ear** – by custom left ear is straight, right ear is gay, both is bi and/or keep 'em guessing.
- **Earl** – bridge of the nose, right between the eyes.
- **Eyebrow** – commonly rejected (pushed out) by the body because it's so close to the bone.
- **Guiche** – through the base of the scrotum between the legs. Not a good choice for cyclists.
- **Labret** – under your lower lip, in the middle.
- **Madison** – front of neck.
- **Madonna** – to the side of the top lip.
- **Navel** – usually a bar rather than a ring.
- **Nipples** – usually horizontal, not least since vertical ones are more obviously out of wack if they stray and go out of line.
- **Nose** – usually to one side and low down on the nostril.
- **Nuchae** – back of neck.
- **Prince Albert** – through the urethra and out the bottom of the glans. Said to have been popular in Victorian times for gentlemen looking for a way of fixing their manhood into their trousers for a better cut. Sadly nobody seems to have recorded what happened to the cut of their trousers when these tethered Victorian penises became aroused.
- **Septum** – the cartilage between the nostrils.
- **Tongue** – expect to lithp a lot for the firtht few dayth.

Here's an idea for you

Sadly piercing is a bit of a hit and miss affair and not every piercer is to be trusted to put a hole in you, let alone risk the health of your crown jewels. So don't just go on the strength of a two minute glance around the piercing parlour; check some references. People with piercings love to talk about it so go onto bulletin boards and Web chat rooms and ask for recommendations of piercers in your area. If you have your eye on a particular piercer ask them to put you in touch with some previous clients as references – if they're proud of their work they should be happy to oblige.

97. It's just a scratch

Getting ink done shouldn't be a spur of the moment decision – good or bad, a tattoo will last a lifetime, so do it properly.

Gangsters, bikers and ex-cons used to hog all the best tattoos, but thanks to David Beckham and the gift of social mobility we can all have one. Certain designs, such as having 'love' and 'hate' on your knuckles, or 'cut here' tattooed across your neck, don't look good in every social situation; but compared to what your parents could get away with tattoowise, more or less anything goes today.

The old joke is that even if your body is your temple, from time to time you need to redecorate it. When you're decorating your house, you prepare. The same applies for your body. We don't mean a bottle of Tequila and a spliff in a tent at a festival. A successful tattoo is never an impulse buy.

First, you need to find the right tattoo artist for you. There are now five times as many studios in the UK as there were a few years ago – about 1500 – but there aren't 1500 good ones. All tattooists are not equal, and if you value your skin, it's best to go to the top-rated studio in your area (or take a day trip to somewhere where there's one you really like). Ask your tattooed friends for advice or check reviews on the internet. The best artists often have a waiting list, so you might need to book a few weeks in advance. This can be an advantage, because it gives you a 'cooling off' period too.

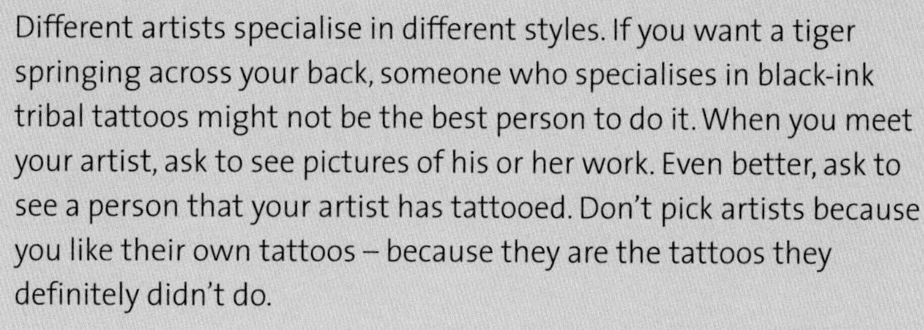

Different artists specialise in different styles. If you want a tiger springing across your back, someone who specialises in black-ink tribal tattoos might not be the best person to do it. When you meet your artist, ask to see pictures of his or her work. Even better, ask to see a person that your artist has tattooed. Don't pick artists because you like their own tattoos – because they are the tattoos they definitely didn't do.

Also, check out the premises. It probably looks a bit like Valhalla, but that's tattoo parlour interior design for you. It's more important to ask questions about hygiene: the equipment must be sterilised in an autoclave (like at the dentist), and a new needle has to be used every time. The best tattoo in the world isn't worth the money if it comes with Hepatitis C.

Let your tattooist help you choose a design. You pick either a 'flash' – a standard design you pick from a book – or a custom piece, in which case have a clear idea what you want, or a picture to copy; don't try and explain a concept to your artist five minutes before your session. The price depends on the design and the size you pick, but a custom piece is charged by the hour. A mid-sized flash from a name artist will still come in at under £100, so they are quite cheap for something that will last a lifetime.

Here's what real men don't let on: it hurts. Some areas more than others so, if you really hate needles, stick to shoulders and biceps rather than bony areas like elbows and shins. Eat before you go to keep your blood sugar high and, if you're really apprehensive, take a painkiller an hour before; but don't get drunk or high because the parlour might refuse to tattoo you until you sober up. If you feel faint tell your tattooist – they're seen it all before so don't be embarrassed. If you want a large design, remember it will take several sessions, so brace yourself.

"Show me a man with a tattoo and I'll show you a man with an interesting past."

Jack London

After the tattoo is finished, your tattoo artist will bandage it or cover it in a sterile dressing, and give you instructions on how to take care of it for the first two weeks. Follow the instructions to the letter. You now have an open wound, and if you don't keep it clean and dry it might get infected; it will certainly mean your tattoo is less vivid or even blotchy. Never, ever, pick at the scab that forms over the tattoo in the first few days, even though you want to show it off as soon as possible.

Be careful whose name you have inked permanently on your skin. If you really must have the name of your significant other, your mate or your children in your tattoo, then for everybody's sake make sure you spell it correctly.

Here's an idea for you

Lots of guys like to get their tattoo done in time for their holiday. A great tattoo turns heads on the beach or at the pool, but fresh tattoos hate being in the sun and the water. Have your holiday tattoo done at least a month before you go, because too much sunshine will permanently fade it. When you're on holiday, use sunblock on the tattooed area: you want your tattoo to last a lifetime.

98. Tantastic fake tans

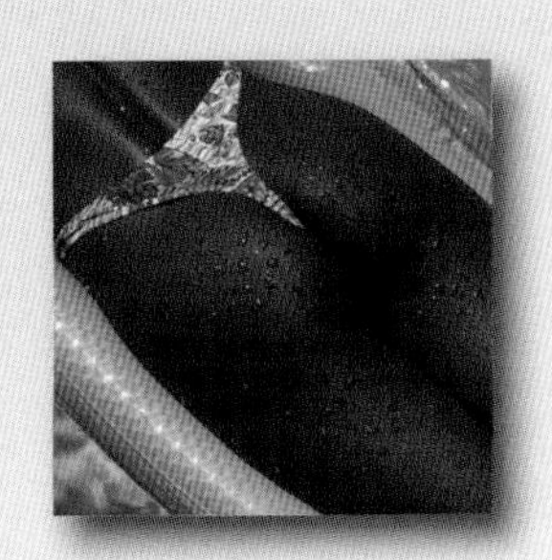

The dappled orange people never cease to raise a snigger in us. Getting away with a fake tan involves more than throwing away the receipt and the packaging.

A tan makes you look slimmer and leaner, by sculpting, shadowing and highlighting muscles. You look fitter and healthier and, most important of all, the boost it gives to your self-confidence will give you that extra edge right from day one of your holiday, not to mention restraining you from dashing out into the sun and becoming the beach lobster. However, sunbathing and sunbeds bring all the joys of skin cancer, premature ageing and that curious barbecued look that only C-list celebrities appear to think is normal.

While it's health irresponsibility to speak well of sunbathing and sunbeds, we can recommend fake tans: they've come a long way. For the best results, have the tan applied in a salon. It will usually last for about five days. If you can't afford that then remember the three golden rules: exfoliate, moisturise, and layer.

Exfoliation is the real key to a convincing fake tan because the difference between natural and ideal colour shows faster the more surface skin rubs off. Take your time over it and keep thinking about how blotches will make you look silly if you get impatient now. Next up is moisturising to give the skin underneath the best chance but don't then rush into application or the moisturiser itself will

interfere with the tan. Leave it twenty minutes or half an hour before you start to apply the first layer of colour.

Use less tanning product where your skin is thicker as the colour will stay longer on these bits anyway. To prevent uneven darkening on bony areas like knees, elbows and ankles, remove excess moisturiser with a damp flannel before applying fake tan. Some experts even recommend avoiding self-tanner on these areas altogether.

Then build up gradually using long even strokes. Keep the application as light as possible because while you can always add more layers later you won't find it as easy to remove. Don't just do the bits you think are going to show, do the lot because this is one all-over tan where you don't have to overexpose yourself and anything you miss is truly going to give you away if errant body parts make a break for the daylight. Get someone else to do your back – uneven 'tanning' on the back is a sure-fire give-away – and don't forget to do your feet. When you're done, get the aforementioned friend to check it out for you – peering over your shoulder at the mirror is not good enough. You need to be 100% sure you are a bronzed god, not a copper-coloured clot.

St. Tropez is generally regarded as the crème de la crème of fake tans, though there are numerous alternatives on offer. Just remember that whatever you do, go for a 'matte' finish. The alternative 'shimmer' only really suits those who think that fashionable evening wear includes a light dusting of glitter and a sequined suit.

The Body Shop once had a campaign in which it declared that 'the only safe tan is a fake tan', which is all well and good but don't forget that a fake tan doesn't itself protect you against the sun. Once you're out there on holiday remember to slap on the SPF with all the care you would if you were exposing your lily-white limbs to the sun – because that's exactly what you are doing.

20

99. Time for action

For the manly man, there's only one rule for jewellery: less is more. The one item of jewellery you really can't do without is an excellent watch.

The choice has never been wider for watch-wearers, and every clothes store seems to have a glass case of fashion watches. That doesn't mean that you should buy a cheap watch every year. Nor does it mean you should let other people buy your watch. Your choice of watch is personal.

You're looking for three things in your timepiece. It has to tell the time properly; it has to say something honest about who you are; and it has to help you look good. This means paying for style and durability as well as engineering. The quality of engineering in even a cheap wind-up watch today is much better than it used to be. If your watch gains a minute a week, how important is this in your life? Look at the clocks in your house. Most of them are wrong.

If you look at some of the abominations on the wrists of your mates, you'd think that telling the time had suddenly become more complicated. Occasionally knowing the date can be useful, as long as you can be bothered to set it on your watch. The rule of thumb for the other dials and functions has to be that if you don't know how to work them, they shouldn't be there. Often they are what retailers know as a 'mug's eyeful' – useless functions stuck on to make something look more expensive.

A classy chronograph (it has a stopwatch function), such as the Omega Seamaster, has clean lines and the accuracy and functionality to back them up.

Here's an idea for you
If you just checked out the cost of a new Rolex and have had to go for a lie down, have you thought about owning a vintage wristwatch from one of the top manufacturers? Some of the classic models from the middle years of the 20th century are works of art, and a 40-year-old top name that has been cared for has many years of life left in it. Don't do this on eBay: a reputable dealer who can provide a history for the watch, or will have restored it personally. Alternatively, ask your grandparents. A forgotten family heirloom might need cleaning, but ultimately it says more about who you are than something you picked out of the Argos catalogue.

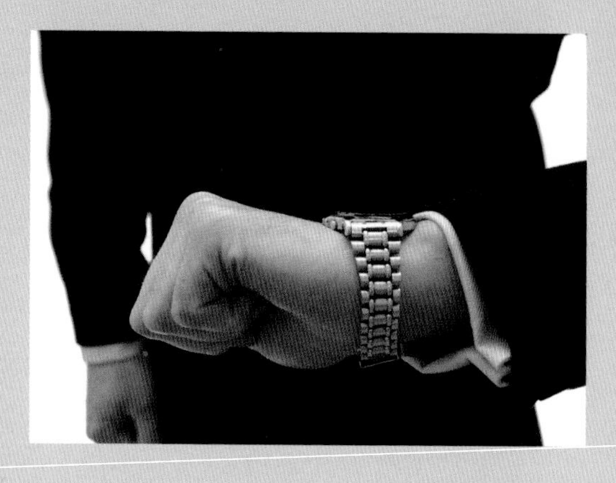

Look at one side-by-side with a cheap imitation, and decide whether you still want to invest in all those little buttons.

Your watch should say something about you. Are you sporty? Casual? A bit of a show-off? A watch can accentuate good attributes, but it won't compensate for bad ones. It also has to be appropriate for the situation. A chunky diving watch looks great underwater and just about ok in the bar, but is ridiculous in a meeting. A heart rate monitor is fine in the gym, but wear it out to dinner and you look like you're part of a medical experiment.

You might want to invest in several watches – they can be very satisfying long-term purchases. You might want to put all your spare cash into one. Either way, your watch will last a long time, so don't follow fashion, and don't buy a watch that will look odd half the time.

For everyday wear, a simple large-face analogue watch with a stainless steel wristband combines satisfying weight with practicality. Many brands now cost less than £100 (Seiko, Tissot and Rotary for example all have great watches in this price range), but more desirable models cost several times that amount. Look for understated elegance (think Swiss Army or Tag Heuer) rather than bling and designer names – this is why gold casings often look naff.

"The way your dad looked at it, this watch was your birthright... so he hid it in the one place he knew he could hide something: his ass. Five long years, he wore this watch up his ass. Then when he died of dysentery, he gave me the watch. I hid this uncomfortable piece of metal up my ass for two years... And now, little man, I give the watch to you".

Captain Koons *(Christopher Walken) in Pulp Fiction*

If you're splashing out, don't think you necessarily need to buy a Rolex; there are plenty of other less obvious brands which are equally – or more – impressive for those in the know. People who aren't in the know will assume your Rolex is a fake anyway.

For evening wear, something a little more subdued, perhaps with a leather strap, is a good alternative. If your daytime watch is a hefty chunk, why not look for a slim watch with an elegant rectangular face? If you don't wear diamonds on your hands, don't even think about them on your watch, and the colour of a leather watch strap should match your belt and shoes.

If you want to look for innovative design, some watchmakers are starting to work with materials like rubber and plastic, or bright colours. There are even some acceptable-looking digital watches out there but, frankly, not many. Consider everything, but buy classic. Everybody you meet, every day for the rest of your life will notice your watch, and most will form some opinion about you based on it. We're not saying that's fair, but it is true.

100. Don't do it yourself

There have never been more people who can make your life easy by doing your chores for you. It may be money well spent.

A friend was recently phoned by her ex.
'Can you come round and see me?' he asked.
'I told you,' she said, *'It's over.'*
'I know. But I don't know how to use the washing machine,' he said.

Mummy's boy? Definitely. Loser? Certainly. But if you face similar problems when faced with complex modern technology like the vacuum cleaner and the iron, it's better to hire help than to humiliate yourself like this. It's a price worth paying.

The most obvious area where hired help will help is in cleaning up your living quarters. A dirty flat might suit you and reflect the amount of time that you habitually put aside for cleaning, but it has disadvantages. No sane girlfriend will set foot inside it, for starters. The problem is that you don't have the inclination or the skill to tidy it – and keep tidying it, week after week after week.

Here's an idea for you
There's an argument that, as an adult, things like tidying, throwing away old newspapers, washing your own clothes, ironing and cooking should not be beyond your capability. It's a strong argument. But how do you learn? You could always pay your cleaner to teach you, ready for when he goes on holiday.

Luckily, there are people to help. They are called 'cleaners', and they advertise in local shops and newspapers. If you're not sure how to hire one – in which case you really are in trouble, aren't you – ask a female to find one for you. If you're expecting her ever to stay the night with you, and she thinks this might be a good idea, she has a stake in your success.

With a cleaner, set your expectations right from the start: politely set out what you would like done every week, every month, or every few months, when you would like your cleaner to call, and how long to stay; whether you want your ironing done, and how much that will cost. If you expect your cleaner to do really grim jobs like taking on the inside of the oven or scrubbing the mildew off your shower, ask in advance and be prepared to pay extra. The job is quite hard enough without you asking for unpaid favours at the last minute. A good cleaner will take the initiative and may start organising your life a little bit. Relax. Go with it. Pay promptly (the average cleaner is not wealthy) and don't try and pretend to your friends that you did it yourself, because no one will believe you.

You wouldn't try and cut your own hair – we hope – so use professional help to take care of other aspects of your appearance. The label on your jacket that looks like a circle with a letter P inside is 'dry clean only'. This doesn't mean that you never clean it; it means that you take it to the dry cleaners, who will return it looking beautiful. When you hand it in, point out where it's dirty and own up to what you spilt on yourself if you want good results. If there are small mends that need to be done, many dry cleaners will do alterations and patches for a few pounds.

"I'm not going to vacuum until Sears makes one you can ride on." **Roseanne Barr**

For bigger sewing jobs, don't hang on to whatever-it-is until you find a friend gullible enough to help you out, or even until you see your mum. Look in the phone book for an alterations tailor, and pay to get the job done properly. Alterations tailors aren't just for hemming trousers: they can work magic. For example, if your shirts are bit puffy and baggy, or the arms are too long, why not have them altered so they fit closer to your body? It's like an instant diet.

Once you start getting people to help you out, there are all sorts of opportunities. If you're going out on a romantic date, why not skip the restaurant? Pay someone to cook for you. Your hired caterer can either cook while you are there, or prepare the food beforehand and deliver it to your door. It's a great way to show off your clean, tidy flat too, and can be about the same price as a flash restaurant (or it can be much more – get a quote).

And finally, if you're short of ideas when you shop for clothes, why not try a personal shopper? Most of the major department stores have them, and there are plenty of professionals who can offer the service on a consultancy basis. You just have to be prepared for someone to look at your wardrobe and say, 'and where are the clothes you actually wear?'

Where it's at...

Note: page numbers in bold take you to *Here's an idea for you*

DEAL
SALE
BARGAIN

Buy *Ultimate Gift Experiences* with **FREE*** high-speed ride for just **£5.00**

This fantastic guide to the UK's best gift experiences and activities comes with a FREE* high-speed passenger ride in a top performance car – worth at least £30. ***Ultimate Gift Experiences*** is also packed with exclusive discounts on many of the activities listed.

From relaxing spa days to hang-gliding and rally driving this book has it all covered, whether you are young or old, a couch potato or gym bunny, a thrill seeker or a lover of luxury. With the help of ***Ultimate Gift Experiences*** the sky's the limit when it comes to planning your next adventure!

To order your copy of ***Ultimate Gift Experiences*** for only **£5.00** (plus post and packaging**) call our offices on +44 (0) 1865 514 888 and quote the promotional code **MMM-UGE**, or send a cheque payable to Infinite Ideas to 36 St. Giles, Oxford, OX1 3LD (don't forget to include the promotional code and your full contact details!).

Alternatively you can order online at ***www.infideas.com*** – just enter the promotional code **MMM-UGE** at the checkout to secure your discount.

*Terms and conditions apply - see book or email ***info@infideas.com*** for more details.
****P&P charges:** UK £2.49 per delivery address, Europe £5.00 per delivery address, Rest of World £8.00 per delivery address.
Offer valid while stocks last.

Spas aren't just for the ladies y'know...

CHAMPNEYS
HEALTH RESORTS

Save 15% on any standard tarriff break with Champneys. It's *the* place to soothe away the stresses of modern day living, hide your self away and reap the benefits of taking time out in complete comfort and with the finest spa treatments around.

Relax in style and indulge in a bit of R&R at one of Champneys four super-stylish health resorts. Experience laid-back luxury at it's finest at the super-chic Tring, their flagship resort and an exquisite world-class spa. Having recently undergone a fabulous refurbishment, this stunning period mansion offers a very sleek new spa and a super-tech gym. Set in 170 acres of Chilterns parkland, it's a truly charming and elegant place to be. Champneys Henlow, a fine country Manor, is a more traditional English retreat with an exquisitely cosy and comfortable atmosphere, while Forest Mere in Hampshire is breathtakingly beautiful. Finally, Champneys Springs in Leicestershire is modern and fresh, with its carp-filled waterways, a superb spa and a striking premiership-standard football pitch.

A Champneys resort is one of the most luxurious places to hide away and be totally spoilt. Luxurious accommodation, elegant surroundings, pampering treats, water therapies, delicious cuisine and the latest fitness trends are all a part of Champneys' spa life, focusing on inner health and outer good looks...there's plenty to leave you feeling completely relaxed.

To receive the 15% discount on all standard tariff breaks Champneys are offering to Manly Man Manual readers visit www.champneys.com and enter promotional code rmm07 into the online reservations section when making a booking.

Valid until the end of December 2009. Cannot be used in conjunction with any other offer.

Esquire
Save over £23

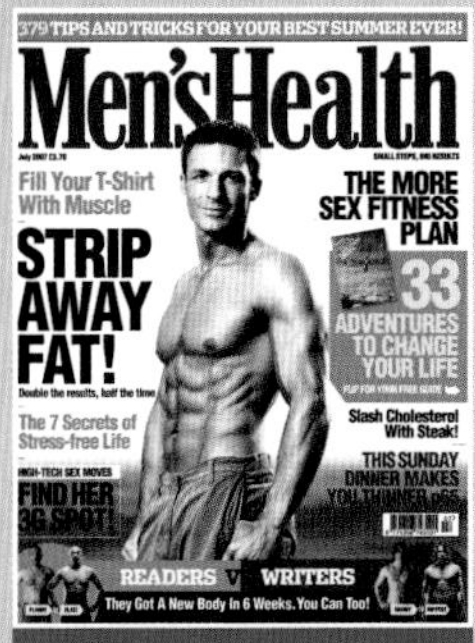

Men's health
Save over £16

Runner's world
Save over £21

Any magazine subscription for £23.99*

Treat yourself or a friend to a subscription to any of these fantastic magazines for ONLY £23.99! Choose from one of their top men's titles on the left.

Alternatively make yourself popular by purchasing a subscription for a loved one from the list below:

Save over £16

HouseBeautiful

Save over £11

SHE

Save over £12

Zest

Save over £14

Call 0870 124 1050** and quote the promotional code 'AE16'.
Lines are open weekdays 8am–9.30pm, Saturdays 8am–4pm.
Alternatively order online, safely and securely, at
www.qualitymagazine.co.uk/AE16

Terms and conditions

Offer valid for UK subscriptions only (excluding BFPO addresses). Acknowledgement of all orders will be sent within 14 days. This offer cannot be used in conjunction with any other National Magazine Company Ltd subscription promotion and closes 30 November 2009. This subscription may not include promotional items packaged with the magazine.

* Initial 12 month non-refundable contract applies. Saving is off the full subscription price. All subscriptions are for 12 issues with the exception of *Men's Health* (11 issues). For subscription enquiries please call 01858 438 838, or visit www.qualitymagazines.co.uk/AE16.

** BT Landline calls to 0870 numbers will cost no more than 10p per minute; calls from mobiles usually cost more, please check with service provider.

Have the ride of a lifetime

Enjoy a driving experience in a high performance car with this special 15% discount with Everyman Motor Racing. They were the first to introduce Formula One Driving Experiences, Ferrari and Supercar Challenges, Mini Cooper Courses and much more.

As the UK's leading operator, established for 25 years, Everyman knows how exciting driving a performance car is. Of course, extraordinary cars demand exceptional supervision and instruction. For your safety and enjoyment, expert tuition is given by leading Association of Racing Schools instructors. Together with their friendly and professional hospitality specialists, they guarantee an experience that is both safe and fun for all.

Everyman is offering all *Manly Man Manual* readers a 15% discount*. Please call 01455 841 670 and quote 'MMM' when booking. Visit www.everymanracing.co.uk for more information.

Terms & Conditions

Participants must have a full current driving licence. This offer is valid until December 2009. Height and weight restrictions apply on some courses – please enquire when booking. Courses run on selected weekdays and Saturdays throughout the year. This offer cannot be combined with any other discounts or promotional offers.

*Offer excludes Formula One.